Why It's OK
to Be Fat

Officially, Western societies are waging a war on obesity. Unofficially, we are waging a war on fat people. Anti-fat sentiment is pervasive, and fat people suffer a host of harms as a result: workforce discrimination, inferior medical care, relentless teasing, and internalized shame. A significant proportion of the population endures such harms. Yet, this is not typically regarded as a serious problem. Most of us aren't quite sure: Is it really OK to be fat? This book argues that it is.

In *Why It's OK to Be Fat*, Rekha Nath convincingly argues that conventional views of fatness in Western societies—as a pathology to be fixed or as a moral failing—are ill-conceived. Combining careful empirical investigation with rigorous moral argumentation, this book debunks popular narratives about weight, health, and life-style choices that underlie the dominant cultural aversion to fatness. It argues that we should view fatness through the lens of social equality, examining the wide-ranging ways that fat individuals fail to be treated as equals. According to Nath, it is high time that we recognize *sizeism*—the systematic ways that our society penalizes fat individuals for their size—as a serious structural injustice, akin to racism, sexism, and homophobia.

For additional online material from the author, related to this book, please see rekhanath.net

Rekha Nath is Associate Professor of Philosophy at the University of Alabama, USA. She works in moral and political philosophy.

Why It's OK: The Ethics and Aesthetics of How We Live

ABOUT THE SERIES:

Philosophers often build cogent arguments for unpopular positions. Recent examples include cases against marriage and pregnancy, for treating animals as our equals, and dismissing some popular art as aesthetically inferior. What philosophers have done less often is to offer compelling arguments for widespread and established human behavior, like getting married, having children, eating animals, and going to the movies. But if one role for philosophy is to help us reflect on our lives and build sound justifications for our beliefs and actions, it seems odd that philosophers would neglect arguments for the lifestyles most people—including many philosophers—actually lead. Unfortunately, philosophers' inattention to normalcy has meant that the ways of life that define our modern societies have gone largely without defense, even as whole literatures have emerged to condemn them.

Why It's OK: The Ethics and Aesthetics of How We Live seeks to remedy that. It's a series of books that provides accessible, sound, and often new and creative arguments for widespread ethical and aesthetic values. Made up of short volumes that assume no previous knowledge of philosophy from the reader, the series recognizes that philosophy is just as important for understanding what we already believe as it is for criticizing the status quo. The series isn't meant to make us complacent about what we value; rather, it helps and challenges us to think more deeply about the values that give our daily lives meaning.

Titles in Series:

Why It's OK to Love Bad Movies
Matthew Strohl

Why It's OK to Not Be Monogamous
Justin L. Clardy

Why It's OK to Trust Science
Keith M. Parsons

Why It's OK to Be a Sports Fan
Alfred Archer and Jake Wojtowicz

Why It's OK Not to Think for Yourself
Jonathan Matheson

Why It's OK to Own a Gun
Ryan W. Davis

Why It's OK to Mind Your Own Business
Justin Tosi and Brandon Warmke

Why It's OK to Be a Gamer
Sarah Malanowski and Nicholas R. Baima

Why It's OK to Be Fat
Rekha Nath

Selected Forthcoming Titles:

Why It's OK to Be a Socialist
Christine Sypnowich

Why It's OK to Be a Moral Failure
Robert B. Talisse

For further information about this series, please visit: www.routledge.com/Why-Its-OK/book-series/WIOK

REKHA NATH

Why It's OK
to Be Fat

Routledge
Taylor & Francis Group

NEW YORK AND LONDON

First published 2025
by Routledge
605 Third Avenue, New York, NY 10158

and by Routledge
4 Park Square, Milton Park, Abingdon, Oxon OX14 4RN

Routledge is an imprint of the Taylor & Francis Group, an informa business

© 2025 Rekha Nath

Library of Congress Cataloging-in-Publication Data
Names: Nath, Rekha, author.
Title: Why it's ok to be fat / Rekha Nath.
Description: New York, NY : Routledge, 2024. |
Series: Why it's ok: the ethics and aesthetics of how we live |
Includes bibliographical references and index.
Identifiers: LCCN 2024007393 (print) | LCCN 2024007394 (ebook) |
ISBN 9780367425494 (hardback) | ISBN 9780367425456 (paperback) |
ISBN 9780367853389 (ebook)
Subjects: LCSH: Obesity–Moral and ethical aspects. |
Overweight persons. | Discrimination against overweight persons.
Classification: LCC RC628 .N27 2024 (print) | LCC RC628 (ebook) |
DDC 616.3/98–dc23/eng/20240408
LC record available at https://lccn.loc.gov/2024007393
LC ebook record available at https://lccn.loc.gov/2024007394

ISBN: 978-0-367-42549-4 (hbk)
ISBN: 978-0-367-42545-6 (pbk)
ISBN: 978-0-367-85338-9 (ebk)

DOI: 10.4324/9780367853389

For additional online material from the author, related to this book, please see rekhanath.net

Typeset in Joanna and Din
by Newgen Publishing UK

Contents

1. BACKGROUND

The term *fatphobic* is sometimes used to describe how we feel about fatness.[1] This term does well in capturing the sense in which we regard fatness as an extremely undesirable trait. Most of us desperately wish to avoid being fat, and we are willing to go to great lengths to do so. In 2018, Americans spent $72.6 billion on weight-loss products and services.[2] From a very young age, the message that it's bad to be fat is ingrained in us. Studies reveal that children as young as three show a preference for a playmate who isn't chubby.[3] Among teenage girls, around one-half report dissatisfaction with their bodies and have engaged in restrictive dieting to control their weight. A survey of over 800 American college students found that one in three agree with the claim that becoming obese would be "one of the worst things that could happen to a person."[4] In a global online survey of over 4000 individuals, 46% said they would prefer to give up one year of life than to be obese, and 15% reported that they would rather their life be shortened by ten years or be severely depressed than be obese.[5]

DOI: 10.4324/9780367853389-1

In this book, I focus on how fatness is generally regarded and treated in industrialized Western societies at present. In particular, I focus on the United States and the United Kingdom because negative attitudes toward and treatment of fat people have been extensively documented in both those societies. However, similar findings have emerged in other Western nations—including Canada, Australia, New Zealand, and Germany—and, increasingly, in non-Western nations as well.[6] The tendency to despise fatness is not universal. For instance, as one anthropologist observes, for women in a Nigerien Arab tribe, fatness is a prized trait that is regarded as a sign of beauty, sexual attractiveness, and prosperity.[7] Historically, there is evidence that in a number of societies, including Western ones, bodies that we would now deem fat were judged to be attractive.[8] In some non-Western societies, as recently as the nineteenth and early twentieth centuries, young women (and, to a lesser extent, young men) deliberately engaged in "fattening rituals" to increase their body size and thereby increase their appeal to romantic partners.[9] Although an aversion to fatness has a long-standing history in the West—for example, finding expression in the slender, sculpted forms heralded by the Ancient Greeks as the aesthetic ideal as well as in the Christian tradition that has long posited a connection between piety and discipline over one's body—negative attitudes toward fatness in Western societies are thought to have become especially pronounced from the nineteenth century onward.[10]

Before going further, let me clarify the terms I use in this book in discussing body size. "Fat" is usually taken to be a pejorative term in our society. That is, to call someone fat typically implies a negative judgment. For instance, when someone asks whether she looks fat in an outfit, she is seeking reassurance that she doesn't since, of course, it would be a bad thing if she did. I'm not using "fat" with that implied negative judgment. Instead, I follow fat studies scholars who have sought to reclaim the word "fat" and who use it as a neutral descriptor to refer to people whose bodies are large.[11] Large in what way? To answer this, we can consult widely employed shared social norms that operate in our society: "fat" refers to those bodies that would generally be regarded as such by most. Conversely, I use the term "thin" to refer to anyone who isn't fat. Using these terms in this way doesn't require universal consensus on who exactly counts as "fat" or "thin," or on precisely which grounds people count as such. This understanding of these terms does, however, suppose that most of us in our society are reasonably adept at using the terms "fat" and "thin" to describe people (just as we are in employing other social classifications such as "tall," "short," "Black," "White," "young," "old," and so on). We can be said to be fluent in using these terms insofar as we are sufficiently well acquainted with the shared standards that apply in the social context that we occupy, which, in turn, enable us to judge which individuals these different terms aptly characterize.

A different way of classifying people according to their body size is based on body mass index (BMI for short). BMI is a measure of a person's weight relative to their height, and it is a measure widely employed in clinical settings. Whereas "fat" and "thin" as defined above are neutral terms, the terms corresponding to BMI categories are not. They are normative terms. As they are used by medical practitioners, public health policymakers, and others, they serve to mark the boundaries of which sized bodies are healthy and which are not. Having a BMI between 18.5 and 25 places a person in the "normal weight" category. Frequently, the BMI classification "normal weight" is used synonymously with "healthy weight." A person with a BMI below 18.5 is officially deemed "underweight." A person who has a BMI above 25 but under 30 is "overweight," and having a BMI at or above 30 means that one is "obese." Obesity is further divided into three distinct classes: "mild obesity" (a BMI over 30 but under 35), "moderate obesity" (a BMI over 35 but under 40), and "severe obesity" (a BMI at or over 40). To give some perspective to these numbers, an average-height American woman of 5'4" counts as overweight if she weighs at least 146 pounds, and she is considered mildly obese at 175 pounds and severely obese at 233 pounds. A man who is 5'11" would be classified as overweight if his weight reaches 179 pounds, mildly obese at 215 pounds, and severely obese at 287 pounds. Not all individuals who qualify either as "overweight" or "obese" also qualify as "fat." An oft-raised example is Arnold Schwarzenegger, who at the peak of his bodybuilding career was mildly obese but, with his huge, defined muscles and low body-fat percentage, wouldn't have been regarded by most around him as "fat." However, there is a good deal of overlap between these two groups.

"Overweight" and "obese" are terms that fat studies scholars find troubling and sometimes refer to as "the o-words."[12] These terms are objected to for unwarrantedly pathologizing those to whom they apply insofar as they medically classify their bodies as unhealthily large. Further, the term "obese" is regarded as problematic for its tendency to invite judgments of disgust and blame toward those to whom it applies. Indeed, as the writer and fat activist Aubrey Gordon observes, the disparaging implications of this term should come as no surprise if we consider that it "is derived from the Latin *obesus*, meaning 'having eaten oneself fat.'"[13] Taking seriously these concerns, I limit my use of these medicalized terms ("underweight," "normal weight," "overweight," and "obese") to when I am engaging with empirical research or with public health and media discourse that relies on these BMI classifications. Otherwise, I use the preferred terms "fat" and "thin."

In the societies that I focus on, in which being fat is over whelmingly regarded as a bad thing, the proportion of the population that is fat has increased dramatically since the 1970s. At present, over two-thirds of American adults are overweight or obese.[14] As a nation, Americans have gotten much larger over the course of the last half-century or so. The obesity rate among American adults has more than tripled since the 1950s.[15] Similar trends are seen in a number of other Western societies, and obesity appears to be on the rise in many other parts of the world too. Obesity is sometimes framed as an "export" from Western societies (especially from the United States) to the rest of the world. In an era of rapid globalization, the charge is that unhealthy diets and sedentary lifestyles associated with the high American obesity rate are spreading across the world. The U.S. may, however, be guilty of exporting much more than that: in recent years, researchers have found that negative attitudes toward fatness that have long been held in Western societies are becoming more prevalent globally.[16]

High and rising obesity rates are widely taken to be a major public health crisis. That it's seen as really unhealthy to be fat—and especially to be very fat—is, of course, a key part of what explains our aversion to fatness. But our aversion to fatness isn't just about health. Being fat offends people's aesthetic sensibilities. Being fat is seen as unattractive, as gross even. We also oppose fatness on the grounds that being fat is an indication of negative character traits, such as being weak-willed and lazy. The pursuit of thinness, bound up as it is with health, fitness, beauty, and discipline, is a moralized endeavor: avoiding fatness is widely viewed as a moral imperative, as something that each of us *should* do by embracing the "right" lifestyle choices.

2. HOW SOCIETY MAKES IT BAD TO BE FAT

Our society's aversion to fatness translates into an aversion to fat people. And so, fat individuals face wide-ranging social disadvantages. These are disadvantages that don't arise for fat people simply by virtue of their being large. Rather, they are consequences of fatness being regarded as a bad thing and of our society not being designed to adequately accommodate larger bodies. The harms begin very early in a person's life. Starting in elementary school, fat children experience weight-based ridicule, teasing, and bullying by their classmates, as well as by their teachers and even their own parents.[17] Children in school are bullied based on their weight more than on the basis of any other factor.[18] Fat children and adolescents find it harder to make friends than their thin peers, and they are more likely to suffer low self-esteem and depression, to worry about their futures, and to experience loneliness.[19] Experiencing weight-based teasing and social rejection has been linked to worse academic performance.[20] Young women who are fat are less likely to attend or graduate from college.[21] Compared to their thinner peers, their parents are less financially supportive of higher-education pursuits, and they may receive less support from educators who harbor anti-fat bias.[22]

The harms continue into adulthood. Fat individuals face pervasive discrimination in the workforce. Compared to thin individuals, they are less likely to be hired and promoted and more likely to receive lower pay for the same work and to be wrongfully terminated.[23] According to a British survey of over 2000 people working in Human Resources, 93% would prefer hiring a normal-weight candidate over an equally qualified obese candidate, and nearly one-half of those surveyed think that obese people are less productive.[24] Fat adults face workplace bullying too. For instance, the cruel humiliations endured by a fat woman working as a teacher included "colleagues [who] sometimes refer to her as 'the walrus,' and make comments such as 'better bring two chairs' when she wants to sit down."[25]

If you are fat, you are likely to be bombarded with messages providing you with a continual reminder that it's bad to be fat. One source of such messaging is government-sponsored public health campaigns.[26] These campaigns let the public know that eating too much or eating "bad" foods makes us fat, and they often reiterate the widely held view that being fat is undesirable and gross. That is one recurrent theme playing out in public health campaigns. These campaigns also reinforce negative stereotypes associated with being fat. For instance, a public health campaign in the state of Georgia targeting childhood obesity depicted glum-looking fat children on large billboards accompanied by demeaning messages: "Big bones didn't make me this way, big meals did" and "WARNING: It's hard to be a little girl if you're not."[27] A New York City anti-obesity campaign wheeled a billboard through low-income neighborhoods, where the city apparently thought its message was most in need of broadcasting, which featured a silhouette of a very large man funneling what appear to be potato chips into his mouth from a sizable bag, with the words "Cut the Junk" written in a huge font and stretched across his substantial stomach (a creative flourish involved carving some of the letters out of "bad" foods—the "C" a half-eaten donut, the "E" made out of a double cheeseburger, and so on, presumably to resolve any doubts about what made this man so fat).[28]

Researchers studying fat stigma point to popular cultural depictions of fat people on TV and in movies—rife with fat jokes and characters playing up common negative stereotypes of fat people—and they conclude that fat people, as a maligned social group, seem to be one of the last acceptable targets of humor and outright ridicule in North America.[29] Our society's obsession with fighting fatness is notably depicted in popular reality television shows such as The Biggest Loser (the American version of which ran its eighteenth season in 2020), on which fat contestants compete with one another to see who can lose the most weight from one week to the next. The Biggest Loser frequently relies on negative tropes about what fat people are like and portrays contestants in demeaning ways. For instance, one consistent theme across seasons involves contestants baring their souls about how they became fat, recounting traumatic and harrowing personal experiences they have endured. The not-so-subtle message that comes through: Fat is dysfunctional. A narrative device the show often relies on is framing these individuals' efforts to slim down as stories of redemption (e.g., having spent years coping with emotional dysfunction through excessive eating, these contestants profess that they are, at long last, ready to take ownership of their problems and to get a grip on themselves by losing massive amounts of weight). *Fat is unruly.*

We live in a society that, increasingly (and rightly so), calls out remarks that have an explicitly racist, sexist, or homophobic tinge. But taking aim at fat people for their body size often does not face the same sanction. In public forums in which most people would avoid making overtly sexist, racist, or homophobic remarks, it is not uncommon to witness instances of downright mean-spirited ridicule and disparagement of fatness being tolerated or even defended. A few years ago, Geoffrey Miller, a psychology professor at the University of New Mexico tweeted, "Dear obese PhD applicants: if you didn't have the willpower to stop eating carbs, you won't have the willpower to do a dissertation #truth."[30]

Besides enduring a constant barrage of anti-fat messaging, a different harm some fat individuals experience concerns the various ways in which our society is not designed to comfortably accommodate their bodies. Some fat people find that seating in workplaces, classrooms, restaurants, movie theaters, or on public transportation is too small for them. At the doctor's office, gowns, beds, or medical equipment may not adequately fit one's body. Then there is the case of the fashion industry often ignoring the existence of many who are fat. Despite the fact that about two-thirds of women in the U.S. are labeled as "plus-size" by the fashion industry (as opposed to wearing "straight-sized" clothes, which usually go up to a U.S. size 14 for women), numerous clothes retailers either fail to carry plus-size clothing at all, or, if they do, the options offered are much more limited than those available to thin women.[31]

I've been emphasizing a certain unity in how fatness is experienced in anti-fat societies like ours: pointing to the numerous ways in which fat people are penalized by a society that is not accepting of their body size. However, in setting out this characterization of what it's like to be fat, I do not want to gloss over important differences in just how being fat tends to be experienced by different fat individuals. One factor accounting for such variance is the matter of how large a person is. As Roxane Gay writes in her book *Hunger: A Memoir of (My) Body*, fat individuals who she refers to as "Lane Bryant fat" (i.e., those who "can still buy clothes at stores like Lane Bryant, which offers sizes up to 26/28") "know some of the challenges of being fat, but they don't know the challenges of being very fat."[32] Elsewhere, on a radio interview, Gay explains that she is very fat, "super morbidly obese" as per the "dehumanizing" official clinical designation assigned to people like her with a BMI over 50.[33] Those at the higher end of the spectrum of fatness face much greater barriers to being accommodated, for instance, to finding clothes that fit and to navigating public spaces. As Gay puts it, "The bigger you are, the smaller your world becomes."[34] Moreover, the larger a fat person is, the harsher the reactions from others one is likely to endure.

How being fat is experienced by a person also interacts with other aspects of one's social identity, such as one's gender, socioeconomic class, race, ethnicity, and sexual orientation. For instance, girls and women typically face far greater pressure to be thin than do their male counterparts. And, in some cases, the penalties associated with being fat vary quite significantly based on a person's class, race, or ethnicity. Such differences, corresponding both to where on the size spectrum a fat person is and how one's size interacts with other dimensions of one's social identity, are important and will be explored in detail later in the book.

3. ARE WE ENTERING AN ERA OF FAT ACCEPTANCE?

In recent years, our society appears to be going through something of a cultural reckoning over the long dominant view that we should all strive to be thin. More folks are starting to question whether engaging in the zealous pursuit of thinness is a worthwhile endeavor. And some are reconsidering our society's long-standing blanket condemnation of fatness.

Let's consider some illustrations. To begin with, although fat-shaming remains pervasive, it has become increasingly common for people engaging in such tactics to be publicly called out for doing so. In 2018, a Victoria's Secret model, Kelly Gale, posted a video on Instagram featuring her and an acquaintance at the popular American fast-food chain In-N-Out Burger. Gale, who has a penchant for posting pictures of herself online in various states of undress, munches on a pear while they discuss how they would never deign to eat the food served at In-N-Out Burger—the establishment that they are (in every sense of the word) patronizing. Then, the model proceeds to engage in a vigorous workout routine right outside the restaurant, clad in revealing fitness gear. The footage of Gale strenuously jumping rope and doing leg lifts is accompanied by such captions as "Do what you gotta do right! No excuses guys" and, with the restaurant sign in focus, "Not gonna pretend that I eat here guys cause I don't." The video wraps up with her receiving, to her great delight, a grocery bag filled with fresh produce for her to feast on. The take-home message of the video is clear: if we put down those shakes and burgers and hit the gym (though, apparently, the sidewalk will do), we too can be svelte, sculpted, and fit like her—and, plainly, this is something we should aspire to.[35]

This video provoked sharp criticism across social media, with many accusing the model of fat-shaming customers at the fast-food establishment. Her in-your-face disdain of those around her indulging in fast food coupled with her need to flaunt her gung-ho workout routine and "clean-eating" habits were perceived by many as condescending and cruel. The largely negative response to Gale's Instagram post reflects a broader social trend of people increasingly using the term "fat-shaming" to call attention to language and behavior that makes (or intends to make) those who are fat feel bad about their size. The Merriam-Webster dictionary reports that the first known use of the term "fat-shaming" was in 2007.[36] These days, the term is squarely in the popular lexicon. A case in point: in 2021, a man wrote to Miss Manners in *The Washington Post* wanting to know whether his wife was wrong to repeatedly fat-shame their pet dog who had put on a few pounds. (Miss Manners affirms her reader's contention that fat-shaming the family pet is a no-no).[37]

Since around 2010, the body-positivity movement has surged in popularity. "Body positivity" does not refer to one single idea. Rather, it is best understood as an umbrella term that encompasses several different ideas as well as forms of activism. Body positivity advocates push back against rigid and unrealistic beauty standards that instill in many of us— especially girls and women—shame and dissatisfaction with our bodies. This movement encourages people, regardless of how their bodies look, to feel good about themselves; to feel confident, beautiful, sexy, and worthy of love; and to find joy and pleasure in physical activity. Arguably, a core tenet of the body-positivity movement is that bodies of all sizes and shapes should be celebrated. Although affirmation of larger bodies has been one central aim of the body-positivity movement, the movement, at times at least, also seeks to challenge conventional beauty standards more generally, drawing critical attention to how Western beauty norms tend to marginalize people of color, people with disabilities, and people who do not conform to traditional gender norms, among others.

The call for body positivity is not new. Indeed, many of the central ideas of body positivity can be traced back to the American fat-acceptance movement that took off in the late 1960s.[38] The terms "body positivity" and "fat acceptance" are sometimes used interchangeably. However, increasingly, the two movements can be seen as having quite different commitments and aims. At its core, fat acceptance is a political movement that opposes the wide-ranging social harms that are imposed on fat people—such as employer discrimination, a lack of accommodation of larger bodies in the design of public spaces, cultural marginalization, and much else. Advocates of fat acceptance seek to dismantle social structures and practices that are rooted in anti-fat bias. Whereas the fat-acceptance movement centers on the distinctive hostilities faced by fat people, proponents of body positivity seek to instill in all individuals (fat or otherwise) greater personal acceptance of their bodies. Body positivity has come to be a movement that's for all individuals who struggle with body insecurities (including conventionally attractive, thin people who feel self-conscious about not being model-skinny). While the contemporary body-positivity movement frequently revolves around beauty, fashion, and self-love, the contemporary fat-acceptance movement has a much broader set of concerns (such as addressing weight-based school bullying and barriers to decent medical care faced by fat patients). So, although the two movements have some overlap, they differ in crucial ways. In recent years, both movements have achieved much greater visibility and wider popular followings. Largely, these advances have occurred in online spaces (on blogs, discussion forums, and social media platforms such as TikTok, Instagram, Twitter, and YouTube).

As these movements have become more mainstream (especially the body-positivity movement), the fashion industry at last seems to be responding to the call that it become more size-inclusive in its offerings. The past decade has seen the emergence of a number of new clothing brands that cater to larger bodies as well as retailers expanding the range of clothing sizes that they offer. What is more, a number of clothing companies have begun to seek models who represent a greater diversity of body sizes and body types. In 2015, two years after launching a body-positive social media movement (#EffYourBeautyStandards), Tess Holliday, at a U.S. size 22, became the largest plus-size model to be signed by a mainstream modeling agency. At that time, no agency had taken on a model who wore clothing larger than a size 20. In 2018, La'Shaunae Steward, who wears a U.S. size 24, was featured in a campaign by the clothing brand Universal Standard. Steward, who has also attracted a sizable body-positive social media following, has been vocal about the importance of diversity and inclusivity in the fashion industry. In recent years, numerous celebrities have used their platforms to call attention to the harms of body-shaming those whose bodies don't conform to conventional beauty standards. Well known for her efforts on this count is fat-positive pop music star Lizzo, who in 2020 became the first Black, plus-size woman to grace the cover of *Vogue* magazine.

Another indication of a cultural shift in the direction of fat acceptance is seen in the changing landscape of the representation of fat characters on television and in movies. Eschewing the usual trends of either having an entire cast without any fat actors or only featuring fat characters that reflect familiar tropes or negative stereotypes (e.g., the hapless, self-deprecating fat friend; the lazy, stupid, and/ or clumsy fat individual; the monstrous fat villain...), several recent television series and films—the shows Shrill and Dietland and the movie Dumplin'—star fat (female) protagonists who, going against the grain, are portrayed as fully fledged human beings.[39] And each of these shows and movie delves into themes of the harms these characters face in navigating a society in which they're taught that their size is a bad thing, and they challenge viewers to critically reflect on stereotypes about fat women in particular. Themes that are common in the online fat-acceptance community, but less so elsewhere, find expression here. For instance, in a particularly dazzling scene of Shrill, the show's main character Annie (played by Aidy Bryant) attends a "fat babe pool party," at which dozens of fat women in colorful bathing suits do, well, exactly what people do at pool parties: swim, dance, frolic, and have fun.[40] Yet, to see a depiction of fat people wearing so little and engaged in a joyful, carefree activity feels daring because it's something we rarely see in our society. The fat women in this scene do not fret about how their bodies look or rush to cover themselves the moment they emerge from the pool, because, as we see in this scene, they look amazing, and they know it.

Perhaps a final indication of our society becoming more accepting of fatness is that in recent years growing numbers of people seem to regard dieting as passé.[41] Companies that had enjoyed great success peddling weight-loss programs and products in previous decades have been revamping themselves in response to this perceived shift in attitudes. In 2015, a brand manager at Lean Cuisine, the purveyor of low-calorie frozen meals, declared that "diets are dead," and he embarked on an ambitious initiative to drop all mention of dieting from product packaging and advertising campaigns.[42] In 2018, the company Weight Watchers decided to change its name to "WW," and it adopted the new tagline "wellness that works."[43] The company explained that its program's traditional focus on weight loss would be replaced by a more holistic approach promoting overall health and well-being. In this spirit, it pledged to do away with its long-standing practice of advertising its program through the use of before-and-after pictures illustrating dramatic weight losses achieved by some. And the ideas of the "Health at Every Size" (HAES) movement, which seeks to decouple the promotion of health from the pursuit of weight loss, have started to gain more attention.[44] Growing numbers of dieticians and medical practitioners are embracing the HAES paradigm.

Given all this, we might wonder: Is our society on the verge of becoming fine with fatness?

4. RESISTANCE TO FAT ACCEPTANCE

No doubt, in recent years, our society has become more accepting of larger bodies in some important ways. But, on the whole, we are quite far from being fine with fatness. Indeed, some indications of our evolving attitudes toward fatness call for further examination. Let's begin with our apparently waning enthusiasm for dieting. As we have seen, major companies that were previously devoted to the promotion of weight loss have been shifting away from that goal. But dieting has not gone away. Instead, it's gone through a savvy cultural rebranding. We now live in the era of *wellness*. We eat "clean" to rid our bodies of toxins we've absorbed from everyday life. We eat like we imagine cavemen did. We refrain from eating between the hours of 7pm and 7am or on days that start with "T." We avoid gluten or dairy or highly processed foods. We wear watches to track each step we take and how many calories we burn on the elliptical machine. We don't do these things to be thin (or so we tell ourselves). We do them in the pursuit of health, fitness, purity, and longevity. We do them to feel energetic and to honor our bodies—treating them like the temples they are. Embracing wellness is seen as an important component of self-care.

But even if weight loss isn't the explicit goal motivating such "wellness journeys," how our bodies look as a result of pursuing wellness certainly does not seem to be irrelevant to most. We might doubt that wellness is really working if we don't achieve that youthful, radiant glow or a more toned, taut physique. Just as with traditional dieting, the moralization of food choices is key to wellness dieting too: foods are labelled "good" and "bad," and we judge ourselves and others for what goes into our mouths.[45] In this way, "wellness" seems to be a wolf in sheep's clothing. It's as much about disciplining bodies as traditional dieting is, despite being couched in a different vocabulary.

In other ways, society genuinely does seem to be moving in the direction of greater acceptance of fatness. But it is worth emphasizing the modest nature of the changes underway. Although it is no longer the case today as it was ten years ago, that not a single major clothing retailer shows their clothes on a model who wears larger than a U.S. size 20, this is still a rare occurrence. As of 2024, only a handful or so of models around that size appear in the campaigns of major clothing brands. Progress has undeniably been made over the past decade in terms of fashion retailers offering an expanded range of plus-size clothing. However, it is less encouraging to discover that the plus-size lines of a number of retailers are only available for purchase online rather than in their stores. This practice seems reminiscent of a theme that emerges in many anecdotes recounted by fat women describing their humiliating dating experiences: men who forge romantic relationships with fat women but refuse to go out on dates with them in public places, lest they endure the horror of being seen by others. *Dear fat customers, we think that you're great and beautiful and we want to profit from selling you fashionable clothes, but can this be our little secret?*

Similarly, while it is a sign of progress that we are starting to see more complex, multidimensional fat characters depicted in a positive light on the screen, on this front too change has been slow. *Dietland*, which aired in 2018 and starred a fat feminist protagonist who gradually over the course of the first season arrives at the radical realization that she need not hate herself for being fat, was not renewed by AMC for a second season due to low viewer ratings. And still today, it is not unusual to come across a TV show or movie that doesn't have a single fat character.

So, the pace of progress is slow. But the perception that we are moving in the direction of fat acceptance at all has met with deep misgivings. This opposition to fat acceptance takes different forms. Central to this opposition is the notion that being fat is dangerous to a person's health, and as such it is seen as obvious that it is not something we should accept. In a 2019 episode of his long-running TV show *Real Time with Bill Maher*, Bill Maher makes a lengthy, impassioned plea to his viewers to join him in regarding fat acceptance as the height of absurdity in our woke age of extreme political correctness. He is incredulous that we find ourselves at a point at which the disastrous health consequences of obesity are taking a toll on millions of Americans, and yet we are talking about the need to become more accepting of fatness?! By comparison, he observes, we don't talk about being accepting of smoking or excessive drinking. Instead, we recognize, sensibly, that those things are bad, and so we think that it's a good thing for people to be shamed out of engaging in those destructive behaviors. Maher argues that this is just what we must do in this case too, remarking that "Fat shaming doesn't need to end. It needs to make a comeback."[46]

Others deem the fat-acceptance movement dangerous for "glorifying obesity" and for giving the mistaken impression to its many often young and impressionable followers that being fat isn't putting them at risk of serious diseases. This perspective is set out by Kiana Docherty in a self-made documentary-style YouTube video, "The Toxic World of Tess Holliday and Fat Activism: Politics, Lies... and Health?," which received over a million views just in the three months after it was first posted toward the end of 2020. A similar viewpoint is expressed by Jillian Michaels, the celebrity trainer well known for her appearances on multiple seasons of *The Biggest Loser*. Michaels takes issue with what she sees as a disturbing trend in the body-positivity movement, which is the celebration of the bodies of fat celebrities such as Lizzo. Michaels says that she is on board with celebrating Lizzo for her music but doesn't understand why people celebrate Lizzo's body, remarking in one interview that "it isn't going to be awesome if she gets diabetes," and in another interview that "there's nothing beautiful about clogged arteries."[47]

To some, pushback against fat acceptance of the sort I just described might sound harsh. And perhaps few share in such anti-fat sentiment. But there is a benign analog to these views that is exceedingly prevalent in our society. In thinking about the cause of fat acceptance, many people seem to oppose outright fat-shaming yet are uncomfortable about going so far as to embrace the idea that there is nothing wrong with being fat at all. On this view, we must work to address two distinct problems, and doing so successfully calls for walking a fine line. On the one hand, it is seen as deplorable that children frequently endure weight-based bullying and that fat people, more generally, are regularly harassed, ridiculed, teased, and shamed because of their size. We should not, proponents of this view contend, be cruel toward fat people. On the other hand, they don't think that our society should condone fatness either.

On the view just set out, rather than resorting to weight-based bullying or fat-shaming tactics, we should do more to assist fat people in acquiring the resources and skills they need to stop being that way. This might call for addressing social problems of access to nutritious food in poorer areas that drive people to subsist mostly on fast food and other foods that tend to be high in calories and low in nutritional value. People should be taught about portion control and how to prepare healthy meals, and they should be educated about how to incorporate regular physical activity into their lives. One prominent advocate of this sort of approach is Kelly Brownell, a clinical researcher at Duke University who has written extensively about the damaging effects of fat stigma but who also maintains a weight-loss clinic devoted to helping obese patients slim down. On this view, talk of "fat acceptance" seems misguided. Instead, we should still oppose fatness but should take care to do so without mistreating fat people. This view, which I take to have problems, will be returned to below.

5. SOME PERSONAL REFLECTIONS

I started thinking about the topic of fat acceptance a few years back when I was in the early stages of writing a paper on social inequality and health. At the time, I listened to an episode of the popular radio program *This American Life* ("Tell Me I'm Fat") that presented different fat people's stories about the indignities, abuses, unsettling realizations, and humiliating experiences they had endured due to being fat in this society. I began reading more about the issue. There was much to read. For several decades now, numerous activists and scholars from wide-ranging academic disciplines have drawn attention to the injustice of how fat people are treated.[48] This theme has been explored in a variety of ways. Some trace the origin of contemporary anti-fat attitudes to racism, sexism, and classism. Others call into question the science and the broader motives behind the "obesity epidemic" that we've been fighting since the 1990s. Still others examine the mechanisms by which anti-fat attitudes are perpetuated and document the far-reaching harms that are produced by anti-fat bias and our obsession with thinness.

As I delved into this literature, however, I was struck by the fact that folks in my own academic discipline, philosophy, were virtually silent about fatness.[49] This omission puzzled me, given the extensive attention philosophers have devoted in recent years to all manner of other, seemingly parallel, social injustices—with much being written from a social justice perspective on ableism, sexism, racism, homophobia, transphobia, and xenophobia. I wondered: *What was I missing?* On the face of it, it seemed to me that body size was yet another trait that had become a basis for a sustained social inequality, as occurs in those other cases. But if that was so, then why weren't philosophers paying more attention to the topic?

Over the past few years, I've gotten to discuss the topic of fat acceptance with a number of philosophers. A theme emerged, one that might shed some light on the question just raised. Overwhelmingly, the folks I talked to were broadly sympathetic to my project in that they resoundingly agreed that anti-fat bias is a neglected social justice issue that deserves more attention. Yet, again and again, people I spoke to expressed their reservations about being wholly accepting of fatness, reservations that manifested themselves in wide-ranging ways. One typical view: "But when it comes down to it, no one is saying that we should be utterly indifferent between being fat or thin, right? Isn't it just obvious that it's better not to be fat?" Frequently, people would cite their health concerns about being fat. Sometimes, their reasoning came down to it perhaps being OK for other people to be fat, but definitely not for they themselves to be that way (e.g., "I have no problem at all with anyone else being fat. But I could never let myself get that way. Eating well and working out is about taking care of myself. When I do those things, I look and feel better, and, yes, part of that involves being in a weight range at which I feel good about myself"). Another person who expressed dismay at all the ways I brought up about our society mistreating fat people went on to remark quite matter-of-factly that personally there was no amount of money he could be paid to be fat. Quite a few folks also made clear that they wouldn't want their own children to be fat and, in some cases, this was an outcome that they had taken con-crete steps to help avoid. These were the matters a lot of people I talked to seemed to be most interested in discussing—not fatness as a social justice issue but rather their own sometimes complicated relationship with the prospect of they or their loved ones being fat.

So, to return to the seemingly puzzling blind spot in the philosophical literature, here's what I've come to conclude. The explanation for that gap is that academic philosophers are people, and people are highly prone to anti-fat bias. Having advanced degrees doesn't make us less immune to that cultural influence. By and large, we don't say much about fat acceptance as a social justice issue, I suspect, because we are subtly (or in some cases not so subtly) reluctant to be wholly accepting of fatness. In this respect, the exchanges I've had with other philosophers mirror those I've had with many others—with friends, family, students, and complete strangers. What I found (though it's hardly much of a discovery) is that people who are thin really care about staying thin, and people who are fat really don't want to remain fat—not just because of what others (would) make of their being fat but also because of how they think and feel about that matter themselves.

In discussing other people's views about fatness, I don't mean to give the impression that I have not been susceptible to the influence of our society's aversion to fatness. I have never been fat.[50] Stating that somehow feels like bragging, which is itself a reflection of dominant cultural views about the value of thinness. At various points in my life, I have felt fat. However, feeling fat is not the same as being fat—not as I understand and use the term "fat." And though I wish I could say otherwise, I have dieted and exercised in the hopes of getting my body to look a certain way, and I have obsessed over my weight. I have done those things on numerous occasions. These days, I don't try to control my body size, something that at first required a fair bit of conscious effort. I've come to realize that thinking about and talking about body size and fat acceptance as a scholarly matter isn't something that is easily done in abstraction from one's experiences, thoughts, and feelings about one's own body. And maybe part of what explains a widespread reluctance in our society to embrace fat acceptance is that doing so feels uncomfortable on a personal level. Engaging in depth with these issues forces us to reckon with our own, often deeply ingrained and subtly manifested, personal biases against fatness.

6. AIMS OF THE BOOK

So, as I see it, here's where things stand today with respect to our attitudes about fatness. Although intolerance of fatness has been called into question in mainstream forums more recently than in previous decades, we nevertheless live in a society that is far from being accepting of fatness. Many, if not most, of us are not quite sure whether it is genuinely OK to be fat. Indeed, it may not be entirely clear to us what it would even mean for us to be accepting of fatness. For instance, what implications might fat acceptance have at the public policy level? Or for how we talk about body size? Or for how we think about our own bodies and what, if anything, we do to control our body size and shape? Resolving these matters is no simple task. Doing so will require exploring a number of issues. These include the relationship between weight and health, the control people have over their weight through their dietary and fitness choices, the effects of fat stigma and of anti-obesity health campaigns, whether there are sound moral reasons for supposing that anyone owes it to others to avoid being fat, and much else. Investigating these issues to enable us to arrive at a reasoned answer to the question of whether it's OK to be fat is what this book sets out to do.

Let me give a preview of what I argue in the chapters to come. It is OK to be fat. A person who is fat does not owe anyone else an explanation or excuse for being fat. What is not OK is how our society regards and treats fat people. It's not just that we fear fat, as the term "fatphobia" suggests. We despise fat. We pity fat. We condemn fat. We hate fat. We find fat shameful. We find fat unattractive. We find fat disgusting. We shudder at the sight of rolls of fat. We recoil from touching the same. We view fat as a sign of weakness, of greediness, of laziness. There is little reason to suppose that these are natural reactions, reactions owing to, say, thousands of years of evolutionary programming. Rather, our culture has trained us to perceive and to respond to fatness in these ways. It is our society, over time and often in subtle ways, that has turned being fat into a mark of shame, an indication of social deviance. And we all partake in reproducing the lessons of our culture. Collectively, we make it very bad to be fat. We never let fat people forget just how much we take issue with bodies like theirs, and we impose severe penalties on them, depriving them of valuable goods and opportunities, all because we disapprove of their size.

Usually, when we talk about social justice issues concerning body weight—specifically, the fact that so many people are fat—we focus on "the obesity epidemic" and how to go about addressing it. In this spirit, we might call for removing soft-drink vending machines from public schools. Or we might call for doing something about the endless stretches of fast-food restaurants, along with bodegas carrying virtually no fresh food, that are mainstays of many poor urban neighborhoods. Perhaps these should be replaced with decent grocery stores. And perhaps more green spaces should be made accessible to residents of those areas. There are legitimate social justice issues linked to these proposals.[51] But these are not the social justice issues this book centrally takes up. This book is about the serious social injustice that we inflict on fat people: the injustice that is the matter of how we view and treat them based on their size.

I approach this issue, in the first instance, by engaging with popular social narratives. Such narratives cast fat people as wronging others for avoidably being fat, or pathologize fatness by framing it as a major health risk, or frame fatness as an indication of a character flaw such as poor willpower. Such narratives are a crucial component of *anti-fat ideology*. Let me explain what I mean by this.

An "ideology" is a system of deeply entrenched beliefs, attitudes, and social meanings that are widely shared in a context.[52] Ideologies matter in the sense that how we collectively represent our social world—through the lens of an ideology—has profound concrete implications for how we interact with one another. Ideology shapes institutional policies, the everyday habits and social roles that we assume, our sense of self, the social scripts that guide our behavior, and much else. Anti-fat ideology does all this. The anti-fat social narratives described above surely play a role in explaining why so many in our society strongly oppose fatness and treat fat people worse than they treat thin people.

As I use "ideology," all ideologies are objectionable, by definition, for two reasons. First, ideology distorts reality by failing to accurately represent to us how things actually are. Second, ideology helps perpetuate systematic injustice. These two reasons are interconnected. As the philosopher Tommie Shelby explains, it is through the mechanism of distorting reality that ideologies play a role in reproducing injustices over time. That is, under the influence of an ideology, many of us misperceive some aspects of our shared social reality, and that misperception is key to our maintaining social structures that unjustly harm some individuals.[53]

Ideology critique, then, has a few aims. One goal is simply to expose the core tenets of an ideology, uncovering and laying bare the constituent parts of an ideology. As the fish who has never left the fishbowl doesn't perceive that it is in water (what else is there?!), we human beings often don't perceive ideologies that deeply shape how we think and act. Those ideologies are so ingrained we don't see them as anything more than how the world, in fact, is, if we see them at all. So, the aim is, as the philosopher Sally Haslanger puts it, "to reveal ideology as such" because when "ideology is invisible to us ... it is necessary to articulate it and make it accessible for critical reflection."[54] A further goal is to reveal the illusory nature of an ideology: to engage in epistemic critique that exposes just how an ideology distorts reality. That epistemic critique, in turn, provides a basis for the moral critique of an ideology that seeks to uncover the moral harms that result from a widespread embrace of a distorted understanding of the world. In giving us a clearer understanding of how things are, ideology critique prompts us to reflect on how things could be different—in particular, how things could be more just.[55]

This book is an exercise in ideology critique—one that takes as its primary subject matter real-world discourse about fatness: how we think and talk about fatness, as well as how that discourse is interwoven in policies, practices, norms, and attitudes that concern how we collectively approach fatness. I work to unmask and to critically examine the core dimensions of anti-fat ideology, piece by piece. In the course of doing so, some of the key questions that I take up are normative: Is it *wrong* to be fat? That is, do I owe it to (certain) others to avoid being fat? If so, on what basis? If not *wrong* to be fat, is it *bad* to be fat? Would I, or others, be better off were I to avoid being fat, and, again, if so, why? And how do the answers to those questions, in turn, bear on the matter of how we should regard and treat fat individuals in virtue of their being fat?

To answer these and other questions, we'll begin by considering what is arguably the cornerstone of anti-fat ideology today. Central to how we view fatness is the notion that carrying "excess weight" (i.e., any weight that places someone above the normal-weight BMI cutoff) poses a serious danger to a person's health, and because so many in our society are fat, from a public health standpoint, this is seen as an issue that we must work hard to combat. It is commonly thought that a key part of working toward the goal of a slimmer, healthier populace is making it clear to the public that it is unacceptable to be fat. However, as Part I of the book (chapters 2 and 3) sets out to show, this reasoning rests on shaky ground. For one thing, the relationship between weight and health is not nearly as straightforward as it is typically portrayed in mainstream public discourse. For another, we know surprisingly little about what works in reducing obesity rates, and we have scant reason to believe that expressing strong social disapproval of fatness furthers that end. As such, this rationale for taking issue with fatness is dubious.

In Part II (chapters 4–6), we turn to a different basis upon which so many people take issue with fatness: they *blame* fat individuals for being fat. Here, we consider different ways that being fat is regarded as not just bad for those who are fat but moreover as doing harm to others. As the media reports with some regularity, obesity is expensive. It is associated with significant healthcare expenses and losses in economic productivity (based on the supposition that obese workers experience worse health). A heavier populace is also taken to be bad for the environment. Food production has damaging effects on the environment, and so excessive consumption linked with larger bodies is thought to hasten our destruction of the Earth. In this part of the book, we examine these claims about the supposedly wrong-making features of being fat.

Also in Part II, we investigate some conceptual matters such as what it would mean for someone to be blameworthy for being fat. In working to answer that question, I tease apart different popular versions of the fat-as-blameworthy charge and consider the merits of each: that being fat is an indication of weakness of will and that fat people exhibit a willful indifference to the harm they may do to others by being fat. Central to the reasoning that fat people are blameworthy is the idea that a person's weight is strongly connected to one's lifestyle choices about diet and exercise. We survey the body of evidence that suggests a considerably more nuanced picture of how much control people tend to have over their weight than the conventional narrative suggests, and we consider when it makes sense to hold people responsible for particular lifestyle choices and their subsequent outcomes.

In Part III (chapters 7 and 8), I turn to the matter of how we should think and talk about fatness. There, I argue for a paradigm shift. Instead of regarding fatness in the negative ways that we currently do, we ought to regard fatness as an oppressed trait. We should approach how fat people are treated in the status quo via the framework of size-based oppression, or sizeism. Sizeism, I contend, is a serious, systematic injustice that we must work to dismantle. Yet, by their very nature, the workings of oppressive systems are typically opaque to us. Chapter 7 seeks to help us better understand the logic of sizeism, in part, by examining some of the key mechanisms concerning how it operates and explaining how its unjust nature is frequently rendered invisible to us.

My analysis in chapters 2–7 reveals that anti-fat ideology is rife with distortions: sometimes there are outright falsehoods, but at many turns and perhaps more insidiously, we find half-truths, glaring omissions, and facts that are interpreted and packaged in misleading ways. If anti-fat ideology deceives us and causes grievous injustice, as I argue it does, then we must change our thinking and change our ways. Chapter 8 concludes by considering just what fat acceptance entails and by briefly exploring how we might go about addressing sizeism. In an online supplement available at rekha.nath.net, the interested reader will find in-depth exploration of some issues that are touched upon only briefly in the book as well as more extensive notes and references.

I am well aware that much of what I go on to argue flies in the face of conventional thinking. To some readers, calling into question the notion that *fat is bad* may seem nothing short of absurd. But that's not surprising. Indeed, that is a reflection of the very nature of ideology: we've been conditioned to adopt the beliefs and attitudes prescribed by the dominant ideology. To those who are skeptical of my project, I ask this. For just a while, try to set aside everything that you have been raised to believe and to feel about fatness up until now. Let's see if we can, if only for a moment, leave the metaphorical fishbowl and allow ourselves to entertain the idea that perhaps things aren't how they have seemed up to this point.

Part I

Promoting Public Health

1. INTRODUCTION

As many see it, it is imperative for us to oppose fatness. On the version of this view that we examine in this chapter, opposing fatness isn't just a matter of our privately held attitudes about being fat. It's about *outwardly expressing* our opposition to fatness. Specifically, this is a position about the appropriate reaction to fatness that should inform public policies, social norms and practices that shape our everyday lives, and our interactions with one another. The reasoning advanced in defense of this position is straightforward. It begins with the claim that the soaring rates of overweight and obesity in our society constitute a public health crisis, which demands a much more serious response than it has yet received. Further, the reasoning continues, we can tackle this pressing problem only by getting everyone to grasp that it's extremely bad to be fat. This argument for expressing an unequivocal opposition to fatness is paternalistic. That is, supposing that it is bad to be fat, this argument relies on the moral supposition that we should do what we can to deter people, for their own sake, from acting in ways that risk making them fat.

This chapter is devoted to critically assessing this argument for why, and how, we should oppose fatness. Doing so

DOI: 10.4324/9780367853389-3

is important because this basis for opposing fatness is a central part of anti-fat ideology. Indeed, the reasoning that fatness should be opposed in this way operates as a widely held, and only infrequently questioned, background assumption that informs our society's response to fatness. I begin by constructing what I take to be the most powerful version of the argument. I then argue that it should be rejected on both empirical and moral grounds.

The argument I will be criticizing assumes both that people's weighing more than they should according to current BMI guidelines is a serious public health concern and that making our population thinner would produce important gains in public health. Neither assumption should be uncritically accepted, as I will show in chapter 3. However, in this chapter, I will grant both assumptions for the sake of argument.

2. WHY THE OBESITY EPIDEMIC DEMANDS AN URGENT RESPONSE

Let's begin by surveying the basic facts typically cited in support of the claim that our nation's expanding waistlines pose nothing short of a public health crisis. To begin with, we are told that being fat kills. Weighing too much greatly increases a person's risk of suffering a host of serious medical conditions including heart disease, diabetes, and certain types of cancer. Back in 2004, a report from the Centers for Disease Control and Prevention (CDC) estimated that each year around 400,000 Americans die prematurely due to being overweight or obese.[1] To put that number into perspective, the annual death toll attributed to cigarette smoking, the leading cause of preventable death in the U.S., has been estimated by the CDC to be over 480,000 in recent years. In the past decade, some have warned that obesity is positioned to soon surpass smoking as the leading cause of preventable deaths in the U.S.[2] From a public health standpoint, the scale of this problem is regarded with grave concern. In the U.S., recent estimates indicate that around 42% of the adult population is obese, and another 31% is overweight.[3] Nearly 15 million American children, close to one in five of those between the ages of two and nineteen, are obese.[4] This is not a uniquely American problem. More than one in every four adults in Canada and the United Kingdom is obese, and about one in every three adults in Australia and New Zealand is obese.[5]

For some time now, we have been told that we are in the grips of an "obesity epidemic." Usually, the term "epidemic" is used to refer to highly contagious infections transmitted from one person to another. Yet, as some see it, framing the issue of excess weight as an epidemic is apt insofar as it helpfully draws attention to the alarming rate at which people are becoming larger.[6] For one thing, the rates of overweight and obesity have risen dramatically in just a few generations. As noted in the previous chapter, over the course of the second half of the twentieth century, the adult obesity rate in the U.S. more than tripled. Since then, the obesity rate among Americans has continued to rise though not quite as sharply as in the decades prior. According to a recent British government report, the adult obesity rate in England has nearly doubled since 1993 when only about 15% of adults were obese.[7] Furthermore, the epidemic terminology is seen by some as fitting in that we are beginning to see the relatively rapid spread of obesity to countries in which it was scarcely witnessed just a few decades ago. Sometimes, obesity is framed as a health problem that exclusively or primarily afflicts the populations of wealthy Western countries. However, according to the World Health Organization (WHO), obesity is on the rise in most societies worldwide—including in many non-Western and poorer societies—and global obesity rates have tripled since 1975.[8] As of 2022, they report that globally about 16% of adults were obese and 43% were overweight.[9] In a 2018 report, the WHO deems childhood obesity "one of the most serious global public health challenges of the 21st century."[10]

3. FAT STIGMA TO THE RESCUE?

Some worry that the current social response to this public health crisis is woefully inadequate. As proponents of this worry see it, too many in our society fail to treat the obesity epidemic as the genuine crisis that it is. In part, this is a concern that, increasingly, being fat is becoming *normalized*. As more of those around us are fat, we each seem to be less aware that we ourselves, or our own children, are fat when that is so. In addition, even when we are so aware, we seem less inclined to take action to shed excess weight. Changes in beauty norms are thought to have played a role in making us more accepting of larger bodies over time. It also appears that the American public has little interest in working to aggressively combat obesity. This is evinced by its mostly lukewarm support for large-scale institutional reforms—e.g., for efforts to drastically alter a "toxic food" environment—the adoption of which many obesity experts regard as necessary to meaningfully address this crisis in the long term.

Against this backdrop, the fat-acceptance movement has been cast as downright dangerous. Opponents of that movement see it as undercutting the public health imperative that we be steadfast in our commitment to dramatically lowering the incidence of overweight and obesity in our population. In their view, it is predictable that the more we come to regard being fat as something that isn't a big deal, the less motivated people will be to try to slim down themselves or to support sweeping social changes needed to fight obesity. So, as these opponents of fat acceptance see it, to counter these disturbing recent trends we are witnessing, the last thing we should do is embrace an approach that fundamentally denies that being fat is a serious problem!

In a 2013 article, "Obesity: Chasing an Elusive Epidemic," the bioethicist Daniel Callahan expresses the sorts of concerns that have just been surveyed. As he sees it, to address this public health crisis, not only must we not be accepting of fatness, but moreover we should actively stigmatize fatness. Callahan suggests that obese people who aren't even aware of their weighing too much need "a shock of recognition," and he reasons that "[o]nly a carefully calibrated effort of public social pressure is likely to awaken them to the reality of their condition."[11] As for motivating people to lose excess weight, he proposes "finding ways to induce people who are overweight or obese to put some uncomfortable questions to themselves," and he recommends that we work to make fat people well aware that they will be perceived as unattractive, face ridicule and discrimination, and be ascribed insulting stereotypes because of their weight.[12] Callahan opposes subjecting overweight and obese children to these stigmatizing tactics, but he suggests that we "apply social pressure on parents to do something about their obese children," aiming to convey to them "that obesity is bad, not to be accepted or delicately evaded or minimized."[13]

One might be concerned about Callahan's weight-stigmatizing proposal on the grounds that setting out to deliberately make fat people feel bad about themselves is cruel. I suspect that Callahan would respond as follows. He would likely acknowledge that his approach seems harsh. But if we look beyond the immediate effects of his weight-stigmatizing proposal, we would see that his approach is less cruel than the alternative. To be accepting of fatness, as he sees it, is akin to throwing up our hands in defeat. To those who are already fat, embracing fat acceptance amounts to telling them, "We're sorry, fat people, you are a lost cause. We won't bother even trying to nudge you toward living a longer, healthier life because in doing so we risk making you feel bad about yourself in the short term." As for those who may become fat unless we steer them away from that path via the proposed tactics, embracing fat acceptance effectively offers them the following rationale for its core message: "Lest we treat you too harshly by instilling in you some self-discipline and a warranted fear of being fat, we'll just leave you alone to make predictably bad choices that set you up for suffering diabetes or heart disease down the road." Ultimately, then, for Callahan, a tough-love approach to tackling our society's weight problem reflects *greater* concern for people's overall health and well-being than the embrace of fat acceptance does.

Whether that response is persuasive depends, in part, on whether stigmatizing tactics can be expected to work. Here, we should ask: By taking a stronger stance against fatness, would we be helping more people lose weight or avoid becoming fat in the first place? On this count, Callahan draws support for his weight-stigmatizing proposal from a parallel example. As he sees it, social pressure was pivotal to reducing the incidence of smoking in our society. Since the 1970s, when society began to cast smoking as a bad thing, as a grave danger to our health but also a filthy and disgusting habit, we have seen an impressive decline in smoking. In 2018, cigarette smoking rates among American adults reached a record low for the past 50 years with fewer than 14% smoking, which marks a 67% decline in smoking rates from 1965.[14] Callahan reflects on how his own personal experiences as a former smoker attest to the useful role that stigma can play: "[t]he force of being shamed and beat upon socially was as persuasive for me to stop smoking as the threats to my health."[15] Based on his reasoning that the two-prong strategy of communicating to smokers society's disapproval of them and adopting public policies that imposed considerable burdens on smokers (e.g., heavily taxing cigarettes and significantly restricting the public areas in which they could smoke) produced tremendous long-term public health benefits, Callahan argues that we should expect similar tactics to help meaningfully combat obesity.

Who is the relevant we who should stigmatize fatness as per this proposal? Callahan doesn't quite say. But the analogy he draws with smoking and his framing of his fat stigma proposal as a "bottom-up approach" would suggest that he is primarily calling on individuals across the board to convey their disapproval of fatness to anyone whom they stand to affect. More generally, though, Callahan seems to support the use of stigmatizing tactics by whoever is in a position to take them up, especially those with the authority and capacity to influence other people's behaviors—which might include the government, public health organizations, medical professionals, and educators. As he sees it, only by embracing this sort of approach might we make strides in reducing the proportion of the population at dangerously high weights.

4. IS FAT STIGMA LIKELY TO DO GOOD?

An initial reaction one might have to the fat stigma proposal just described is that Callahan is hardly suggesting a novel strategy. Indeed, on reflection, it would seem that we already are doing as he prescribes and, moreover, that we have been doing so for some time now. In any case, our fundamental aim is to consider whether fat stigma (a term I'll use interchangeably with "weight stigma," the term more often used in the social-scientific literature) should be embraced. To answer this question, it would be helpful to consider whether fat stigma is working, or could be expected to work, in the way envisioned by its advocates. So, is there support for the cost-benefit assessment gestured at above—that is, can we reasonably expect short-term harms fat stigma produces by making fat people feel bad about themselves to be outweighed by long-term health benefits it might produce for those it helps to avoid being fat (either by not becoming fat or by not remaining fat)? Because fat stigma has been prevalent in our society for some time now, researchers have been able to study in depth just how it seems to affect people. Before turning to the findings of this literature, it will be useful to say a bit more about what I mean by "stigma."

Different definitions of "stigma" have been proposed. For our purposes, people are stigmatized when they are regarded and treated by others as much lesser in virtue of being a certain way. This "way" might involve having some trait or exhibiting some behavior. According to the sociologist Erving Goffman in his seminal work on stigma, the stigmatized person has a "discrediting attribute" and as a result suffers "a spoiled identity."[16] Belonging to a stigmatized group makes a person susceptible to enduring wide-ranging social disadvantages. Because stigma is a multifaceted and varied phenomenon, social scientists who study its effects have usually done so by investigating just one dimension of stigma at a time—for instance, looking at how people are affected by workplace discrimination or by experiencing humiliation for having a stigmatized trait. Nevertheless, the studies tell us a lot.

The consensus view in the literature on weight stigma is that it doesn't help. Actually, it's worse than that. Let's start with its alleged benefits. In general, weight stigma doesn't help fat people lose weight. Moreover, it appears to be counterproductive. In one study that tracked more than 6000 individuals for four years, those who reported experiencing weight discrimination were more likely to become obese or remain obese than those who did not.[17] A number of studies have shown that fat individuals who experience, or who perceive experiencing, weight stigma are more likely to engage in behaviors that are counterproductive to sustained weight loss, such as binge eating and avoidance of exercise.[18] For instance, one study found that overweight children who felt more self-conscious about their bodies were less likely to engage in physical activity.[19] Several studies show that exposing individuals who identify as fat to weight-stigmatizing messages drives them to eat more and may specifically drive indulgence in high-sugar and high-fat foods.[20] So, contrary to what some suppose, making people feel bad about themselves for being fat does not make them more likely to lose and keep off weight. That fat-shaming doesn't help and does great harm to fat people shouldn't come as a big surprise. Indeed, these findings align with what many fat people have been saying for decades now.

It might be thought that the main way that weight stigma could improve society's health is not by helping those who are already fat but rather by making it less likely that others will become fat. By analogy, most of the decline in smoking over the past 50 years can be attributed to fewer people, especially teenagers, taking up smoking rather than to people quitting. Has weight stigma helped in this way? As the statistics surveyed above make clear, there hasn't been any decline in obesity rates in recent years. However, in measuring successes in obesity prevention efforts, it might be better to focus specifically on trends in childhood obesity. That is because many people become fat early in life, and fat children and adolescents are much more likely to be fat adults.[21] But childhood obesity has not declined in recent years.

Still, while childhood obesity rates nearly tripled from the 1970s to the early 2000s, since then they seem to be increasing at a much slower pace.[22] Might weight stigma be the reason why? It's hard to say. We don't know how these trends would have looked in the absence of weight stigma. Perhaps childhood obesity rates would have continued to rise more steeply if not for weight stigma. But perhaps not. In any event, weight stigma has been prevalent in our society for decades now, and we haven't seen any decline in childhood obesity.

So far, the case for weight stigma doing good overall rests on shaky ground. Available evidence suggests it doesn't help people who are fat become thinner and might actually make them heavier. And there is no solid proof indicating that it helps prevent obesity. But there is one other way that stigma might help. Most obesity experts think that substantially reducing obesity rates would require significant structural interventions—for instance, regulating food advertising, improving access to nutritious foods, taxing soft drinks, and reconfiguring the physical design of public spaces to make recreational activity meaningfully accessible to more people.[23] Yet, as observed earlier, there isn't robust public support for such changes. So, might weight stigma get the public to accept the urgency of fighting obesity and thereby help bring about the sort of sweeping structural changes that could make a real difference?

It doesn't appear that weight stigma would help in this way either. Indeed, stigmatizing fatness would seem to make the public *less* rather than *more* inclined to support institutional measures that could make a difference. Why is this? Rebecca Puhl, a trained clinical psychologist and professor at the University of Connecticut, who has written extensively on obesity policy and weight stigma, offers an explanation. That "[o]besity is dismissed as a personal failing," she and a co-author suggest, influences how our society responds to high obesity rates.[24] At the core of fat stigma is the assumption that it is people's own fault for letting themselves (or their children) weigh too much. That assumption leads many to suppose that reducing the incidence of obesity is an imperative that falls on fat people themselves (or, in the case of fat children, on their parents), and *not* on society. This insight, these researchers continue, can help make sense of the half-hearted social response to addressing obesity that we have seen in recent years, against the backdrop of significant weight stigma: "Rather than working on a comprehensive plan to address the obesity epidemic, policymakers have mainly focused efforts on education of those afflicted."[25] This hypothesis seems reasonable. Why should we expect reinforcing the message that it is individuals' own fault for weighing too much to increase public support for significant structural changes?[26] Rather, we might expect stigmatizing fat people to make society *less* likely to implement sweeping structural changes—even if such changes offer the most promising route to reducing obesity rates.[27]

5. STIGMA DOES SERIOUS HARM TO PEOPLE'S HEALTH AND WELL-BEING

Not only does subjecting fat people to weight stigma seem to make it less likely that they will become thin, but, moreover, weight stigma appears to seriously harm their physical and mental health in many ways. One longitudinal study tracking more than 18,000 individuals for at least eight years found that those who reported experiencing weight discrimination had a lower life expectancy than those who didn't.[28] Numerous studies indicate that people who experience weight stigma are more likely to suffer depression and low self-esteem.[29] According to one large-scale study, obese people who reported experiencing weight-based discrimination were much more likely to be diagnosed with a mood or anxiety disorder.[30] Mounting evidence suggests that experiencing weight stigma is both psychologically and physiologically stressful for a person, and stress is thought to be a crucial pathway by which weight stigma negatively affects health.[31] Perceiving oneself to have a lower social status and experiencing prolonged stress are both factors that appear to affect the body's pattern of fat distribution in specific ways that increase a person's risk of suffering certain obesity-related diseases.[32] Indeed, the stress caused by weight stigma is conjectured to play a role in increasing obese individuals' susceptibility to medical conditions frequently associated with obesity, such as high blood pressure, type 2 diabetes, and heart disease.[33]

Although the evidence just surveyed suggests that weight stigma harms people's health in a number of different ways, scientific understanding of precisely how it might do so is in its early stages. In part, this is because the topic of weight stigma has only begun to attract more serious attention from researchers in the last few decades. However, the preliminary findings on the detrimental effects of weight stigma are in line with a larger body of evidence pointing to the damaging health consequences of other forms of stigma that have been studied more extensively.[34]

A different way weight stigma harms the health of fat individuals concerns how they are treated in healthcare settings.[35] The vast majority of doctors and nurses endorse negative stereotypes about obese patients and report holding negative attitudes about them. Studies show that medical practitioners spend less time overall with patients who are obese, and they spend less time providing obese patients with health-promoting education. Fat patients, in turn, widely report feeling disrespected by medical professionals and being made to feel bad about their weight in clinical settings.[36] As a result, people who are fat are less likely to seek out preventative healthcare and are more likely to cancel or delay making medical appointments. In many instances, doctors and nurses are hyper-focused on the weight of their fat patients, and this can have disastrous implications for those patients' health. Anecdotally, horror stories abound of fat patients facing life-threatening situations that could have been averted but for medical professionals who failed to explore plausible diagnoses of their health problems that were unrelated to their weight—diagnoses that very likely would have been explored for thin patients presenting with the same symptoms and complaints.[37]

Against a backdrop of pervasive weight stigma, it has been well documented that overweight and obese individuals face significant workforce discrimination.[38] Being fat implies a wage penalty in our society—one that's especially pronounced for women.[39] It makes a person less likely to be hired, more likely to be fired, and less likely to receive a pay raise or promotion. These economic harms translate into yet another way that weight stigma harms health: it can make a person poorer by negatively affecting one's earnings and one's social mobility, and lower socioeconomic status, in turn, is strongly associated with worse health.[40]

So far, we have focused on those harmed most acutely by weight stigma, namely, fat people. But it harms thin people too. For thin people (as with fat people), weight stigma may drive an excessive and unhealthy preoccupation with weight; eating disorders and disordered eating; a compulsive need to exercise or to achieve a physique that is unattainable for most (e.g., the coveted "thigh gap" some women strive for); negative body image and low self-esteem.[41] Inculcating people with an extreme fear of being fat can lead some individuals who otherwise would have embraced healthy habits and maintained a clinically healthy weight to become unhealthily thin. Now, it's plausible enough that weight stigma may benefit some people in the way envisioned by its proponents. That is, some individuals may adopt healthy habits that enable them to become or stay thin because of the stigma associated with being fat. Even so, the available evidence strongly suggests that far more people—likely a majority of fat people, and many thin people too—are harmed by fat stigma and that the harms they suffer are frequently severe.

6. FAT STIGMA LIKELY WORSENS SOCIAL INEQUALITIES

So far, fat stigma does not seem defensible by appeal to cost-benefit reasoning. There is scant evidence that fat stigma does any good, and plenty of evidence that it does a lot of harm.

But even if fat stigma were to produce significant health benefits of the sort its defenders envision, a further reason to oppose it concerns the problematic ways it tends to interact with extant social inequalities.

To foreground this worry, let's consider some basic facts about the variance in obesity rates between different segments of the American population.[42] It's often thought that obesity is especially prevalent among poor people and people of color. There is some truth to that, but those associations are oversimplified. For women, socioeconomic status is a significant predictor of obesity. But it's not so much that poor women are far more likely to be obese than women who aren't poor. Rather, rich women are much less likely to be obese than either middle-class or poor women.[43] Obesity rates are also far lower among women who graduate from college than among those who don't. Things are different for men, for whom overall obesity rates don't markedly differ based on income or education level.

In the United States, there are racial and ethnic disparities in the prevalence of obesity, but they too seem to be almost entirely explained by differences among women. At least this is so when we compare Whites, Blacks, and Hispanics.[44] Across these three groups, obesity rates are similar for men. Not so for women. Obesity rates are much higher among Black and Hispanic women than among White women. In fact, Black women of any income level have a higher obesity rate than that of any other cohort disaggregated by race/ethnicity, class, and gender. As is true of American women generally, Black women are more likely to be obese if they are poor (the obesity rate among poor Black women is 55%). Mexican-American women who aren't rich are also much more likely to be obese than their non-rich White counterparts. For White men, obesity rates are similar regardless of socioeconomic status. Among Black and Hispanic men, however, obesity is somewhat more prevalent among those in higher-income brackets. Across the board, obesity rates are significantly lower among Asian Americans—less than half that of any other racial or ethnic group discussed above.[45]

There are a few reasons why these associations matter. For one thing, if weight stigma helped decrease obesity rates over time (which, were that to happen, would likely occur through prevention), then that benefit would tend to be disproportionately enjoyed by members of relatively privileged social groups. Conversely, we might expect the harms that weight stigma produces to be disproportionately borne by relatively socially marginalized individuals. These projections are based in part on the well-established finding that public health campaigns aimed at modifying individual behaviors tend to disproportionately benefit well-off members of society while disproportionately burdening the already socially disadvantaged.[46] For instance, this has happened in the case of smoking, which Callahan cites as a social success story. In the decades-long fight to reduce tobacco use in the U.S., smoking rates have declined significantly among rich and middle-class Americans but much less among the poor.[47]

But it's not just that already disadvantaged groups would likely benefit less (if at all) from weight stigma than the well off. It's that stigmatizing tactics would tend to impose on them, more so than on others, a net harm. Members of certain disadvantaged groups, such as poor women of color, are more likely to become obese and to remain obese than others. As such, these individuals, more than others in society, would be especially susceptible to enduring anti-fat vitriol and mistreatment, and for many of them that might be so for much of their lives. In practice, then, if weight stigma stands to do any good, we might expect its benefits to come at the cost of deepening inequalities between society's well-off and worse-off members. Specifically, weight stigma might worsen the overall health and well-being of already badly-off segments of the population without providing the majority of those individuals with any compensating benefits, and it would do this for the sake of producing benefits primarily for already better-off individuals.

In other ways too, weight stigma interacts with existing social inequalities, inequalities along the lines of class, race and ethnicity, and gender. Given the popular link between obesity and poverty that exists in the public imagination, expressing opposition to obesity often takes the form of criticizing poor people for making unhealthy lifestyle choices or pitying poor people for their blighted social circumstances or defective cultural values that drive their "bad" choices. The parallel case of smoking may, again, be instructive here. Over the decades, as smoking is increasingly regarded as something that mostly poor people do, it has also widely come to be seen as a repulsive habit. That's unlikely to be a mere coincidence. Rather, the changing demographics in smoking have almost certainly played some role in fostering those harsh cultural attitudes toward smoking and smokers. Like society's disdain for smoking, society's disdain for fat bodies and for the dietary habits commonly supposed to be the key culprit for producing them—e.g., near-daily fast-food consumption—may well serve as a means of expressing classist attitudes: whether consciously or not, many take issue with what they view as gross, unhealthy habits embraced by poor and ignorant people, from whom they wish to separate themselves. Being anti-fat, then, may well be a way of being anti-poor and of reinforcing reductive negative stereotypes about poor people.

Similarly, that there are higher obesity rates among people of color—and, moreover, that this is an association that is widely thought to hold—sets the scene for the racial undertones that characterize much anti-fat rhetoric.[48] In *The Obesity Myth*, legal scholar Paul Campos offers one striking illustration of this, drawing attention to the gratuitous use of racialized anti-fat imagery employed in an article on the obesity epidemic by Greg Critser in a 2000 issue of the popular magazine *Harper's*. In that article, "Let Them Eat Fat," in the course of discussing what he views as disturbingly high childhood obesity rates, Critser describes a scene he witnesses at his neighborhood Winchell's one morning (after informing us that, along with McDonald's, "Winchell's Donut stores" are among "the places where the high-risk population indulges in high-risk behavior"):

> Mami placates Miguelito with a giant apple fritter. Papi tells a joke and pours ounce upon ounce of sugar and cream into his 20-ounce coffee. Viewed through the lens of obesity, as I am inclined to do, the scene is not so *feliz*.[49]

Cloaked in the guise of social concern about obesity apparently gives one license to appeal to racist language and imagery that is downright offensive. Of course, many well-to-do, non-Hispanic White Americans are obese too. In fact, low-income Mexican-American men are slightly *less* likely to be obese than rich, non-Hispanic White men.[50] Yet, as so often seems to happen when social elites raise concern about obesity, the author of this article chooses to focus on, to his mind, the distasteful habits of poorer fat individuals belonging to marginalized racial or ethnic minority groups. Playing up this racial dimension of weight stigma is, indeed, a favored narrative of the mainstream media more generally. In *What's Wrong with Fat?*, the sociologist Abigail Saguy examines how these biases surface in media coverage of obesity. She found that news "articles mentioning the poor, blacks, or Latinos were ... more likely to discuss individual blame and sociocultural factors," than those that didn't. In doing so, the articles that focused on those groups were more likely to, for instance, paint a picture of the gluttonous habits of fat people who belong to these marginalized groups or to criticize "minority ethnic culture" such that "ethnic minorities are depicted as backward or ignorant and as needing to be educated in proper food choices and preparation."[51] Taking issue with fatness, then, can serve as a vehicle for the socially privileged to criticize and to play up negatively stereotyped portrayals of the lifestyles choices of poorer minorities.[52]

Fat stigma interacts with gender in a distinct morally troubling way. Overall, rates of obesity and overweight do not markedly differ between American men and women. However, as noted above, rich women are much less likely to be obese than poorer women. Against a backdrop of fat stigma, plenty of evidence reveals that women suffer far harsher social penalties for being fat than men do.[53] One study of American CEOs estimated that at least one-half of male top executives were overweight or obese compared to as few as one in ten female top executives.[54] Women who are fat are less likely than thin women to get married or to attend college.[55] Fat men don't appear to be penalized in these particular ways.[56] Fat women also earn significantly less than thin women, a wage penalty that obtains but is less pronounced for men.[57] It's not just that women face harsher penalties when they are perceived as weighing too much, but moreover the weight-control standards imposed on women are more stringent. Essentially, women begin to face social penalties in the workforce and pertaining to their romantic prospects when they are slightly overweight, penalties that become much more severe the larger they are, while men face weight-based penalties in these domains only when they are obese.[58] The particularly harsh weight-based penalties suffered by women are thought to play a role in explaining why poorer women are more likely to be fat than richer women: women who are fat have a much harder time socially advancing. Conversely, it's plausible to suppose that rich women stay thin, in part, due to the immense social pressure on them to be that way—certainly, many of them have good reason to believe that some of the social privileges they enjoy are tied to their thinness.

That fat stigma likely worsens social inequalities in these various ways—based on socioeconomic class, race, and gender—gives us further reason still to oppose it.

7. WHAT OF FIGHTING FATNESS IN MORE BENIGN WAYS?

The case against using fat stigma as a public health tool has been undermined in several ways. To recap: We have little basis for expecting fat stigma to produce the projected benefits. Besides not helping, fat stigma likely causes harm. The harms it causes can be devastating and tend to be disproportionately borne by already marginalized individuals. Still, even if we are convinced that we shouldn't embrace weight stigma as a public health tool, we might wonder if there are *some* ways of signaling disapproval of fatness that would be conducive to promoting public health and would avoid producing the objectionable harms of harsher, stigmatizing tactics.

Rather than trying to make fat people feel bad about themselves, it might seem that a justified anti-fat campaign should instead focus on education efforts, aimed at providing the public with a clear understanding of the health risks of excess weight and of the practical steps they can take to avoid being fat. Such a campaign might equip individuals with tools to facilitate positive lifestyle changes—for instance, offering community cooking classes. Fundamentally, such a campaign might seek to empower people to make better personal choices, namely, choices to help them avoid being fat, without at the same time subjecting those who are fat to harsh social penalties.

We have reason to be cautious about this sort of approach. In spite of trying to ensure that such an anti-fat campaign wouldn't be overtly stigmatizing, it might still inadvertently harm fat people. In particular, there's a real worry that even if such a campaign were to avoid contributing to the problematic tendency for fat people to be regarded and treated with explicit animus, it might still bolster people's *implicit bias* against those who are fat. And a rise in implicit anti-fat bias, in turn, could help sustain or even worsen the wide-ranging social disadvantages that fat people endure in the status quo.

To motivate this worry, let me clarify just what implicit bias is, as well as why it might be reinforced by an anti-fat campaign of the sort under consideration. "Implicit bias" of the kind we'll focus on refers to how our thoughts, feelings, beliefs, and other attitudes can cause us to perceive people who belong to some social groups in more or less favorable terms without being consciously aware of our doing so.[59] These biases, in turn, can affect how we behave.[60] Operating under the subconscious influence of our implicit biases, we are susceptible to treating people differently without intending to or even realizing we are doing so. Implicit bias is a well-documented phenomenon that numerous studies suggest we are all prone to exhibiting. Part of why we are so susceptible to exhibiting implicit bias is that we mostly cannot help but absorb dominant prejudices, narratives, and stereotypes from our surrounding cultural environment.

Since implicit bias operates below the level of conscious awareness, it isn't measured by asking people to report their attitudes about different social groups. Instead, the main way implicit bias is measured is through tests that assess how closely people associate two distinct concepts with one another. Usually, in these tests, a person is tasked with matching particular words or images corresponding to a given social trait (e.g., "man," "woman," "masculine," or "feminine") with other words that indicate either a positive or a negative evaluation (e.g., "good," "bad," "intelligent," or "stupid"). So, for example, on a racial implicit-bias test, a person might be asked to match pictures of Black people with the words "good" and "bad" respectively, and then to do the same with pictures of White people. If it repeatedly takes someone without explicitly held racial bias longer to perform a match—say, matching a picture of a Black person with the word "good" than it does to match a picture of a White person with that same term—that can be presumptive evidence of implicitly held anti-Black bias.

A recent study examining how, at a population level, common biases (both explicit and implicit) are shifting over time reached some interesting conclusions about weight bias that bear on our present assessment of a non-stigmatizing social campaign against fatness. Drawing on over four million tests and surveys carried out from 2007 to 2016, two

Harvard psychology researchers tracked changes in explicit and implicit attitudes toward a number of different traits—concerning sexual orientation, race, skin tone, age, disability, and body weight.[61] Over the span of that decade, for each of those traits, they found a decline in people's explicitly endorsed biases, though explicit weight bias decreased less than explicit biases concerning any of the other traits. For all the traits except for weight, implicitly biased attitudes declined or remained stable. But implicit weight bias indicating favorable attitudes toward thin people and unfavorable attitudes toward fat people rose dramatically. Between 2004 and 2010, implicit anti-fat bias increased by 40%, after which it continued to rise but at a slower rate. What might have accounted for this rise in implicit weight bias at a time when people's implicit biases against all the other less-favored social groups were falling or at least remaining steady? Putting forth their best guess, the study's authors write:

> We think the increasing attention to the health benefits of lower body weight and concerns about the obesity epidemic may be responsible for the increase in bias. Additionally, the perception that body weight is always under one's own control ... may lead to harsher attitudes toward those who are overweight.[62]

So, their hypothesis is that the recent rise in implicit weight bias may be due to more people coming to endorse the following two claims: (1) It's unhealthy to be fat, and (2) People have control over their weight. If that hypothesis is correct, that would lend support to the concern that virtually any anti-fat campaign (even one eschewing overtly stigmatizing tactics) would likely increase, or at least help sustain, implicit anti-fat bias in the population. Indeed, it's hard to see how any such campaign could avoid reinforcing both of those claims. The first claim, that being fat poses a health risk and thus should be avoided, seems foundational to any fat-fighting campaign. As for the second claim, central to the proposal that such a campaign use educational tools to promote public health is the reasoning that people can achieve a healthier weight via behavioral changes, and that focus on behavioral change, in turn, underscores the notion that people have control over their weight: by reiterating the message that they can avoid being unhealthily large by choosing to act differently.

If it seems plausible that virtually any anti-fat campaign would tend to strengthen people's implicit anti-fat bias, do we further have good reason to expect that to lead to harmful consequences for fat individuals? As we have already seen, in the status quo, fat people suffer wide-ranging social disadvantages. Weight-based discrimination in the workforce and in healthcare contexts is significant and has been well established. The extent to which implicit weight bias (when teased apart from explicit weight bias and perhaps other factors yet) contributes to the disadvantages that fat people suffer is not known. However, the effects of implicit bias exhibited toward other socially disadvantaged groups, especially women and racial minorities, have been studied more extensively, and in those cases implicit bias is thought to play an important role in sustaining the systematically disadvantaged position of those groups. So, that provides us with some reason for supposing that implicit bias might well do real harm to fat individuals too.

Another reason to be concerned about the harms fat people might suffer due to implicit weight bias has to do with just how widely it is held. Researchers have found high levels of implicit weight bias in the broader population, cutting across social groups: such bias is exhibited by men, women, fat people, thin people, young people, and old people. People who report not consciously holding negative attitudes about fat people often exhibit high levels of implicit anti-fat bias. Because this bias is so pervasive, it threatens to have negative consequences for fat people in numerous domains. What is more, implicit anti-fat bias has been documented in specific domains in which fat people are particularly vulnerable to being harmed by those biases translating into unfavorable treatment. For instance, health professionals specializing in obesity treatment (including doctors, nurses, and nutritionists) exhibit strong implicit weight bias even when they report not explicitly endorsing negative attitudes about fat people.[63] At least on a subconscious level, medical professionals have been shown to judge obese individuals to be bad people and to associate obese individuals with damaging stereotypes such as their being lazy, stupid, and worthless.[64] Such implicit bias might well result in obese patients being treated worse by those very medical professionals charged with promoting their health. What is more, against a backdrop of pervasive implicit anti-fat bias, our society would seem to be even less inclined to take steps to address the systematic disadvantages fat people have long faced and likely will continue to face without a concerted social effort to counter anti-fat bias.

Still, one might wonder whether an anti-fat campaign of the sort under consideration, unlike a weight-stigmatizing approach, would tend to produce meaningful public health benefits. There is reason to think not. Numerous interventions of this kind—i.e., non-shaming obesity-fighting initiatives that try to get individuals to make healthier choices through education efforts—have been implemented in many different communities over the years. Simply put, no high-quality evidence indicates that any such intervention has had a non-negligible impact on reducing obesity rates.[65]

8. CONCLUSION

The arguments this chapter has advanced against using fat stigma as a public health tool do not necessarily provide a basis for taking issue with *all* tactics that might be used to fight fatness for this purpose. There might be ways of fighting fatness that would avoid seriously harming fat people and thus avoid giving rise to some of the concerns that I've raised. Whether there are such tactics that would, on the one hand, avoid those concerns, and, on the other hand, produce important health benefits, is an empirical question. I see no reason to dismiss outright the possibility of there being some such tactics. But what such tactics are is something I don't think we have a clear idea of yet. Countless attempts to reduce population-level obesity rates by changing individual behavior have been tried and have failed. As such, we have some reason to expect that any effective tactics would be quite different from anything that we have tested on a large scale to date. In any case, because fat stigma is so severe at present, an abundance of caution would need to be exercised in adopting any tactics that signal disapproval of fatness, which risk (even if only inadvertently) contributing to stigma.

Based on what we know about the costs and (projected or actual) benefits of anti-fat campaigns, it is wrong-headed to downplay the burdens such campaigns impose on fat people, treating them as if they were relatively minor costs that are likely to be outweighed by significant gains in the years to come. In fact, the costs at issue are serious ones that harm hundreds of millions of people in our society, and we do not have good reason to believe that they are going away anytime soon. Indeed, for the foreseeable future at least, the wide-ranging social harms inflicted on fat people that have been discussed—including outright discrimination, social exclusion, and being made to feel inferior—can be expected to persist, and to do so for a majority of our population. In light of this, it seems especially troubling to insist that from the standpoint of promoting our society's overall health and well-being, the *real* action lies in working to eliminate fatness while turning a blind eye to the serious harms that we avoidably impose on fat people in the status quo. Even if it were true that our society is waging its war on obesity out of genuine concern for people's health, a clear-headed, factually informed assessment of the consequences of this strategy shows it to be woefully misguided.

3

1. INTRODUCTION

Our society's dominant approach to weight as a public health issue supposes it to be, in one sense, a very simple problem to solve, and, in another sense, a very difficult problem to solve. Let's begin with how it is framed as a simple problem. It's bad to be fat. Fat people would be a lot healthier if they became thin. We all know what fat people need to do to stop being fat: eat less and move more. Put those assumptions together, and it's plain as day what must be done to address this public health crisis. We just need to get fat people to eat less and move more. Yet, for decades now, we've failed to curtail high and rising rates of overweight and obesity. This brings us to what makes the problem quite vexing despite that initial impression of simplicity. Although we know just what needs to change, it's been really hard to figure out how to get most fat people to adopt and stick with the requisite lifestyle changes to avoid being fat. So, the thorny public health challenge that confronts us can be understood as a matter of uptake: How to get most people to do the things we know they must do to be thin? Perhaps, it's thought, the answer lies in finding just the right social messaging or in figuring out how to lean on people just so to elicit the desired behavioral changes.

DOI: 10.4324/9780367853389-4

In the previous chapter, the dominant understanding of fatness as a public health problem that I've just sketched was presumed to be more or less correct. And based on that presumption, we considered the merits of, arguably, the most popular way our society has sought to address the uptake problem: i.e., applying ever-greater social pressure on people to avoid being fat—pressure that often takes the form of stigmatizing fatness. I argued that doing so isn't justified: it doesn't work, it seriously harms fat people, and there are other moral objections to weight-stigmatizing tactics. The chapter ended by entertaining the prospects of a different way of trying to solve the problem—namely, by employing non-stigmatizing means of nudging people toward the sorts of lifestyle choices that would help them achieve a healthy weight.

But what if the very basic understanding of weight as a public health issue that prompts us to seek such remedies isn't justified? In this chapter, we will critically examine the dominant understanding of fatness as a public health problem, assessing in turn each of the key assumptions that it relies on. These assumptions and the conclusion that they support are as follows:

1. It is really unhealthy to be fat.
2. Fat people would be much healthier if they became and stayed thin.
3. We know what fat people need to do to become and stay thin: eat less and move more.
4. Getting fat people to try harder to be thin by making those commonsense lifestyle changes will produce significant public health benefits.
5. *Conclusion.* So, from a public health standpoint, we just need to figure out how to get fat people to try harder

to be thin by adopting and sticking with those lifestyle changes (eating less and moving more).

The four sections that follow (sections 2–5) explore the merits of these four assumptions in turn. In section 6, I discuss two important alternatives to the mainstream approach: treating excess weight with surgery or with drugs. Overall, this chapter argues that the conventional understanding of weight as a public health issue is seriously flawed. It oversimplifies complex empirical matters, and it generalizes inappropriately. In some cases, it presumes that we know quite a bit more than we actually do. In other cases, it ignores entirely or downplays the relevance of scientific and social-scientific data that should inform our reasoning. The conventional way that we think about fatness isn't just wrong. It is dangerous. How we frame fatness as a public health matter does not amount to mere empty rhetoric. On the contrary, it profoundly shapes what our society does in response to this perceived problem. And, based on what we know, we have every reason to believe that the dominant understanding of fatness is worsening our society's health.

2. THE HEALTH RISKS OF BEING FAT

In this section, we turn to the first bedrock assumption of how we typically approach fatness: It is really unhealthy to be fat. That is a message that we hear all the time. Being fat isn't just a minor health issue, we're told, but quite a serious one. To dare to call into question this assumption can meet with serious ire from public health experts. And much of the pushback we see against the fat-acceptance movement comes from those who cast the movement as dangerous for daring to suggest that fat people can be healthy. Most of us, I suspect, have a cursory understanding of why carrying excess weight may be bad for us. But beyond that, there is much that we tend to be less sure about. Is it true that being fat is categorically bad for our health? Just *how* bad is it for a person to be above a normal weight? Is the suggestion that a person can be "fit but fat" a complete myth?

Let's start with the relationship between excess weight and health. Much of what is known at present about why it might be unhealthy to be fat is based on associations that have emerged in cohort studies, specifically, associations between, on the one hand, excess weight and, on the other hand, higher rates of particular diseases and higher mortality rates. In a cohort study, researchers work with a data set, usually involving a large number of subjects, that enables them to sort these subjects into different cohorts (e.g., into the BMI categories of normal weight, overweight, and obese) and to investigate whether those different cohorts differ in other salient respects (e.g., whether those in one BMI category had more heart attacks over the past decade than those in others). Of the adverse health outcomes linked to being fat, the link between excess weight and diabetes is by far the starkest. One study found that when compared to normal-weight individuals, overweight individuals were three times more likely to develop diabetes, and obese individuals with a BMI of at least 35 were about 20 times more likely than normal-weight individuals to develop diabetes.[1] In addition, over 85% of people with type 2 diabetes are overweight or obese. Carrying excess weight heightens the risk of cardiovascular disease, with one study estimating the risk of heart failure to be twice as high for obese individuals as compared to normal-weight individuals.[2] The risk of developing a handful of different cancers is also twice as high for obese individuals than for normal-weight individuals.[3] To give some context to these statistics, smokers are 15 to 30 times more likely to get lung cancer than non-smokers.[4]

In addition, it's well established that people who carry excess weight are more likely than those who don't to have certain "risk factors" that translate into a person being at greater risk of developing diseases associated with higher weights. These risk factors include high blood pressure, high blood sugar, low HDL ("good") cholesterol, high LDL ("bad") cholesterol, and high triglyceride levels. Someone who has more of these risk factors is deemed to have a "cardiometabolic risk profile" that significantly increases their risk of heart disease or diabetes. These risk factors thus help explain, at least to some extent, why being fat can make a person more susceptible to developing some diseases.

Researchers have also found that excess weight can shorten one's life. But there has been quite a bit of variance in these findings. For one thing, there isn't consensus about how much excess weight a person must carry to be at heightened risk of premature death. For another, across different studies, estimates vary widely concerning the extent to which excess weight shortens life expectancy. According to a 2013 review and meta-analysis of nearly a hundred studies on this matter, when compared to those in all other BMI groups (including normal-weight individuals), overweight individuals lived the longest.[5] Furthermore, this review and meta-analysis indicated that people who were mildly obese (with a BMI below 35) didn't have a much higher mortality rate than normal-weight people; only above a BMI of 35 (at which point a person qualifies as moderately obese) did obesity appear to be clearly linked to premature death.

However, other rigorous studies from around the same time reached different conclusions. For instance, a 2009 analysis of 57 studies concluded that being overweight might reduce a person's life expectancy by up to two years and that being mildly obese was linked to a decreased life expectancy of two to four years.[6]

One point of consensus in this field of research is that severe obesity (having a BMI of 40 or more) is linked to lower life expectancy. A 2014 study, which has been the largest-scale attempt to date to examine the relationship between severe obesity and mortality, concluded based on the pooled results of 20 studies that individuals with BMIs in the 40 to 45 range live 6.5 years less, on average, than normal-weight individuals.[7] For people with BMIs in the 55 to 60 range, this study found a reduction in life expectancy of nearly 14 years.[8] Its authors concluded that being at the higher end of the severe-obesity spectrum lowers one's expected life span by a comparable amount as being a smoker does for a normal-weight adult.[9]

The just-described findings are based on cohort studies. Such studies only establish correlation and not causation. Do we have reason to further suppose that having a higher BMI, at least at some levels, is causally linked to lower mortality? We do. As we have seen, we know that carrying excess weight makes a person more likely to have certain health problems and associated risk factors. What is more, researchers have started to gain a more sophisticated understanding of the biological mechanisms that might explain just why carrying excess weight would harm one's health. Fat is an active substance, and when a person gains large amounts of fat this can trigger numerous changes in the body. To take one example, gaining excess fat can cause increased production of certain hormones, and the rise of one such hormone, estrogen, in obese women is thought to play a key role in explaining their greater risk of getting breast cancer.[10] Higher levels of body fat also contribute to higher insulin levels in the bloodstream, which over time increases a person's resistance to insulin, and that, in turn, sharply increases the risk of diabetes.[11] As for heart disease, part of the explanation is that higher levels of "bad" (LDL) cholesterol and triglycerides in the bloodstream, which are linked to being obese, help form plaque that lines the blood vessels and that forces the heart to work harder.[12] In addition, having more body fat is linked to systemic inflammation, which is thought to be another contributing factor in heart disease.[13] In fact, systemic inflammation seems to play a key role in causing or exacerbating several other obesity-related conditions too, including certain cancers and diabetes.[14]

So, it is reasonably well established that there is an association between high BMI and poor health outcomes, and there is some mechanistic understanding of how excess weight might contribute to those poor health outcomes. Still, it is not obvious to what extent fatness causes the various health problems at issue. Indeed, in those cases in which fat people are at a greater risk of developing and dying from certain diseases, it is unclear that excess weight is the sole, or even a primary, cause of that heightened risk. As we saw in chapter 2, there is compelling evidence that experiencing weight stigma can make fat individuals more susceptible to contracting obesity-related conditions such as type 2 diabetes and heart disease. Furthermore, being fat is known to correlate with other factors, such as poor diet and low fitness, and these other factors can negatively affect health in their own right. Let us explore how these factors seem to influence health outcomes independently of weight.

Let's begin with diet. Back in the 1950s, the American medical researcher Ancel Keys hypothesized that following what is now commonly referred to as the "Mediterranean diet"—a diet that involves olive oil as a main source of fat; the consumption of plenty of fruits, vegetables, legumes, and fish; and limited consumption of red meat, sweets, and highly processed foods—might lower the risk of heart disease. In countries in which the Mediterranean diet characterized how most people ate, Keys noticed that there were lower rates of heart disease than in other countries. The large-scale, cross-country cohort studies he conducted on this matter provided some evidence that a Mediterranean diet might be good for heart health.[15] But since Greek and Finnish men (two of the cohorts Keys studied) differed in numerous ways besides dietary habits, it was a matter of speculation that diet could explain why the former had fewer heart attacks than the latter.

However, in the early 2000s, a landmark effort was undertaken to further understanding of the potential benefits of the Mediterranean diet. This was the PREDIMED study, and it is the largest randomized controlled trial carried out to date examining how the Mediterranean diet seems to affect the risk of cardiovascular disease and diabetes.[16] This type of study is the gold standard of epidemiological research. In this case, 7000 individuals in Spain, who at the start of the study didn't have cardiovascular disease but were at high risk for it, were randomly assigned to one of two groups. For nearly five years, one group followed a Mediterranean diet, and the other group followed a low-fat diet. These individuals were not dieting in the traditional sense in that they were not instructed to restrict their overall caloric intake. At the end of this study, the adherents of the Mediterranean diet had a 30% lower risk of cardiovascular disease.[17] In a separate study of a subset of PREDIMED subjects, researchers tracked over 400 individuals who didn't initially have diabetes and were at high risk for cardiovascular disease.[18] Again, some were randomly assigned to follow a Mediterranean diet and others a low-fat diet. After around four years, adherents of the Mediterranean diet were 52% less likely to get diabetes than those following the low-fat diet. For both heart disease and diabetes, the comparative health benefits of the Mediterranean diet couldn't be plausibly explained by changes in people's body weights or levels of physical activity (neither of which changed significantly, and there weren't meaningful differences in either factor between the two cohorts who were following different diets). These studies strongly suggest that diet, independently of weight, may matter quite a bit in affecting a person's risk of obesity-linked diseases.

Exercise, however, may be even more important to health than diet. The health benefits of exercise have been well documented for a long time. Overall, it appears that obese individuals don't tend to be as physically active as normal-weight individuals.[19] As such, it might be that some of the increased mortality risk associated with having a higher BMI is explained by low fitness rather than by high weight. The majority of studies assessing the mortality risks associated with different BMI categories, including those discussed above, do not account for this possibility. This omission is generally owing to the fact that researchers are relying on data sets that don't include information about the physical activity or fitness levels of the studied populations. However, there are several dozen large-scale cohort studies that disaggregate subjects based on BMI and fitness. One such study, notable for its especially high number of subjects—over 300,000 European adults who didn't have cardiovascular disease or cancer at the start of the 12-year period over which they were followed—examined whether obesity or physical inactivity was linked to higher mortality.[20] A key finding was that being "very inactive" (compared to being only "moderately inactive") was twice as likely to kill a person as was being obese (when compared to not being obese). Numerous other studies corroborate the general finding that the more physically active a person is, the greater one's longevity.

Still, it seems that even being very physically active doesn't eliminate, though it may significantly reduce, fat people's heightened risk of developing certain serious health conditions linked to obesity, such as diabetes. However, achieving a high level of fitness might do just that. That is, a person's fitness level, which is a factor connected to but distinct from how much physical activity one engages in, seems to bear even more so on overall health. Sometimes referred to in the literature as "aerobic fitness" or "cardiorespiratory fitness," fitness is essentially a matter of a person's endurance for performing sustained, difficult physical activity. For the purposes of studying its health impact, a person's fitness level is usually measured through a treadmill test that gauges how efficiently one's body uses oxygen while engaged in intense exercise. A 2014 meta-analysis, which was the first meta-analysis of its kind to assess the overall findings of studies on the relative contributions fitness and BMI each had on mortality rates, found that fit people across all BMI categories had similar mortality rates to one another, while unfit individuals regardless of BMI had a mortality risk double that of fit individuals.[21] And a 2010 systematic review of 36 studies found that fit, obese individuals were less likely to die prematurely than were unfit, normal-weight individuals.[22] Like much else on the science of weight and health, whether fitness is a better predictor of life expectancy than BMI, and, indeed, whether achieving high fitness entirely eliminates the higher mortality rate linked to obesity, are not settled matters.[23] However, there is consensus among experts that fitness and physical activity both matter a great deal to our health and that achieving a high level of fitness, in particular, seems to substantially reduce the health risks associated with excess weight.[24]

Besides the established associations between diet and fitness, on the one hand, and risk of serious disease and mortality, on the other, important strides have also been made in understanding how these "lifestyle interventions" (as they're sometimes referred to in this literature) may improve people's health. Glenn Gaesser, a professor of exercise physiology at Arizona State University, has long argued that if we care about improving people's health, we should place much less emphasis on weight and much more on diet and exercise. In a 2011 co-authored paper, he summarizes the findings of around a hundred studies, mostly from the previous decade, that document the wide-ranging biological mechanisms triggered by a more nutrient-dense diet and exercise, which go some way toward explaining the considerable health benefits experienced by overweight and obese people who adopt those lifestyle habits even when they don't lose weight.[25] One significant contribution of this paper is its explication of how adopting those lifestyle interventions can produce sweeping improvements in the risk factors discussed above that predict obese individuals' higher risk of diabetes and cardiovascular disease. For instance, engaging in aerobic exercise or strength training decreases blood pressure and inflammation, and increased fiber intake reduces diabetics' total cholesterol and triglyceride levels. Indeed, study after study shows that overweight and obese individuals who had, or were at risk of having, type 2 diabetes or cardiovascular disease experienced substantial health benefits from adopting a more nutritional diet or starting an exercise program, even when those lifestyle changes weren't accompanied by weight loss.

So, it appears that through diet and exercise a person who is fat may be able to significantly mitigate, if not escape entirely, key negative health outcomes associated with being fat—both obesity-linked diseases themselves and risk factors that predict susceptibility to those diseases. If this is the case, then fatness *per se* should not be condemned as unhealthy, certainly not to the extent that it currently is. Quite clearly, fatness can and does come apart from these other factors, poor diet and low fitness, that may play at least as important a role in accounting for the health problems at issue.

That being fat is unhealthy has been called into question in other ways too. First, a number of fat people are "metabolically healthy," which means that they don't exhibit the characteristic cardiometabolic abnormalities (high blood pressure, insulin resistance, high cholesterol, systemic inflammation, etc.) that are linked to obesity and that increase one's risk of cardiovascular disease, stroke, and diabetes. One large-scale study estimated that as many as 50% of overweight individuals and 30% of obese individuals may be metabolically healthy, which would suggest that they are no more likely than healthy, normal-weight individuals to develop those serious conditions.[26]

Second, BMI classifies individuals as too heavy for their height based only on their weight and thus without further taking into account the particularities of what makes someone heavy. Yet those particularities can bear on whether being heavy is linked to health problems. For one thing, a person's "body composition" matters: being heavy in virtue of having significant lean body mass (as a serious weightlifter might) isn't linked to poor health. By contrast, having a high proportion of body fat can be.[27] For another, having a lot of fat doesn't always seem to be linked to poor health. Where the fat is located matters. Having a lot of fat around the major organs ("visceral fat") greatly increases a person's risk of serious obesity-related diseases. But having large accumulations of fat deposits just below the surface of the skin ("subcutaneous fat"), especially around the thighs and buttocks, doesn't seem to carry that risk. It may even confer health benefits. Some studies link having greater fat deposits in those lower-body regions to a lower risk of heart disease and diabetes.[28] In general, carrying a lot of fat around the middle of the body is linked to a higher risk of obesity-related conditions. And there's quite compelling evidence that for normal-weight, overweight, and mildly obese individuals, their waist circumference better predicts their risk for obesity-related diseases than does their BMI.[29] There also seems to be considerable interpersonal variance with respect to how heavy someone would need to be (measured by BMI) for their risk of certain diseases, such as type 2 diabetes, to become elevated.[30]

So, as it bears on health, being fat may be neutral or even beneficial in some cases. However, as concerns some of the findings just described, it would be premature to draw firm conclusions to that effect. In the case of "metabolically healthy obese" individuals, some studies suggest that in the long term they are still more likely than metabolically healthy normal-weight individuals to develop risk factors linked to cardiovascular diseases and diabetes.[31] But even if a not-insignificant segment of the obese population avoids developing serious health problems, what should we conclude from that? Here, an analogy with smoking might be helpful. About one in three smokers isn't killed by a smoking-related condition, a fact that may be explained by genetic variance in how smoking affects different people.[32] However, we don't currently have the means to easily identify which individuals in the population appear to be more or less immune from the harms of smoking. It seems reasonable enough to claim that smoking is unhealthy, notwithstanding the fact that quite a few smokers may not be seriously harmed by it. Similarly, it would seem reasonable to judge excess weight to be a health risk. Furthermore, up to this point, in assessing whether it's unhealthy to be fat, I have limited my focus to the most serious, widespread chronic diseases associated with obesity. But there are health conditions that obese individuals who are in excellent cardiometabolic health nevertheless are at greater risk of developing—for instance, sleep apnea and osteoarthritis.[33] As for the findings described above concerning body composition and body fat distribution, they seem to be generally accepted. And so, being above a normal weight shouldn't in itself be treated as an indication that a person faces heightened risk of serious disease.

Overall, can we reasonably conclude that it is really unhealthy to be fat? To conclude as much would be, at best, to greatly oversimplify a complex matter. The science on weight and health admits of considerable nuance, and there's a good deal about this relationship that we just don't know. Taking the body of evidence we have surveyed as a whole, we can confidently conclude a few things. Being above a normal weight is *not* bad for people across the board—certainly not always, and not obviously in general either. There is, however, fairly strong evidence that being severely obese meaningfully increases one's risk for experiencing serious health problems and significantly lowers life expectancy. As best we can tell, moderate obesity is associated with increased risk for health problems and higher mortality but much less so than is severe obesity. Being mildly obese may decrease life expectancy slightly, and being overweight may not shorten one's life at all.

According to recent estimates, about 30% of American adults are overweight, and a majority of obese adults in North America qualify as mildly obese.[34] Around 9% of American adults are severely obese.[35] Certainly, in absolute terms that is a lot of people. Yet, in relative terms, that latter cohort for whom serious health risks linked to carrying excess weight have been firmly established is not so great. Often, the more than 70% of the population who are over a normal weight are cast as being at a significantly heightened risk of premature death due to their excess weight. That is a very misleading portrayal.

In any case, BMI should be treated as a blunt tool that, at best, may serve as a proxy for other factors that are much more reliable indicators of a person's health. A number of factors—such as one's body composition, where on one's body one carries fat, which types of food one eats, and how much one exercises or one's fitness level—are relevant to whether, and to what extent, being fat is linked to poor health. Frequently, in the popular imagination, being fat is seen as akin to a ticking time bomb: it's taken to be only a matter of time before a fat person will be afflicted with a deadly condition as a result of carrying excess weight. Clearly, that is not so.

3. SHOULD FAT PEOPLE EXPECT TO GREATLY IMPROVE THEIR HEALTH BY BECOMING THIN?

Let us turn to the second assumption of our society's dominant framing of weight as a public health issue: *Fat people would be much healthier if they became and stayed thin.* Given the findings surveyed in the previous section, we have some presumptive support for this assumption. We know that normal-weight individuals are less likely than obese individuals to suffer from type 2 diabetes, heart disease, and some cancers, and we know that normal-weight individuals tend to live longer than obese individuals. There is also a good deal of evidence that can help explain why people who are obese, in general, have a higher risk of developing these conditions, a risk that is especially pronounced for those with severe obesity. To be sure, a number of factors appear to mediate the association between higher BMI and poor health—notably, improvements in diet and fitness may significantly reduce fat individuals' risk of developing obesity-related health problems. Still, available evidence suggests that carrying excess weight (in particular, excess fat) is linked to health problems in its own right. And so, it would seem reasonable to suppose that obese individuals (and maybe overweight individuals too) would likely enjoy substantial health improvements by becoming thin. However, there is more to the story.[36]

Let us begin by considering life expectancy. Does significant weight loss achieved by fat individuals tend to prolong their lives? The short answer is that we just don't really know: if it does, then we don't yet have solid evidence to back that up. It's not that the relationship between weight loss and mortality hasn't been studied. It has been, and quite extensively at that. But, as most experts on this topic contend, there is a dearth of high-quality evidence on the matter. The majority of studies over a few decades examining the relationship between weight loss and mortality reveal an association that baffles most researchers: among individuals with comparable starting BMIs, those who lose weight consistently have a *higher* mortality rate than those who don't. These studies are all cohort studies involving large numbers of people who are tracked over many years. Among other shortcomings, most of these studies don't distinguish between intentional and unintentional weight loss, and that is a problem because unintended weight loss is usually a sign of a serious underlying health condition.

In a 2009 paper, a team of researchers conducted a review and meta-analysis of data pooled from 26 studies tracking weight loss and mortality rates for overweight and obese individuals.[37] When they restricted their analysis to studies involving intentional weight loss, they found that overall, overweight and obese individuals who intentionally lost weight didn't live any longer or shorter than their counterparts whose weights remained the same. However, further investigation revealed that obese individuals who were classified as "unhealthy" (based on having cardiometabolic risk factors) experienced a slight decrease in mortality rates if they lost weight. But for metabolically healthy obese individuals, as well as for overweight individuals across the board, losing weight was linked to a slight rise in mortality rates. What is the takeaway from these findings? One point of consensus among those who study this matter is that we can't infer too much from the just-described body of evidence. Largely, that is because most of the studies are based on very few data points. For instance, in many of these studies, researchers know nothing about any given subject's weight-loss trajectory beyond the person's weight at just two different intervals (e.g., we might know that Mary-Sue was 180 pounds in 1990 and 150 pounds in 2000, but we would have no idea how long that weight loss was sustained).

But there has been one long-term, large-scale randomized controlled trial that has investigated how weight loss undertaken by fat people may affect longevity (as well as cardiovascular health). This is the "Look AHEAD" trial, which epidemiologists widely regard as the most rigorous longitudinal study to date examining how weight loss achieved through diet and exercise affects mortality and cardiovascular health.[38] A total of 5145 overweight or obese American adults who were, on average, in their late fifties and had type 2 diabetes were randomly assigned to either the intervention group, which was instructed to diet and exercise with the aim of losing and keeping off at least 7% of their initial body weight, or to the control group, which received diabetic support and education but was not prescribed weight loss.[39] Over the nearly ten-year period in which researchers tracked the two groups, the key question they set out to answer was whether those in the intervention group (i.e., the weight-loss group) would be less likely than those in the control group to die from cardiovascular causes or to experience non-fatal heart attacks or strokes (heart disease is the most common cause of death among diabetics).

Those in the intervention group lost and kept off more weight than those in the control group—by the end of the first year, on average, they had lost close to 9% of their starting body weight (compared to less than 1% for the control group). By the end of the study, members of the intervention group had, on average, lost and kept off 6% of their initial body weights compared to the control group, whose average sustained weight loss was 3.5%.[40] Yet, despite the greater weight loss achieved by those in the intervention group, those folks fared no better with respect to any of the major health outcomes that were measured. Specifically, their risk of suffering a heart attack, stroke, or cardiovascular-related death was not meaningfully lower than those in the control group. A different study drawing on data from the Look AHEAD trial investigated whether, 16 years from the outset of the study, individuals in the intervention group were less likely to die from any cause of death. No statistically significant difference in mortality rates between the two groups was found.[41]

So, as with the body of cohort studies on this matter, this study too provides no support for the supposition that fat people can expect to live longer by losing weight. Nor does it help support the hypothesis that sustained weight loss tends to improve the cardiovascular health of overweight or obese people. Indeed, no rigorous large-scale study to date has demonstrated that when fat people lose weight, they tend to experience meaningful long-term improvements in their health and longevity. We simply do not know whether the second assumption—that fat people would be much healthier if they became and stayed thin—is true.

4. WE DON'T KNOW HOW TO MAKE FAT PEOPLE THIN

A concern that might be raised about the Look AHEAD study is that it can't provide much insight into whether weight loss produces significant health benefits for overweight or obese individuals because those in the intervention group didn't lose all that much weight. As far as we can tell from the available data, very few, if any, individuals in the intervention group even came close to reaching and staying at a normal weight. For instance, a woman of 5'4" who initially weighed 210 pounds and had a BMI of 36, which was the average BMI among subjects, would have had to lose 31% of her body weight, some 65 pounds, to get down to a normal weight of 145 pounds. Yet, if she lost the average amount of weight for members of her cohort, that would have amounted to a weight loss of just 13 pounds and would have moved her from the moderately obese category to the high end of the mildly obese category. If the vast majority of individuals in the intervention group failed to reach a clinically healthy weight, then perhaps *that* explains why they didn't experience significant health improvements.

In light of this concern, to better assess whether fat people would enjoy major health benefits from weight loss, it would seem that what's needed is a large-scale study that, over the span of several years, compares one group of overweight and obese individuals who lose and keep off *all* of their excess weight by making the standard lifestyle changes with another cohort of otherwise similar overweight and obese individuals whose weight remains stable over that same period. But we shouldn't hold our breath for such a study to be conducted anytime soon. We have little reason to expect a large number of initially overweight and obese individuals to lose and keep off enough weight via lifestyle changes to be in the normal-weight category for years.

The foregoing reflections set the scene for this section's main aim. This is to investigate the third assumption of the mainstream public health approach to fatness: *We know what fat people need to do to become and stay thin, which is to eat less and move more.* I will argue that this assumption should be flatly rejected. In particular, I'll argue that we do not know what works *in the real world* to make most fat people thin. The fact of the matter is that for the great majority of fat people, we have no clue what life-style program they should embrace to have a realistic chance of becoming and staying thin. Indeed, in the field of obesity research, it has been well known for years now that only rarely do overweight and obese individuals who follow the standard diet and exercise advice manage to achieve the sought-after outcome of becoming and staying thin in the long run.

In recent years, one may have heard the claim that upwards of 95% of weight-loss attempts made by overweight and obese individuals are destined to fail. Some contemporary weight researchers have vigorously contested this claim. Two researchers who have done so are Rena Wing and James Hill, who teamed up in the 1990s to establish the "National Weight Control Registry," which is a database collecting information about thousands of people who have successfully lost and kept off large amounts of weight through behavioral changes. In a widely cited 2001 paper, these researchers dispute the notion that almost all weight-loss attempts fail, arguing that "the picture is much more optimistic, with perhaps greater than 20% of overweight/obese persons able to achieve success."[42] They base that estimate on a single, small study that found by phone survey of 500 adults randomly selected from the general population that just over 20% of the 228 overweight individuals polled had reported success in their weight-loss efforts.[43]

Now, we cannot draw general conclusions from a single, small study—especially from one that relies on self-reported data, which is notoriously unreliable. To get a better overall sense of how successful overweight and obese people's weight-loss attempts tend to be, we would need higher quality data that involves more people. Over the last 15 or so years, several scholars have engaged in rigorous attempts to investigate this matter. To begin with, a team of U.K.-based researchers set out to investigate the likelihood of obese individuals reaching a normal weight. They embarked on one of the largest longitudinal studies to date to track changes in body weight among the general population, following 176,000 obese adults for nine years during which time each participant's BMI was measured on at least three different occasions. Among their key findings, published in a 2015 paper, were that women who were mildly obese at the start of the study had a 1 in 124 chance of reaching a normal weight in any given year, while mildly obese men had only a 1 in 210 chance of achieving that same outcome.[44] For those at higher levels of obesity, the odds were worse still. For instance, women with an initial BMI of at least 40 had no better than a 1 in 608 chance in any given year of reaching a normal weight. To clarify: it was not the case that *all* of the obese subjects in this study were actually *trying* to lose weight. Even so, the study's findings do reveal just how exceedingly rare it seems to be for *any* obese adult to achieve that outcome.

If we turn to studies that focus only on the success rates of deliberate weight-loss attempts, people's odds of achieving and maintaining significant weight losses don't seem to be much better. A 2007 systematic review and meta-analysis of randomized controlled trials carried out over the decade prior looked at how much weight overweight or obese adults lost and kept off for at least one year.[45] Analyzing the findings of 80 studies tracking the weight losses of participants of diet and/or exercise weight-loss programs revealed that the *most successful* weight losses were achieved by individuals who embarked on very low-calorie diets. Those folks, on average, lost 16% of their initial body weight about six months into their diets. And three years from when they started their diets, they had sustained an average weight loss of about 5% of their starting weights. Two things are worth underscoring here. One, all the other groups who variously engaged in other types of diets, exercise alone, or some combination of dieting and exercise, lost and kept off less (and, in some cases, considerably less) weight than the group whose results I've just described. Second, to reach a normal weight, most obese individuals would need to lose more than 16% of their starting weights, which was the peak weight loss initially achieved (though not sustained) by those whose weight-loss efforts were, on average, the most successful.

A different 2007 paper that also systematically reviewed studies measuring dieters' weight-loss successes (and failures) provides further insight into people's ability to maintain weight losses over time.[46] The lead author of this paper, Traci Mann, is a psychologist at the University of Minnesota who has written extensively on health and dieting. In carrying out this review, she and her team were interested in studying the longer-term effects of dieting, and to this end they sought out studies that followed dieters for a minimum of two years from when they began a diet. They were able to find only seven randomized controlled trials that had been conducted since 1985 that tracked dieters' weight-loss outcomes for at least that long. Across those studies, which tracked subjects anywhere from two and a half to six years, broadly similar conclusions to those of the review just considered emerged concerning just how little weight dieters seem to keep off over time: the average weight loss that subjects had maintained at their final follow-ups with researchers was just 2.4 pounds.

But it's not just that this review found that most people don't lose much weight by dieting (though, plainly, that is so). As Mann's team explains, the overall body of scientific evidence on weight loss and dieting makes abundantly clear that after achieving an initial weight loss on a diet (as most dieters do), nearly all dieters go on to see some of the weight they lost creep back on. The more time that elapses after a person initially loses the weight, the more of that lost weight tends to be regained.[47] Indeed, study after study reveals the strikingly similar trajectory of most overweight and obese people's weight-loss attempts through behavioral modifications. In the first six or so months of trying to slim down, the greatest amount of weight is lost. Around this point, most people hit a plateau: despite their continued efforts to shed more pounds, the scale just won't budge. Then, for most, the regain period begins. How much of the lost weight eventually returns and how fast regain happens varies from person to person, but nearly everyone who loses much weight (usually any more than 5% of their starting weight) through behavioral modifications gains quite a bit of it back in the months and years that follow.

Let's return to the relatively optimistic projection of weight-loss efforts made by the researchers who started the National Weight Control Registry: that at least 20% of overweight and obese individuals' weight-loss efforts might be expected to succeed in the long term. We may wonder what accounts for the relatively high success rate (which, notice, still tells us that some 80% of weight-loss attempts fail!) in the study that they cite when many dozens of other studies over decades suggest that exceedingly few people sustain a significant weight loss over time. The answer comes down to how Wing and Hill define "success." They propose that "successful long-term weight loss maintenance" entails a person "intentionally losing at least 10% of initial body weight and keeping it off for at least 1 year."[48]

The practice of studies tracking dieters' weight-loss outcomes for such a short timeframe as one year is not uncommon; rather, it seems to be the norm. Yet, given what we have considered above concerning the typical trajectory of weight-loss attempts, defining success as Wing and Hill (and many others) do is problematic. It sets the bar low. It deems people's weight losses successful at a point that tends to be followed by weight regain for just about everybody who loses much weight at all. In assessing the success of people's weight-loss efforts, we should be concerned fundamentally with how well people do in losing and keeping off weight *in the long run*. And on this count, we haven't yet identified a safe, practical method that would enable most fat people to lose and keep off substantial amounts of weight in the long term. Certainly, most people who try to slim down by following the standardly prescribed lifestyle changes don't succeed in the long term in achieving anything more than a very modest weight loss at best.

My claim that we don't know how to make most fat people thin will strike some readers as preposterous. Of course we do, one might protest, returning to the original refrain: *Eat less, move more*. It's that simple. In response, let me clarify my claim. Granted, for the majority of overweight or obese individuals, it is, strictly speaking, possible for them to reach and maintain a normal weight by making changes to their dietary and exercise habits.[49] Indeed, if almost any fat person were confined to a laboratory setting and forced to abide by a restricted low-calorie diet for months without any opportunities for straying from it, one would almost certainly lose weight and keep that weight off while being made to stick to that regimen. Based on this thought experiment, it can be easy enough to suppose that achieving that same result—making a fat person become and stay thin—outside of a draconian lab setting just requires those with excess weight to get themselves to stick with those same diet and exercise habits that would enable them to achieve a normal weight in the lab.

There's just one problem with this way of seeing things: *In the real world*, it almost never works! For decades now, doctors and public health officials have continued to insist on and dispense this standard prescription of *eat less and move more*. Millions of fat people desperately try to slim down by following that advice. Yet weight-loss efforts aren't any more successful today than they were over half a century ago when the now reasonably well-known statistic of the greater-than-95% failure rate of weight-loss attempts first surfaced. That we have a pretty good idea of what would work in an experimental setting to make fat people thin is beside the point. What matters is that such knowledge has not translated into a workable *real-life* solution, one that can be expected to give many, if not most, fat people a meaningful shot of reaching and maintaining a normal weight.

So, the third assumption—that we know what fat people must do to become and stay thin, namely, eat less and move more—is false. For the overwhelming majority, that prescription doesn't work. If that is so, then the upshot of the previous section, that we don't really know whether making fat people thin would greatly improve their health, is somewhat moot: not only don't we know whether becoming thin would help them, we don't know how to make most fat people thin anyway. From the standpoint of public health promotion, we shouldn't dogmatically focus on the fact that most fat people could become thin if they were confined and monitored for months in a lab setting. Rather, we should focus on what is known about feasible strategies that would actually be health promoting in the real world. And, clearly, in the real world, instructing fat people to eat less and move more just doesn't work in helping most of them become and stay thin.

5. SHOULD FAT PEOPLE EXPECT TO GREATLY IMPROVE THEIR HEALTH BY *TRYING TO* BECOME THIN?

Let us turn to the fourth and final assumption: *Getting fat people to try harder to be thin by making those commonsense lifestyle changes (eating less and moving more) will produce significant public health benefits.* I'll start by explaining why it might seem beneficial to advise fat people to strive to be thin by eating less and moving more in spite of the problems raised in the previous sections. Then I will show that the opposite is closer to the truth.

Even if most fat people won't succeed in losing all (or even much) of their excess weight, it's frequently thought that anyone who is fat should still try to reach a normal weight via lifestyle changes. This is based on the supposition that their health would be improved by such an effort. As we saw in section 2, improving diet and fitness can yield impressive health benefits for people independently of weight loss. Also, there is a good deal of evidence pointing to wide-ranging health benefits associated with modest weight reduction, of just 5–10% of one's starting weight, for those who weigh too much. For instance, although the major conclusion of the Look AHEAD trial was that weight loss for fat individuals didn't reduce the risk of major cardiovascular events or lower mortality from cardiovascular causes, further studies drawing on that data set found weight loss to be linked to a number of other health improvements including lower incidence of sleep apnea, severe chronic kidney disease, knee pain, and mobility-related disability.[50]

Perhaps the most impressive benefits of modest weight loss, though, are those concerning diabetes prevention. A 2006 study conducted by the Diabetes Prevention Program Research Group—a well-regarded randomized controlled trial with over a thousand subjects with an average initial BMI of about 34—found that for every 2.2 pounds that a person lost, their risk of developing diabetes decreased by 16%.[51] Although nearly everyone struggles mightily to maintain significant weight losses over time—as the previous section showed—sustaining a modest weight loss in the long term appears to be feasible for many overweight and obese individuals. So, even if most fat people's weight-loss efforts won't make them thin, those efforts may still do them good both by prompting the adoption of healthier habits and by producing modest weight loss.

Initially, then, it might seem that for most fat people, working hard to become thin would be a health-promoting strategy. However, initial appearances can be deceiving. One problem is that for many fat people, trying to become thin can be at odds with adopting and sticking with health-promoting behaviors in the long term. Consider an example. If you're not fat, suppose that you are. You are constantly bombarded with the message that you need to lose a lot of weight if you wish to escape all manner of life-threatening medical conditions. This scares you into action. You commit yourself to the goal of achieving a clinically healthy weight, and in service of that goal, you make lifestyle changes: increasing your consumption of fruits and vegetables, cutting back on soda and fast food, and exercising more regularly. Over the following year, despite assiduously adhering to this diet and fitness regime, your weight loss comes to a sudden halt after just a few months. All told, at the end of the year, you lose and keep off 15 pounds, falling far short of the 50 pounds that you set out to lose so that you would reach a normal weight.

Based on what we know, you have almost certainly improved your health in meaningful ways by making those lifestyle changes and by modestly reducing your weight. But you likely don't feel that your efforts have been a success. Indeed, since you adopted those lifestyle changes as a means of helping you reach a normal weight (rather than as a means of directly improving your health, regardless of how doing so affected your weight), it would be quite natural for you to feel disappointed at that one-year mark. That's because whatever health improvements your efforts produced, you are still fat. And your sense of personal failure is confirmed by how others perceive you. Based on how your body looks, others around you—including, most likely, your own doctor—regard you as still having a whole lot more weight to lose before you'll be healthy. Having not even come close to your goal weight, your weight-loss efforts may strike you as futile. As a result, you might abandon the habits you'd embraced over the past year. That would seem a perfectly understandable reaction. Why stick with them? After all, despite those habits actually being health promoting, they haven't helped you get close to attaining your goal (and the one that society emphasizes as crucial for your health): to stop being fat.

It's not just that weight-loss efforts made in pursuit of thinness might *discourage* healthy behaviors. Even worse, they might *encourage* unhealthy behaviors. We know that some fat individuals who desperately want to be thin resort to patently unhealthy means to help them achieve that goal. A variety of unhealthy strategies purport to facilitate more dramatic weight loss than safer, healthier methods often do. For example, to control their weight, many people take up smoking; abuse diet pills, illegal drugs such as cocaine or amphetamines, or laxatives; regularly vomit after meals; or, for months, follow dangerously low-calorie, nutritionally deficient diets, sometimes doing so while exercising for hours a day. Disturbingly, it is not unusual to hear of people losing huge amounts of weight by following such bizarre but popular fad diets as the "cookie diet" (on which a person eats nothing but cookies, sometimes supplemented by a single daily meal of lean protein and vegetables, until reaching one's desired weight). In recent years, popular diet pills used to trigger rapid weight loss have been linked to fatalities, and the use of many diet pills increases the risk of suffering a heart attack, stroke, or psychotic episode.[52] On this basis, then, it is a mistake to suppose that weight-loss efforts and healthy habits always, or even generally, go hand in hand.

It is also a mistake to suppose that by trying to lose a substantial amount of weight, a person thereby improves her chances of achieving and sustaining at least a modest weight loss. In fact, people pursuing the goal of substantial weight loss may be *less* likely, not *more* likely, to achieve and sustain a modest weight loss. Part of the reason for this has to do with how people's weight-loss expectations seem to affect their success in reducing their weight. One study that tracked several hundred obese women enrolled in weight-loss programs found that individuals who had more ambitious weight-loss expectations at the outset were more likely to prematurely quit their weight-loss programs once underway.[53] Most likely, that happens because losing much less weight than one sets out to, despite trying very hard, can leave a person feeling frustrated and defeated, which, in turn, can lead one to abandon the project wholesale.

Worse yet, it appears that many people who try to lose weight end up *heavier* in the long run, when compared to people who start out at similar weights but don't attempt to lose weight. On this matter, we can return to the review of dieting and weight loss studies by Traci Mann and co-authors discussed in the previous section. Those researchers examined ten observational studies (in which subjects are observed without any interventions made by researchers) that compared the weight trajectories of dieters and non-dieters over the span of a few years. In seven of them, the dieters ended up heavier than they were before dieting, and, in general, the dieters gained more weight over time than the non-dieters did. Pooling together data from eight observational studies that followed dieters for several years (but didn't also track a comparable group of non-dieters as the just-described set of studies did), the researchers found that, on average, 41% of dieters weighed *more* four to five years after dieting than they had before starting their diets.[54] What is more, it's suspected that these studies *underestimate* the tendency for dieting to make people heavier in the long term. That is because they only include data about the weight-loss trajectories of those study participants who follow up with researchers, and it's likely that the numerous participants in these studies who don't follow up with researchers have been less successful in maintaining their weight losses than the ones who do.[55]

As we have seen, the tendency for weight gain to follow deliberately undertaken weight loss is exceedingly common. In the scientific literature, this ubiquitous phenomenon is called "weight cycling." Numerous large-scale observational studies have found weight cycling to be associated with a variety of negative health consequences including higher mortality and an increased risk of cardiovascular disease.[56] Whether weight cycling causes poor health outcomes, however, has not been established.[57] Still, these findings might provide at least a weak reason for being cautious about weight-loss attempts.

So, the fourth assumption of the dominant public health approach to weight—that getting fat people to try harder to be thin via the standardly prescribed lifestyle changes will produce significant public health benefits—should be rejected. For a sizable majority of fat people, following the standard advice is likely to harm them. Pursuing thinness can disincentivize long-term adherence to healthy lifestyle behaviors and can make people less likely to maintain beneficial modest weight losses. Pursuing thinness can incentivize unhealthy weight-control behaviors, such as crash-dieting or using dangerous diet pills. Pursuing thinness seems to, perversely, make people heavier in the long term, and the weight cycling that nearly always accompanies deliberate weight-loss attempts might have adverse health effects.

6. WHAT ABOUT WEIGHT-LOSS SURGERY OR DRUGS?

At present, drugs and bariatric surgery are the only weight-loss methods that reliably produce sustained, substantial weight loss in many people. Let's consider what is known about each, starting with bariatric surgery. I'll focus on the two most popular types of bariatric surgery, gastric bypass and sleeve gastrectomy.[58] In the U.S., bariatric surgery typically costs between $15,000 to $35,000, with most health insurance companies only covering these procedures for patients who either have a BMI over 40 or have a BMI over 35 and an obesity-related medical condition. Even with insurance coverage, bariatric patients frequently shoulder some out-of-pocket costs and may require time off work to recover post-surgery. As such, many people who might want to undergo the surgery won't be able to afford it.

No other weight-loss method produces the substantial long-term weight losses experienced by the average bariatric patient. Following surgery, weight loss peaks in the first two years, and patients typically lose 20 to 30% of their starting weight. One large-scale study found that among patients with an initial BMI over 35, a significant majority who had gastric bypass surgery—over 70%—maintained a weight loss of at least 20% a decade after the surgery.[59] Still, it's rare for bariatric patients to reach a normal weight. And one study found that about one in five bariatric patients do not achieve a clinically significant weight loss, which is defined as losing at least 50% of one's excess weight in the year following the surgery.[60] Compared to otherwise similar obese individuals who don't undergo the surgery, numerous studies indicate that bariatric patients experience meaningful health improvements. These include higher life expectancy (with some studies finding that severely obese, middle-aged individuals who have the surgery, on average, live around three years longer than those who don't, and other studies finding life expectancy gains of over six years for that demographic) and a lower risk of cardiovascular disease, type 2 diabetes, and cancer.[61]

Although bariatric surgery has become safer in recent years, it still carries a very small risk of major complications in its immediate aftermath. These complications include heart attack, blood clot, and, in fewer than 1% of cases, death.[62] Post-surgery, patients must abide by stringent dietary constraints— such as adhering to a very low-calorie diet, only eating small portions at a time, and avoiding certain types of foods—for the rest of their lives. Not surprisingly, a number of studies find that this proves a challenge for most bariatric patients.[63] Due to the drastic ways the surgery changes the digestive system, long-term nutritional deficiencies are a common side effect. One-third to one-half of bariatric patients have anemia two years after the surgery, and all who undergo the surgery are at significantly heightened risk of suffering a fracture due to reduced bone mineral density.[64] The long-term effects of bariatric surgery beyond ten years aren't well known.

Until fairly recently, there weren't any safe prescription weight-loss drugs that produced particularly impressive, sustained weight losses for the average user. That has changed with the latest class of weight-loss drugs to hit the market. This class includes Wegovy, which is specifically marketed for weight loss, and Ozempic, which is approved for diabetes but is currently being prescribed off-label for weight loss. These drugs, which have the active ingredient "semaglutide," help people lose weight by dramatically reducing their appetite. In a randomized controlled study of nearly 2000 overweight or obese subjects (with an average initial BMI of 38), taking a weekly dose of semaglutide over 68 weeks produced an average weight loss of just under 15%, with nearly one in three individuals taking semaglutide sustaining a weight loss of at least 20%.[65] Another high-quality study suggests that weight loss on semaglutide peaks at around the 1.5-year mark and that continued weekly use of the drug enables maintenance of a 15% weight loss, on average, at the two-year mark.[66] Once people stop taking semaglutide, they typically regain much of the weight they lost while on it.[67] Over a two-year period, compared to subjects taking a placebo, subjects on semaglutide experienced improvements across a range of cardiometabolic risk factors: they had lower blood pressure, lower cholesterol and triglycerides, decreased systemic inflammation, and improved blood sugar control.[68]

Still, these drugs aren't for everyone. It's not uncommon for patients taking semaglutide to experience gastrointestinal side effects such as nausea, vomiting, and diarrhea, side effects that in some cases are severe.[69] Relatively little is known at present about the drugs' safety and efficacy beyond two years (though that is not unusual for new pharmaceuticals). To be eligible for a Wegovy prescription in the U.S., a patient must either have a BMI above 30 or a BMI of at least 27 and a weight-related medical condition. Currently, obtaining full or even partial coverage of Wegovy from health insurance companies is proving a challenge even for many who meet those eligibility criteria. And with a price tag of around $1300 for a monthly supply, Wegovy is prohibitively expensive for many who are eager to take it (similar drugs such as Ozempic and Mounjaro are pricey too, retailing for around $900 per month). At these prices, maintaining a significant weight loss over time with the help of these drugs would require paying around $10,000 a year for the rest of one's life.

Quite unlike the standard prescription of *eat less and move more*, weight-loss surgery and drugs do seem to help many people lose a good deal of weight and become healthier. However, that's not to say that all, or even most, who use these methods will lose much weight or enjoy substantial long-term health benefits. Indeed, it is worth underscoring that many fat people who lose weight via surgery or drugs are unlikely to reach a normal weight. And, at present, neither option is effectively within the reach of many fat people. Still, if surgery and drugs offer a viable means for some fat individuals to lose weight and become much healthier, then a shift in mainstream discourse on weight might be called for. Perhaps, instead of dispensing the ineffective, harmful advice to fat people that they try to be thin via lifestyle changes, we should devote greater resources to making these alternative weight-loss methods safer, more effective, and meaningfully accessible to those who make an informed decision to use them. This isn't to suggest that, all things considered, we should embrace a public health paradigm that prescribes weight-loss surgery or drugs to fat people across the board. Among other things, how promoting those weight-loss methods might reinforce or worsen fat stigma requires examination. We'll return to this issue in chapter 8.

7. CONCLUSION

Based on the best available evidence, there is a massive gulf between, on the one hand, what would seem to promote people's health in relation to obesity-related concerns, and, on the other hand, what most in our society believe would do so. If you ask the average person, most would scoff at the idea that a fat person who eats a nutritious diet, is physically active, and has modestly reduced her weight could be healthy. And it is widely believed that significant weight loss is feasible for most to achieve through relatively easy behavioral changes. These aren't just views held by the typical layperson but are also widely held by medical practitioners. Doctors and nurses frequently admonish obese patients for not losing enough weight, and they downplay the value of beneficial lifestyle changes for patients for whom they fail to produce substantial weight loss. *Being fat is the problem*, indeed, is the key message propagated by public health agencies, the mainstream media, and the multibillion-dollar weight-loss industry.

The real public health challenge that we face as concerns high rates of overweight and obesity isn't about figuring out how to get fat individuals to eat less and move more so that they become thin. Rather, the real challenge is working out how to redirect attention and resources to public health matters that we are positioned to meaningfully address. And a key part of doing that involves figuring out how to counter the mistaken and dangerous anti-fat narratives that have long dominated public discourse about weight, the persistence of which continues to do untold damage to the health and well-being of millions of people.

Part II

Fat-blaming

4

1. INTRODUCTION

Thus far, our focus has been on arguments for expressing opposition to fatness (and, by extension, to fat people) that are grounded in forward-looking considerations: considerations concerning the good that might be produced by taking that stance. In this chapter, we turn to arguments for that same conclusion that are grounded in backward-looking considerations: considerations concerning the idea that fat people are blameworthy for what they have done (or not done) in connection to their being fat. According to those arguments, responding negatively to fat individuals isn't about trying to bring about some positive outcome, such as improving their health. Rather, it is thought that fat people are blameworthy and that they deserve to be socially sanctioned because others have a legitimate moral complaint against them for being fat.

Many in our society blame fat people for being fat. Let's think about what this means.[1] Blaming has two components. First, when I blame someone for something, I make a moral judgment. If I blame you, I judge you to have committed a moral offense. Second, blaming involves a negative reaction on the part of the person doing the blaming that is directed toward the person being blamed. Specifically, it

DOI: 10.4324/9780367853389-6

involves a reaction that, as the philosopher Angela Smith puts it, "expresses protest" to a person for a perceived moral offense they have committed.[2] Blaming is a means of holding a blameworthy party to account, by drawing attention to and registering disapproval for what they have done.

Consider some of the harsh ways that fat people are treated. And we should make no mistake: their treatment is harsh. It is often conveyed to fat people that others regard them with disdain, scorn, and resentment. They are shamed, taunted, harassed, ridiculed, humiliated, and bullied. Strangers gawk at them or shake their heads with disapproval, or even disgust. In public areas, fat people are frequently addressed rudely or ignored entirely. Blatant weight-based discrimination in the workforce is legally permissible and widely practiced. Further, our society seems to take little interest in accommodating very large bodies in social spaces. When fat people have trouble fitting into too-small areas, such as on airplanes, they are regularly met with unmasked contempt. Many think that this is just as it should be. As they see it, if fat people don't like how they are treated, well, that's too bad; it's their fault for being that way, and if they want things to be different then it's incumbent on them to stop being fat.

These harsh reactions might, in part, reflect a tough-love approach (that is, an approach on which some folks set out to make navigating social spaces utterly miserable for fat people for the ostensibly well-meaning purpose of nudging them to make healthier choices and to thereby become better off). However, in this chapter, I set aside that sort of forward-looking rationale for them, which we have already considered in previous chapters. Instead, my focus is on the backward-looking rationale that sometimes explains these harsh reactions: a rationale on which these reactions are understood as a means by which some individuals express to fat people their protest of them, communicating to them their strong disapproval of their being fat.

In what follows, the main question I seek to answer is whether fat-blaming—in some of the forms that it takes, or in some forms that it might take—can be justified. Answering this question, in turn, requires taking up two other queries.

1.1 Judging as blameworthy

The first query about whether blaming fat people is justified concerns whether fat people are, in fact, blameworthy. A person is blameworthy for something if, and only if: (a) she has done something morally wrong,[3] and (b) she is objectionably implicated in the wrongdoing at issue—that is, her acting wrongly reflects some morally objectionable aspect of what she's like as a person, such as a reprehensible motive or a character flaw, that is manifested in her wrongful act.

Suppose you learn that your grandmother's lawyer, Harris, is a con man who tricks his elderly clients into transferring their hard-won, paltry life savings to his offshore bank account. He is motivated by greed. Although he is financially well off, his affinity for luxury goods drives his quest to become wealthier still. He is well aware of the devastating consequences his actions have for his victims, but he doesn't care about that. This is a clear-cut case. Harris is blameworthy. It's easy to see how both conditions for establishing his blameworthiness are satisfied. For one thing, he acts wrongly in stealing from his clients. For another, Harris is objectionably implicated in that wrongdoing: his motives for so acting and his lack of concern for the suffering his actions cause others make him a despicable person.

For fat people to qualify as blameworthy for being fat, then, (a) they must be doing something morally wrong in connection to being fat, and (b) there must be some criticizable aspect of what they are like that is manifested in that wrongdoing. Are both those things true of fat people? That is what would have to be shown if fat people are, in fact, blameworthy for being fat.

Before proceeding, let me make some terminological points. So far, I've been speaking of fat people being blameworthy *for being fat*. But strictly speaking, on the just-presented account, a fat person wouldn't be blameworthy for being fat. Rather, a fat person would be blameworthy for some objectionable aspect of herself (an attitude, a character trait, a motive, etc.) that is manifested in some wrongful conduct she commits that is linked to her being fat. That way of putting it is a real mouthful. So, for ease of language, I'll often refer to fat people being blameworthy, or being blamed, "for being fat." I'll sometimes use the term "fat-blaming," or I'll just talk about blaming fat people. In all these cases, unless otherwise specified, these turns of phrase should be understood as referring to fat people being blameworthy for, or being blamed for, their being objectionably implicated in some moral wrongdoing that is connected to their being fat.

1.2 Expressing blame

This bring us to the second issue that must be investigated to determine whether, and if so how, blaming fat people would be justified. If we assume that fat people *are* blameworthy, then what sorts of outwardly expressed blaming reactions would be a fitting response to their transgressions? These two components of blaming—one's being blameworthy and others expressing blame toward them—are inextricably tied. What would qualify as a fitting blaming reaction in a particular case depends on the nature of the blameworthy party's wrongdoing, on the nature of how one is objectionably implicated in that wrongdoing, and perhaps on other factors as well (e.g., whether one has already personally reckoned with their wrongdoing or tried to make amends for it). So, for instance, we suppose that, all else equal, a murderer deserves much harsher condemnation than someone who commits petty theft. Similarly, when it comes to how we judge people for committing the same wrongful act—say, taking the life of an innocent person—we suppose that a much harsher penalty is fitting for an individual who commits first-degree murder (i.e., carefully planning to deliberately kill someone) than for an individual who commits involuntary manslaughter (i.e., killing someone without intending to do so).

1.3 Roadmap

I will argue that fat-blaming is nearly always unjustified. That is, I will argue that there is almost never a sound moral basis for blaming fat individuals in connection to their being fat. There are, however, popular narratives that would, if true, support the judgment that fat people are often blameworthy—narratives that can sound plausible and scientifically respectable but that, in reality, are neither. Indeed, those narratives cast fat people in such a negative light that it's little surprise that so many believe that they deserve to be treated in highly punitive ways.

Because these popular narratives that seek to explain why fat people are blameworthy hold such powerful sway, my strategy in arguing that fat-blaming is nearly always unjustified is to engage with them directly. As we have seen, the enterprise of blaming is complex and multifaceted. What is more, in the case of fat-blaming there are several distinct accusations advanced against fat people concerning why they are blameworthy. As such, it will take me some time to defend my conclusion that fat-blaming is unjustified. This chapter and the next two chapters are devoted to this task. Together, these chapters answer three questions that are crucial to assessing the case for fat-blaming:

(1) Are fat people doing anything morally wrong by being fat? If so, what?
(2) If fat people are doing something morally wrong by being fat, are they objectionably implicated in that wrongdoing?
(3) If it's blameworthy to be fat, then what sorts of blaming reactions toward fat people might be warranted?

Here's how we will proceed. In the next section, I take up Questions 1 and 2, considering just what it is that fat people are blamed for. There, I clarify the nature of the wrongdoing that they are accused of committing, and I discuss two popular views concerning why they are thought to be objectionably implicated in that wrongdoing. Following that, I consider proposed explanations of why it is wrong to be fat. I argue that none provides a sound basis for concluding that fat people, in general, are doing anything wrong by being fat. Chapter 4 argues, then, that Question 1 should be answered in the negative. In chapters 5 and 6, I take up Questions 2 and 3. I begin with Question 2: If we grant the mistaken assumption that it is generally wrong to be fat, are fat individuals objectionably implicated in that wrongdoing? I argue that, in general, they are not. Then, we turn to Question 3: If it's blameworthy to be fat (which may be true of some individuals), then what sorts of blaming reactions might be justifiably directed toward those individuals? In such cases, almost none of the blaming reactions that are typically directed at fat people would be justified. Overall, these three chapters argue that we shouldn't blame fat people.

2. WHAT ARE FAT PEOPLE BLAMED FOR?

What exactly about a person's being fat might make one blameworthy? To help answer this question, let's consider a few real-life illustrations of fat-blaming:

Case 1. Just before take-off aboard a flight, a woman is on the phone complaining loudly for several minutes about the indignity of occupying the middle seat between two fat passengers whom she derisively calls "pigs." She says, "I don't know how I'm going to do this for the next four hours … because they're squishing me." She continues, "I'm stuck, but at least they'll keep me warm." When some of this woman's fellow passengers rebuke her for making these mean-spirited remarks, she proceeds to inform them, "I eat salad, okay?"[4]

Case 2. Members of a group calling itself the Overweight Haters Ltd hand out cards to fat commuters on the London Tube to let them know precisely why their being fat is despicable. These cards feature large-print text that reads, "It's really not glandular, it's your gluttony. … Our organisation hates and resents fat people. We object to the enormous amount of food resources you consume while half the world starves. We disapprove of your wasting NHS [National Health Service] money to treat your selfish greed. ... And we do not understand why you fail to grasp that by eating less you will be better off, slimmer, happy and find a partner who is not a perverted chubby-lover, or even find a partner at all. We also object that the beatiful [sic] pig is used as an insult. You are not a pig. You are a fat, ugly human."[5]

Case 3. In an opinion piece, a journalist rails against a proposed government measure that would require food manufacturers to reduce portion sizes and lower the fat content of certain unhealthy foods: "It's greed that makes you fat. Not ignorance about the dangers of junk food. Like all normal-sized people, I have to work hard to stay trim. Everyone knows endless burgers and crisps, washed down with litres of fizzy drink, are bad for you. But fatties lack the willpower to stop eating. ... this initiative suggests the fatties waddling about our streets are the Government's fault—they're all victims, as though those giant sausage rolls automatically fly off the hot plate and into their open mouths. We don't need more laws to ram home the harsh truth about gluttony—just common sense and strength of character."[6]

Even by the standards of our fat-hating culture, the anti-fat animus on display in these examples may be extreme. Still, I take these examples to be instructive insofar as they reflect grievances about fat people that seem to be quite widely shared. These cases give us an idea of what the conduct that fat people are being blamed for might be. Specifically, they appear to be blamed for failing to make lifestyle changes that would enable them to avoid being fat. Being fat, it's usually thought, isn't something that just happens to a person but rather is a person's own doing. Indeed, it is frequently assumed that most people can, through their lifestyle choices, avoid becoming or remaining fat. This supposition is implicitly affirmed by the airline passenger who announces to others that she eats salad (read: "Fellow fat passengers, if you regularly opted for salad like I do, then you wouldn't be so large"). It also finds expression in the anti-fat diatribe of the Overweight Haters. They suggest that people might be off the hook for being fat were their fatness caused by glandular problems. But they further seem to outright deny that such medical causes, in fact, explain why anyone, or perhaps almost anyone, is fat. So, these reflections help us make some progress toward answering Question 1 ("Are fat people doing anything morally wrong by being fat? If so, what?"). The wrongful conduct that fat people—at least those who don't have medical conditions making it literally impossible for them to lose weight—are blamed for is a failure to do what it would take to avoid being fat.

Still, if that's the conduct that fat people are blamed for, we should further ask: What would make it wrong for a person to not do what it would take to avoid being fat? If it's wrong to avoidably be fat, that would mean I have a moral obligation—that I owe it to others—to not be fat. The fat-blaming cases above suggest that disapproval of fat people is sometimes grounded in considerations that don't have anything to do with morality. For instance, the airline passenger in Case 1 apparently finds fat people repulsive—to her, they're "pigs," and she seems distressed by the prospect of their flesh touching her. In Case 2, the Overweight Haters' condemnation of fat people is, in part, grounded in their finding fat people "ugly" and in the reasoning that fat people would be "better off," "happier," and enjoy more promising romantic prospects were they to stop being fat. These considerations don't help ground a legitimate *moral* complaint about people's fatness. We don't owe it to others to conform to conventional standards of beauty or sexual attractiveness; and even if true that a fat person's life would go better for her were she to lose weight, that would give her a *prudential*, not a *moral*, reason to avoid being fat.

Perhaps a more promising basis for thinking that individuals have a moral obligation to watch their weight is gestured at by the Overweight Haters in their admonishment of fat people for using up valuable public healthcare resources that they wouldn't require if they weren't fat. Their reasoning seems to be that, by weighing too much, fat people wrongfully harm others—specifically, their fellow taxpayers. Parallel reasoning might underlie the airline passenger's complaint: she feels wrongfully harmed by those fat passengers who, as she sees it, encroach on *her* space and thereby make her less comfortable. In the next section, we'll turn to a more sophisticated formulation of this view that fat people wrongfully harm others.

But for now, let's turn to *Question 2*, which concerns the second dimension of blameworthiness. Assuming for the sake of argument that fat people are doing something wrong by being fat, do we have any good reason for further supposing that they are objectionably implicated in that wrongdoing? Fat-blamers (i.e., those who blame fat people for being fat) suppose that most fat individuals' failure to avoid being fat reflects some deficiency that can be meaningfully attributed to them. Put otherwise, fat-blamers criticize fat individuals for some morally objectionable aspect of what they are like that is taken to be manifested in their failure to slim down. The wrongdoing of being fat is supposed by fat-blamers to be *on* fat individuals, so to speak: that criticizable conduct is taken to flow from their *agency* in the right sort of way to make it meaningfully attributable to them. Recall the Harris case. In that case, our judgment of the lawyer as blameworthy for the wrongful act of ripping off his elderly clients was explained, in part, by that act stemming from his agency: his committing that act freely, with full awareness of the relevant consequences of the act, and the act reflecting his motive of greed and his lack of concern for his victims' well-being. But not all wrongful acts can be explained in this way.

Consider the case of Jones, who is also a lawyer who diverts into his personal bank account a large amount of money belonging to his vulnerable, elderly clients, money that he's been entrusted with investing for them. Jones, however, does this unknowingly, due to a few mistaken keystrokes in the course of making some online financial transactions. Suppose this mishap wasn't owing to carelessness on Jones's part—rather, it was an error he couldn't have reasonably anticipated. How should we judge Jones for taking his clients' money without their consent? In general, this is a wrongful act: people ought not behave this way (namely, taking others' money without their consent). Jones is causally responsible for carrying out this wrongful act and for the outcome it produces. And upon discovering what he's done, it is surely on him to rectify the matter. However, he isn't blameworthy for taking the money. That's because his act causing this wrongful harm isn't the product of his agency, not in any meaningful sense: he acted unwittingly (without knowledge of what he was doing and without intending to harm anyone), and he didn't show a lack of care for others; it was just dumb luck that his action caused such great harm, and it's an error that anyone could've made. As such, Jones is not objectionably implicated in the wrongdoing he commits.

In this respect, Jones crucially differs from Harris, whom we aptly judge a villain for acting with malicious intent in deliberately plotting to steal from his clients.

The Jones case illustrates how acting wrongly and being objectionably implicated in acting wrongly can come apart. It's worth elaborating on each of the two distinct moral evaluations involved in assessing a person's blameworthiness for an action. Let's begin with the first, which concerns whether someone has done something wrong. Here we are assessing the moral status of a type of action (such as stealing) from the perspective of those who stand to be negatively affected by it. In the case of stealing, based on the harm that stealing can cause to its victims, we conclude that, in general, it's wrong to steal. Importantly, in judging the moral status of types of actions (based on what might make them wrongful from the standpoint of affected parties), we are not considering the particularities of any given individual who might commit such acts. The second evaluation—which concerns whether someone is objectionably implicated in a wrongful act—does attend to those particularities: it calls for consideration of various aspects of a person (such as her motives, knowledge, values, etc.) that connect her to a wrongful act that she commits. So, whereas the first evaluation is general (in the sense that it concerns the types of actions that individuals are, in general, obligated to refrain from performing), the second evaluation is specific (in the sense that it concerns aspects of a particular person and their circumstances that relate to why they acted as they did). Engaging in these two distinct forms of moral evaluation, we conclude that Jones performed an act of "innocent wrongdoing"—that is, he acted wrongly without being blameworthy for so acting.

Let's return to the question of how fat individuals are related to the wrongful conduct of failing to do what it would take for them to avoid being fat (assuming, for the sake of argument, that this conduct is wrongful). Is a fat person who could avoid being fat like Harris, who knowingly and freely elects to do wrong by others? Perhaps, like Harris, a fat person's wrongful conduct reveals to us something objectionable about the sort of person that she is—a deficiency in her values, her character, her motives, her concerns, or the like. Alternatively, is a fat person who could avoid being fat like Jones, who isn't objectionably implicated in the wrongdoing that he commits? Perhaps, like Jones, a person's being fat doesn't reflect anything meaningful about what one is like that would make one blameworthy for the supposedly wrongful conduct at issue.

If we consider fat-blaming as it occurs in the three cases above, it is clear that fat-blamers take fat people to be actively, objectionably implicated in their being fat—making them more like Harris than Jones. In the popular imagination, there seem to be two main explanations for why fat people fail to make "better" lifestyle choices and for why they are thus blameworthy for that failure. First, fat people are sometimes accused of being weak-willed. So, for instance, in *Case 3*, we are told that "fatties lack the willpower to stop eating," and they need "strength of character" of the sort exhibited by thin people who "work hard to stay trim." Second, it is sometimes supposed that people are fat owing to their "gluttony" or "greed" (as is asserted in *Cases* 2 and 3). On this charge, it's assumed that fat people could easily enough slim down, they know they should, and they know how to do so, but, it's thought, they don't take such steps because they wholeheartedly embrace their excessively indulgent lifestyles that make them fat. Fat people who behave in this way are criticized for having bad values: by selfishly affirming their hedonistic ways, they fail to accord due weight to the moral imperative of fat avoidance.

So, there are at least a couple of different ways that a person might be objectionably implicated in connection to being fat: through weakness of will or through bad values. These aren't competing accusations. Some fat people may be weak-willed, and some others may have bad values. Those who blame fat people tend to assume that most fat people are objectionably implicated in being fat in at least one of these ways.[7]

3. WHY MIGHT IT BE WRONG TO BE FAT?

Let us now return to the matter of why it might be wrong to be fat (for those who can avoid being fat). The suggestion raised in the previous section was that it might be wrong to be fat because being that way *does harm to others*. In a 2012 online opinion piece, "Weigh More, Pay More," the well-known moral philosopher and public intellectual Peter Singer argues along these lines. He writes: "Is a person's weight his or her own business? Should we simply become more accepting of diverse body shapes? I don't think so. Obesity is an ethical issue, because an increase in weight by some imposes costs on others."[8]

Singer discusses several costs that he takes fat individuals to impose on others. His main example concerns airlines having to spend considerably more in transporting heavier passengers because doing so requires burning more jet fuel. That problem generalizes, he explains: "When people get larger and heavier, fewer of them fit onto a bus or train, which increases the costs of public transport." It can also be expensive to accommodate fat people when doing so calls for reconfiguring various physical spaces, furniture, equipment, and much else. For instance, to attend to much larger patients, Singer observes that hospitals "now must order stronger beds and operating tables" and "build extra-large toilets." Then, there are the costs of treating obesity-linked medical conditions (e.g., diabetes, cardiovascular disease, and joint problems). He cites a statistic revealing how staggeringly high the cost of treating such conditions is, noting that each year, "in the United States and Canada, overweight or obese people accounted for $127 billion in additional health-care expenditure." To make matters even worse, Singer laments, fat people contribute much less to the economy than thin people do. The just-mentioned study on healthcare costs, Singer notes, also found that each year in the United States and Canada, "the costs of lost productivity, both among those still working and among those unable to work at all because of obesity, totaled $115 billion." Finally, Singer explains how being fat is bad for the planet too: "An increase in the use of jet fuel is not just a matter of financial cost; it also implies an environmental cost, as higher greenhouse-gas emissions exacerbate global warming."

Singer is far from alone in drawing attention to various social costs of obesity. Quantifying such costs appears to be of growing interest to researchers, and in the last few decades numerous studies have been published on this matter. One recent study attempts to quantify just how bad obesity is for the planet, concluding that 1.6% of all human-produced global emissions may be due to obesity, with the world's adult obese population—about 609 million individuals—collectively emitting an extra 700 megatons of carbon each year ("extra" meaning above and beyond what they would emit if they were of a normal weight).[9] The study's authors discuss three main mechanisms by which they take obese individuals to disproportionately contribute to global warming. First, in addition to echoing the aforementioned point that transporting heavier passengers requires greater fossil fuel use, the researchers also assume that obese people emit more than others because they are more likely to drive rather than to walk short distances. Second, these researchers explain that heavier people use more oxygen to perform basic bodily functions, and that, in turn, is linked to expelling more carbon dioxide into the atmosphere. Third, it is assumed that obese individuals eat 30% more food than normal-weight individuals, and so they contribute more to the emissions-heavy food production sector than thin people do. Based on these assumptions, the study's authors estimate the carbon footprint of obese individuals to be about 20% greater, on average, than that of normal-weight individuals. Frequently, empirical findings of this sort are picked up by the main-stream media and framed in moralized terms, reiterating the popular notion that obese people make things worse for others. The study just discussed was widely cited by global news outlets, with one typical article in *The Times* opening thusly: "If you can't stay slim for yourself, maybe you should lose weight for the planet."[10]

Let's pause to clarify the moral complaint about obesity that is raised by Singer and others. The complaint is that fat people, in virtue of their size, generate potentially significant costs that others are made to bear. Usually, when industry expenses increase (as when rising obesity rates cost airlines or hospitals), that translates into higher prices for consumers across the board. That means that thin people, who don't contribute to the added costs, must pay more for plane and train tickets, healthcare, and so on. However, that some people generate higher costs that are passed on to others doesn't fully capture the moral complaint. We can notice that other cases in which individuals generate added costs that are, in part, imposed on others, don't invoke a parallel moral complaint. For instance, we don't tend to react similarly to having to share in the higher healthcare costs of treating a child with leukemia or to those incurred by a restaurant that must build a wheelchair ramp to accommodate disabled customers. The moral complaint Singer and others raise about fat people is predicated on the claim that, unlike the child with leukemia or the person born with a disability, most fat people can avoid being fat and thus can avoid generating higher costs. Specifically, it's thought that most fat people can avoid being fat by making better lifestyle choices—choices that they can be reasonably expected to make. And so, it seems unfair that people who aren't fat be made to bear the costs produced by fat people's failure to take reasonable steps to avoid being fat.

To be clear, Singer isn't interested in the backward-looking endeavor of criticizing fat people for their past wrongdoing. He doesn't support penalizing fat people on the grounds that they deserve to be punished or because doing so would fittingly express social disapproval toward them. For Singer, as a consequentialist, the proper moral response to the matter of fat individuals harming others in virtue of their weight is to be guided by, and only by, forward-looking considerations about how we might make things better for everyone. With that aim in mind, he calls for measures that would make people bear higher costs for becoming or remaining fat, such as taxing "foods that are disproportionately implicated in obesity" and charging heavier people more to fly.

One purpose of such measures, Singer explains, would be to deter people from becoming fat (and thus from producing the harms at issue). However, based on the empirical evidence we considered in chapters 2 and 3, it is questionable whether the proposed financial penalties would help reduce obesity rates by much, if at all. A second purpose of these measures that Singer discusses would be to make fat people (and consumers of certain unhealthy foods) personally bear a greater share of the social costs of obesity rather than passing those costs on to others. But by the lights of Singer's consequentialist framework, it is not obvious why doing that would make things better. That is, we might wonder why it would be morally preferable for those extra costs to be borne by fat people, rather than by those best positioned to bear added financial costs (such as society's richest). In any case, the focus of this chapter is on whether it might be wrong for fat people to be fat based on backward-looking moral considerations. And no doubt, for proponents of some non-consequentialist moral frameworks (such as one that values fairness), it might seem a good thing to make folks who avoidably generate added costs of this sort to personally bear them. As such, I wish to explore whether Singer's analysis of how fat individuals harm others might help ground a legitimate moral complaint about people avoidably being fat, one that could explain why it is wrong to be fat.

4. FAT PEOPLE DON'T IMPOSE WRONGFUL ECONOMIC HARMS ON OTHERS

Do the above considerations appealed to by Singer (and others) provide us with a sound moral basis for taking issue with people for being fat? I will argue that they do not. In this section, I focus on the charge that fat people impose wrongful economic harms on others—in particular, based on their higher healthcare expenses and their lower productivity. The next section takes up the charge that they wrongfully harm the environment.

To begin with, we should notice that this case for why it's wrong to be fat relies on a number of broad generalizations and stereotypes about what is implied by someone's being fat. For one thing, as concerns the charge that fat people generate added healthcare costs, being fat is not a reliable indicator of poor health. As we saw in chapter 3, the relationship between a person's BMI and health status is not straightforward. A number of variables—such as whether a person's higher BMI is due to greater muscle mass or to excess fat, where on one's body one carries excess fat, and one's level of aerobic fitness—might significantly affect whether, and to what extent, being fat adversely affects a person's health. Also, certain healthy habits, such as eating a nutritious diet and regularly exercising, may be better predictors of a person's health status than weight, especially as pertains to one's risk for obesity-related diseases. What is more, being fat doesn't make someone a less productive employee. So, the claim that fat people generate added economic costs by being fat, at best, might provide a basis for taking issue with *some* fat people but certainly not all or even most.

The empirical basis for this charge against fat people is questionable in other ways too. Initially, the claim that obese people have higher healthcare expenses seems plausible. Numerous studies carried out over several decades confirm that obese individuals, on average, have higher annual healthcare expenditures than normal-weight individuals (such studies are wide-ranging in their estimates of how much higher, with some as low as $732 and others as high as $3508).[11] Available evidence also furnishes a plausible basis for *why* obese people's annual healthcare expenses tend to be higher: people who are obese are more likely than those who aren't to have chronic diseases, to be hospitalized, and to have ongoing pharmaceutical drug needs.[12]

However, if we consider estimates of the average healthcare resources that people use over the course of their lifetimes rather than on an annual basis, then it's less clear that obese people cost more than others. Indeed, one widely cited study suggests just the opposite: namely, that over a lifetime, obese individuals use *fewer* healthcare resources than non-obese individuals. This study's authors arrive at that conclusion based on projections of the diseases (and associated healthcare expenses) that obese individuals would likely have if they weren't obese and thus lived somewhat longer.[13]

I do not claim that the empirical issue of whether obese people use more healthcare resources than they would if they weren't obese has been decisively settled.[14] I merely wish to show that the widely touted claim that they do cost society more in this way isn't nearly as well substantiated as we might expect it to be. For the sake of argument, though, let's suppose in what follows that Singer's factual suppositions about the costs obese people generate check out, i.e., that it's true that obese people cost society more than others based on their higher healthcare expenses and lower productivity. As the bioethicist Christopher Mayes argues, even if that were so, we wouldn't necessarily be warranted in accusing obese people of costing society more, all things considered. That's because if we're engaged in the exercise of quantifying a person's net costs to society, a question arises of just how we should carry out that assessment. Depending on how we calculate different people's net costs to society, it might be that society gains overall from many of its members being obese. Citing a recent estimate of the weight-loss industry's worth at $139.5 billion, Mayes suggests that the sorts of obesity-related costs discussed by Singer might well be "neutralized by the gains of industries associated with causing or curing obesity."[15]

The point here, as before, is not to suggest that we can definitively conclude based on these further facts that obese individuals don't impose a net economic burden on society. Rather, it is to demonstrate that settling that issue isn't so easy to do. It would require addressing the conceptual matter of just how we should go about measuring an individual's net impact on society, and that is a matter that tends to be ignored by those who raise this complaint about obese people.

But even if upon resolving that conceptual matter we find that we have good reason to conclude that fat people impose a net financial burden on society, it wouldn't follow that it would be wrong for fat people to impose the relevant costs on others. Up until now we have been assuming that individuals have a moral obligation to avoid acting in ways that foreseeably risk imposing costs on others. But why should we assume this? In general, for any action φ, it doesn't seem to follow from "φ-ing risks harming others" that "φ-ing is wrong." And in the particular case at hand, it's not at all obvious that each of us owes it to others to make health-promoting lifestyle choices. For instance, I hardly seem to be wronging others by, say, failing to regularly do the crossword puzzle (or to perform similar mentally strenuous activities) to lower my risk of dementia. Likewise, we might be skeptical that individuals would be violating a duty to others by failing to get at least six hours of sleep most nights, by being chronically stressed due to working long hours, or by not maintaining any close social relationships. Yet all of those behaviors might translate into higher healthcare costs, which would be shared by others.

Parallel reflections apply to lifestyle choices we make in domains other than health.[16] For instance, it doesn't seem that I owe it to others to maximize my productive contributions to society. Imagine that quitting my job as a high-powered attorney to pursue my dream of basket-weaving would predictably result in depriving my fellow citizens of significant tax revenue for years to come. That wouldn't imply that I would be wronging others by doing so. To suppose otherwise would be to hold people to an implausible moral standard, one that would be unduly restrictive of their personal freedom.

Thus, I am not generally obligated to refrain from making lifestyle choices that would foreseeably risk negatively affecting others. Sometimes I am. For example, plainly, I am obligated to not throw large rocks from an overpass onto a busy freeway below, though I derive amusement from doing so. However, a balance must be struck between, on the one hand, respecting individuals' freedom to pursue their favored aims and, on the other hand, limiting individuals' ability to act in ways that harm, or risk harming, others. Just how we are to adjudicate between these two competing ends when they come into conflict depends on the details. To establish that it's wrong to be fat, based on the costs that being fat might produce for others, we need a principled explanation of why individuals don't have the right to impose those specific costs on others, even though they are free to act in various other ways that might also negatively affect others.[17] Can such a principled explanation be found?

Some in the public health ethics literature appeal to the value of *solidarity* to explain why, at least in some instances, individuals might be obligated to make certain health-promoting lifestyle choices to avoid burdening their fellow citizens.[18] The idea that solidarity grounds such an obligation takes as its starting point a construal of society as a cooperative scheme that benefits all of its members. Given that each of us benefits from belonging to society, in the spirit of solidarity, each of us might be obligated to do our part in sustaining this cooperative enterprise. The reasoning here is simple: it seems wrong for a person to enjoy the benefits of social cooperation and yet to do nothing in return, or even worse, to act in ways that make things worse for others. But again, there are only certain sorts of burdens we are to avoid imposing on others by appeal to this rationale. How do we work out which those are?

The bioethicists Ben Davies and Julian Savulescu propose that in a society characterized by relations of solidarity, individuals can be expected to act in certain health-promoting ways to avoid burdening their fellow citizens.[19] But on their view, there are important constraints on just when it would be reasonable to demand that people do so. For one thing, we can only reasonably demand that our fellow citizens engage in healthy behaviors that would be "realistically adoptable" for them.[20] Sometimes, acting in a health-promoting way might clash with fulfilling personal obligations, e.g., as for the individual whose only means to provide for his family is to do grueling work that takes an immense toll on his health.[21] In this case, it wouldn't be reasonable to expect such a person to quit his job for the sake of his health. In addition, Davies and Savulescu argue, individuals can only be held responsible for embracing health-promoting behaviors when they are equipped to autonomously choose to do so. This requires that one be well informed about what concrete steps to take to become healthier; that one be able to rationally reflect about the matter; and that one be provided with "considerable support" to make the prescribed behavioral changes.[22] Furthermore, these authors emphasize, it is only reasonable to call on people to make a good-faith effort to engage in healthier behaviors. We cannot reasonably demand that they succeed in those efforts.[23] On this account, the value of solidarity explains not only why, in some cases, individuals have an obligation to look after their health but also why, in other cases, the prerequisites for that obligation are not fulfilled. As the authors themselves put it, "Solidarity is a two-way street."[24]

Does Davies and Savulescu's proposal provide a plausible basis for supposing that obese people are shirking an obligation they have to their fellow citizens? This depends on whether society is doing its part to meaningfully enable its members to autonomously make healthier choices to avoid being obese. There is ample evidence that our society is failing in this regard (which I only gesture at here but will discuss at length in the next chapter). For instance, consider the ubiquity of inexpensive fast food that some individuals get accustomed to regularly eating, coupled with aggressive food industry marketing tactics that drive many toward those foods. This can make it very hard for some to avoid being obese, especially those who are genetically susceptible to obesity. For some individuals, being meaningfully equipped to make healthier lifestyle choices that would enable them to avoid being obese would likely require significant infrastructural changes. For example, it would likely require ensuring that all members of society have effective access to affordable, tasty, nutritious foods as well as strictly regulating predatory fast-food advertising tactics, particularly those that target young children. So, on the proposed account of solidarity-based obligations, there would be little basis for accusing obese people of wrong-doing for failing to do their part to avoid being obese. What is more, even if this account did yield the verdict that obese individuals have a solidarity-based obligation to make healthier weight-related choices, these individuals would only be required to *strive for* a supposedly healthy weight rather than to *achieve* such a weight.

There's further reason yet for why fat people shouldn't be criticized on this basis. Besides our society failing to meaning-fully enable people to make better lifestyle choices pertaining to their weight, our society is implicated in producing some of the very costs that fat people are accused of imposing on others. Let me explain. For one thing, as discussed in chapter 2, pervasive weight stigma worsens fat people's health. Fat individuals receive inferior medical care due, in part, to the high levels of anti-fat bias exhibited by medical professionals. And experiencing stigma on a day-to-day basis takes a toll on people's physical and mental health. Anti-fat bias also contributes to fat people enduring workforce pen-alties, e.g., being less likely to be hired or promoted, being more likely to be fired, and receiving lower wages for the same work as thin people—penalties that are especially steep for women. Being fat is linked to worse educational outcomes for girls and women, who receive less financial support to attend college. To reproach fat people for burdening others on account of being less healthy and less productive, when society has a hand in making fat people worse off in these ways, would not merely be morally unjustified, it would be morally egregious.

Overall, then, the charge that fat people wrongfully impose economic costs on others should be rejected. Both the key empirical and moral premises this charge rests on are questionable.

5. FAT PEOPLE SHOULDN'T BE BLAMED FOR CLIMATE CHANGE

Let's now turn to the charge of environmental harm: that fat people are wronging others because their weight is bad for the planet. As with the previous charge that accuses fat people of wrongfully imposing economic harms on others, this charge too may rely on unwarranted generalizations. It assumes that fat individuals eat more and drive more than their thin counterparts. Even if it's true that fat people, on average, eat more and drive more than thin people, it doesn't follow that any given fat person eats a lot or is sedentary. Yet, fat-blamers often unfairly generalize in just this way. In addition, the concerns raised in the last section, calling into question the plausibility of demanding that fat people reduce their weight in the absence of meaningful social support for that endeavor, apply here too. So, we already have some preliminary basis for finding the charge of environmental harm raised against fat people to be questionable. However, for the sake of argument, let's set aside those problems and focus on the aspect of this charge that might seem the most morally plausible: its supposition that we should take issue with individuals for acting in ways that avoidably contribute to accelerating the warming of our already dangerously hot planet. Here, I take for granted that addressing global warming is among the most morally pressing issues that humanity currently faces and that doing so requires radically scaling back our collective greenhouse gas emissions. Still, even if fat people do disproportionately contribute to global warming in the aforementioned ways, I argue that they shouldn't be condemned on that basis.

From a big-picture perspective, drawing attention to fat people for their excessive contributions to global warming seems a petty distraction. Others bear a much greater share of responsibility for high emissions. Indeed, the emissions of the world's wealthiest individuals eclipse the contributions of the rest of humanity. According to a 2020 Oxfam report "Confronting Carbon Inequality," the world's richest 1% of individuals, some 63 million people, are responsible for an incredible 15% of the total man-made emissions produced over the last few decades.[25] This group emits more than twice as much as the three billion individuals who are the poorest 50% of the global population.[26] Heating and cooling their massive homes, regularly vacationing on private jets and yachts, and buying luxury goods in abundance are part of what makes them super-emitters compared to the rest of us. The excess per capita emissions produced by the super-wealthy (those in the top 1%) are about 91 times greater than those attributed to obese individuals. By comparison, obese people, on average, don't even emit twice as much as normal-weight people according to the study discussed in section 3. The marginal increase in jet fuel use associated with an obese passenger who flies a few times a year (relative to a non-obese passenger) that Singer is concerned about is but a drop in the bucket of global emissions when measured up against the extra jet fuel burned by a super-wealthy person who flies her private jet on a weekly basis (relative to a person of average financial means).

Now, it is true that the food production and transportation sector is a major source of emissions, accounting for around one-third of global emissions.[27] And so it might seem plausible to criticize people who eat more than others for thereby increasing consumer demand for the products of one of the economy's most emissions-intensive sectors. However, once we look at the bigger picture, drawing attention to the harm that fat people (might) do by eating more than thin people, again, seems a petty distraction. Here, we can consider some further facts about how our food system is linked to harmful emissions. A shockingly high proportion of the food supply in the United States—between 30 and 40%, or some 133 billion pounds—ends up being thrown out each year.[28] And food that is not eaten produces even greater emissions than the food we eat because as that food decomposes in landfills over time, it releases methane, an especially potent greenhouse gas. Globally, food waste is estimated to account for 8% of all emissions.[29] So, it looks like any extra emissions associated with fat people eating more than thin people are dwarfed by the emissions linked to all the food that *no one* is eating.

Instead of reproaching ordinary individuals for having slightly inflated carbon footprints compared to their peers, perhaps we should direct our condemnation toward corporations and governments that have done so much more to cause global warming.[30] Against this suggestion, one might protest that there is plenty of room at the table for condemning *all* those who needlessly hasten climate change—corporations, governments, and ordinary individuals with excessively large carbon footprints. But even if one takes this stance, we have little reason to single out fat individuals for their role in worsening climate change. After all, excess emissions are linked to all manner of things that many folks in well-off societies regularly do: frequently flying for business; taking road-trips, cruises, or travelling the world;

shopping online; playing a competitive sport and eating copiously to fuel one's training; consuming meat, coffee, and chocolate; having kids or pets; playing computer games for hours on end; using a dryer instead of a clothesline; leaving lots of lights turned on; not composting household food scraps; not planting trees; keeping one's home extra-warm in the winter or extra-cool in the summer; frivolously purchasing new clothes and shoes; living in an old or poorly insulated home. The list goes on and on.

So, fat people could be condemned for being fat. However, in that case, it would be arbitrary to draw special attention to fat individuals for their contributions to climate change. Indeed, if fat individuals are blamed on this basis, then parallel condemnation should be extended to the vast majority of ordinary individuals in well-off societies for engaging in similar wrongdoing. At best, then, fat people might be blameworthy on this count—but only for committing a transgression comparable to transgressions that most of us, including most thin people, commit.

6. CONCLUSION

The chapter began by setting out a philosophical account of blaming, an account that can help us identify and tease apart the different fundamental constituent parts of fat-blaming as it occurs in our society. To work out whether fat-blaming is justified, I explained, requires answering three questions. The main task of this chapter has been to answer the first of those three questions: Are fat people doing anything morally wrong by being fat? If so, what?

To that end, we have examined what might seem to be the most promising grounds for supposing that it is morally wrong to be fat: namely, that by being fat, a person risks harming others in non-trivial ways. Especially, that's thought to occur in virtue of the high healthcare costs of treating obesity-related medical conditions and the environmental consequences of fat people using more resources. If initially that reasoning seems compelling, I have shown that it doesn't hold up under scrutiny. First, that reasoning relies on dubious empirical claims. If one accuses individuals of doing harm, one should be confident that those accused are actually doing the relevant harm. Yet, in the case at hand, it is far from clear that such confidence is justified. Second, even if fat people cause the harms in question, it wouldn't follow that they have an obligation to avoid being fat. That's because for any action φ, it doesn't follow from "φ-ing risks harming others" that "φ-ing is wrong." A further argument would be needed to bridge that gap. And the solidarity-based argument, which might seem a promising candidate for bridging that gap, doesn't succeed at that.

Third, blaming fat people for harming others on the grounds we've considered is hypocritical. For one thing, those who blame fat people on that basis tend to ignore the fact that others in society play a non-negligible role in helping to produce the harms that fat people are accused of wrongfully producing. What is more, we typically don't blame other groups of people for producing parallel harms to those fat people are regularly blamed for bringing about. Indeed, if we set aside all the other problems with the foregoing case for why it's wrong to be fat, at best, to blame fat people for harming others is a glaring instance of cherry-picking. In popular discourse, alarm is frequently raised about the steep costs that fat people impose on the healthcare system. But where are the parallel exhortations of, say, those working high-powered jobs and subjecting themselves to health risks associated with sleep deprivation and chronic stress? Or, of extreme athletes engaging in risky behaviors? Similarly, fat people are blamed for accelerating global warming and for wasteful consumption, but many others who produce much greater excess emissions and more wastefully consume resources are not.

So, at least based on the arguments that we have considered in this chapter, there doesn't seem to be a sound moral basis for concluding that, in general, it's wrong for people to be fat. If that is so, then the case for blaming people for being fat wouldn't get off the ground: the first of the two necessary conditions for establishing their blameworthiness would fail to be satisfied.

1. INTRODUCTION

In chapter 4, I argued that blaming fat people for being fat is unwarranted because there is nothing morally wrong with being fat. But in this chapter, I will make the contrary assumption. I will assume, for the sake of argument, that there *is* something morally wrong with being fat. From that assumption alone, we cannot infer that fat people are blame-worthy for being fat. As I noted in chapter 4, drawing that inference would require further showing that fat people are objectionably implicated in being fat—for instance, due to weakness of will or bad values. And I will argue that, for the vast majority of fat people, this further condition is not satis-fied. Most fat people are not fat because of weakness of will or bad values.

In this chapter, I will focus on the claim that many fat people are fat because they are weak-willed. That claim is widely believed. Fat people are thought to have poor self-control that leads them to make bad lifestyle choices, namely, eating too much or exercising too little. That supposition is common. Indeed, some think it is obviously correct. But whether it is true is an empirical question. And the empirical

DOI: 10.4324/9780367853389-7

evidence is clear: in general, fat people are not fat because they are weak-willed.

Section 2 addresses conceptual questions. What exactly does weakness of will involve? When, and why, might someone be blameworthy for exhibiting weakness of will? Answering those questions will enable us to clarify just what fat people are being blamed for, and why, when they are accused of being weak-willed. Section 3 considers whether people *remain* fat because they are weak-willed, and section 4 considers whether people *become* fat because they are weak-willed.

2. BLAMING FAT PEOPLE FOR BEING WEAK-WILLED

Let's consider what it means to be *weak-willed*.[1] Weakness of will arises in cases in which a person is pulled between competing desires concerning how to act, and owing to weakness, one isn't able to get oneself to act as one thinks one should, all things considered. Take, for instance, a college student who is watching a gripping crime series on Netflix. He believes he shouldn't watch more than one episode since he must wake up very early to take an important exam. But the show is captivating, and he just can't stop himself from binge-watching late into the night. The reason the weak-willed person can't get himself to act in accordance with his own considered judgment is poor self-control. "Self-control" refers to a person's capacity to steer oneself, to exert the discipline that's needed to resist temptations when they arise. The weak-willed person gives in to temptations that he genuinely wishes to resist but cannot resist because he lacks sufficient self-control. So, the weak-willed individual is sometimes unable to get himself to act in accordance with his own better judgment of how he should act.

When might a person be blameworthy for being weak-willed? To recall, it would only be appropriate to deem a person blameworthy if he has done something morally wrong. As such, a weak-willed person might be blameworthy if he fails to do the right thing due to his weakness. Sometimes, in exhibiting weakness of will, a person only fails himself. That's the case for the above-described Netflix-binger who only lets himself down by staying up too late owing to his weakness. But consider a variant of that case. Let's now imagine a person who, against his better judgment, stays up very late watching Netflix, and in doing so doesn't just fail himself. Rather, as a result of staying up until the wee morning hours, he oversleeps and misses his daughter's debut piano recital. He was fully aware that his daughter would be crushed by his absence at her recital, and, accordingly, he knew that he shouldn't stay up late. Yet, he was so weak in the moment that he couldn't tear himself away from the TV. Plausibly, the father is blameworthy for missing his daughter's recital. Underlying that intuition is the judgment that he should have been able to exercise greater self-control, of the sort that would have enabled him to have done the right thing.

But we might wonder, what accounts for the judgment that the father should have been capable of exhibiting greater self-control? We might make this judgment based on our own personal reflections about what it'd be like for us in a situation like the one that the father faced. Most of us are intimately familiar with this sort of case. Specifically, we know what it's like to turn off the TV and pull ourselves away from a riveting show when we recognize that we have very good reason, all things considered, to do so. It can be hard. Still, despite it requiring some willpower to switch off the TV, most of us regularly get ourselves to do just that. So, we negatively judge the Netflix-binging father based on the reasoning that it's not *so* hard to resist the temptation to binge-watch a show late into the night.

Consider a different case. Sean, a rookie cop, knows the secret location where a confidential informant—a young mother about to testify in a high-profile case against a drug kingpin—is being kept. He is kidnapped by a henchman of the drug lord who presses him to reveal the location. Sean knows that if he does so, it's all but guaranteed that the informant will be killed and the state's case against the drug lord will fall apart. Through several rounds of severe beatings, he stoically keeps silent. But the tactics become increasingly brutal. Brandishing pliers, his captor threatens to pull out his fingernails one by one if he does not comply. Worn down mentally and in agonizing physical pain, Sean feels the pliers clamp down on one of his nails. He cannot bring himself to hold out any longer and divulges the informant's location. Shortly thereafter, the informant is murdered, and Sean is released.

Now, we wouldn't conclude that Sean exhibited faulty self-control for eventually giving in to his captor's demands. He didn't behave like the Netflix-binging father who could have gotten himself to do the right thing had he just exerted a normal measure of self-control. Indeed, almost anyone in Sean's situation—facing the imminent threat of having their fingernails pulled out—would have acted as he did. In those circumstances, very few people would be able to override the powerful human impulse we all have to protect ourselves from grievous bodily harm. To resist and endure such gruesome acts of violence would, for Sean (as for almost anyone in those circumstances), require nothing short of an iron will. And that is so even if he had excellent reason to believe that his efforts to keep the informant safe by remaining silent would succeed. Given the extremely trying nature of his circumstances, Sean is not blameworthy for the wrongful act he commits.[2]

The foregoing reflections suggest a general principle about when it would (and wouldn't) be appropriate to judge someone blameworthy for committing wrongdoing when one could have done the right thing had one summoned greater willpower: if it would take *extraordinary* willpower for a person to get oneself to do the right thing, one's failure to do the right thing shouldn't be judged blameworthy. This is because when it comes to judging whether someone is blameworthy for acting wrongly, it doesn't seem reasonable to expect a person to exert extraordinary self-control—of the sort that most individuals in similar circumstances wouldn't be able to exert—to get oneself to comply with moral demands. Hence, although we can plausibly suppose that Sean was bound by a stringent moral obligation not to reveal the informant's location (an obligation that he himself felt the force of), it wouldn't be fitting to blame him for ultimately giving up that information. Granted, Sean's revealing the informant's location leads to devastating, tragic consequences. Yet, given the immense costs resisting would have implied for him, he wouldn't be justifiably condemned for the wrongful harm that befalls the informant as a direct consequence of his failure to resist. The blameworthy failure of the weak-willed person, then, is a failure to exhibit *normal* self-control to get oneself to do the right thing.

These reflections concerning what weakness of will involves and when someone might be blameworthy for being weak-willed can help shed light on why fat people are blamed for being weak-willed. Those who blame fat people on this basis suppose that for the vast majority of us, it isn't all that hard to avoid being fat—certainly, it is assumed, fat avoidance doesn't require anything like extraordinary willpower. And so, it is frequently supposed that many fat people are fat because they fail to exercise normal self-control.

Now, a proponent of this line of reasoning can grant that fat avoidance might well take *some* effort for many, if not most, people. Certainly, one need not suppose that it is easy for most folks to avoid being fat. What is more, one can acknowledge that working to lose a lot of weight by radically changing one's diet and exercise habits might *feel* like a serious sacrifice for a fat person (just as it might feel extremely difficult for the Netflix-binger to turn off the TV when it gets late). But, the reasoning continues, that is just as we should expect: people who have allowed themselves to be excessively indulgent for a long time might well have to endure a trying adjustment period before they become accustomed to eating appropriately sized portions (and types of foods) and exercising regularly. Yet, that the sacrifices entailed by fat-avoidance efforts feel so great to these folks is itself taken to be an indication of fat individuals lacking proper self-control in the first place—and that, in turn, is seen as something that is their own fault. So, it's thought, those individuals can be, and should have been, more disciplined all along. Armed with normal self-control, fat avoidance would be well within the reach of most fat people, requiring nothing more than relatively modest sacrifices. And so, it's supposed, doing what is required to be thin calls for most fat individuals doing nothing more than developing and acting on a normal sense of self-control.

We judged the Netflix-binger as weak-willed based on the reasoning that most of us with normal self-control can pry ourselves away from the TV. The judgment that most fat people are weak-willed is based on parallel reasoning. The notion that most fat people could avoid being fat if only they exercised normal self-control assumes that most fat people and most thin people are roughly similar regarding how hard it is for them to avoid being fat. More specifically, the idea here is that the majority of us, fat and thin alike, are similarly positioned to make the same sorts of "weight-affecting choices," i.e., choices about what we eat and how much we exercise. This is to suppose: (1) that we all grapple with temptations that are experienced in roughly similar ways—for instance, wanting to overeat or to skip the gym, and (2) that in the face of such temptations, most thin people exert discipline and resist acting in ways that would make them fat, while most fat people do not. Thin people, on this line of reasoning, simply make better weight-affecting choices more consistently than fat people do. If that's so, then it would seem that most fat people could avoid being fat if only they had proper self-control of the sort generally exhibited by thin people.

In summary, the weakness-of-will charge supposes that most fat people are unable to resist temptations owing to an internal willpower deficiency. If we assume that there's something morally wrong with being fat, then we would be justified in blaming individuals who are fat because they are weak-willed. In particular, it's supposed that it's reasonable to expect people to exhibit normal self-control. Further, it's supposed that exhibiting normal self-control is all that's needed for people—thin and fat alike—to get themselves to act in ways that would enable them to avoid being fat. But that reasoning is flawed, as I will now explain.

3. DO PEOPLE REMAIN FAT BECAUSE THEY'RE WEAK-WILLED?

Available evidence gives us ample basis for rejecting the supposition that most fat people would be thin if only they exerted similar willpower to that exerted by most thin people. In fact, it appears that for some, perhaps many, fat people, becoming and staying thin would prove to be extremely hard. For such individuals, putting forth the effort that fat avoidance would require would call for exhibiting nothing short of *extraordinary* willpower—willpower greater than that which can be reasonably expected of anyone. Therefore, the widespread tendency in our society for fat individuals to be regarded as weak-willed for their failure to slim down is unwarranted.

Losing a large amount of weight through lifestyle changes tends to be no easy feat. Yet, as hard as doing so can be, for just about all who manage it, maintaining a substantial weight loss over time is even more difficult. This is because for most people, significant weight loss profoundly alters their internal biochemistry in ways that push their bodies to regain the weight they have lost. At least, that is what some 60 years of scientific research on weight loss suggests. In what follows, I'll discuss key findings on this matter.[3]

One relevant factor is that losing a lot of weight generally causes a person's metabolism to dramatically slow. A slower metabolism makes it harder to sustain a weight loss because it means that, to avoid gaining weight, a person must eat less than she could if she had a higher metabolism. Consider a recent study that gathered data from a rather unusual group of subjects: former contestants of the popular weight-loss reality television show, *The Biggest Loser*.[4] The show's premise is simple. At the start of each season, around a dozen contestants begin their "weight-loss journeys," competing over the coming months to see who loses the most weight and thus becomes the season's winner. At the start of the season, all 14 individuals in the study were obese, weighing 328 pounds on average, and they all had normal metabolisms at that point. Following restrictive diets and working out strenuously for hours a day produced the sought-after results. By the end of the grueling 30-week competition, all these individuals had lost a lot of weight, an average of 128 pounds. After losing so much weight, their metabolisms had slowed drastically, dropping to rates quite a bit lower than would be expected based on their new lower weights. Their daily energy requirements were about 275 calories fewer than would be predicted for someone of that body size with a normal metabolism.

The *Biggest Loser* study also revealed that even years after losing a lot of weight, people's slow metabolisms don't seem to recover (and may actually become more sluggish yet as time goes on). Indeed, six years after the competition ended, the 14 individuals participating in the study all had much slower metabolisms and were, on average, burning 500 fewer calories a day than would be expected if they had normal metabolisms at their respective body sizes.[5] A 500-calorie "metabolic penalty" can be significant: for the majority of normal-weight adults, suffering such a penalty would translate to having to eat 20 to 25% fewer calories than would typically be required to maintain one's weight.

Especially surprising to the researchers was that the subjects' metabolisms remained abnormally low six years after the competition despite the fact that, by then, all but one of them had regained some of the weight they had lost. Most had regained much of what they had lost, with five of the fourteen individuals ending up heavier than before the contest or within just

1% of their starting weight.[6] Such weight gain would predict that their metabolisms would correspondingly bounce back to normal levels. But nothing of that sort happened. Six years out, the subjects' metabolisms were *even lower* than they had been at the peak of their weight loss, right at the end of the competition. One man, Danny Cahill, was the worst off in the group in terms of the damaging effects weight loss had on his metabolism. Just before the competition, Cahill weighed 430 pounds. He lost an astonishing amount of weight, getting down to 191 pounds and emerging as the season's winner.[7] Six years later, he had regained around 100 pounds. Far from that weight gain reinvigorating his sluggish metabolism, his metabolism stayed so slow that, to maintain his new weight of 295 pounds, Cahill had to eat 800 calories fewer a day than a man of that weight with a normal metabolism would.[8]

So, after losing a lot of weight, one may well end up with a seriously slow metabolism that doesn't recalibrate to normal levels over time. But one might wonder: In virtue of having a super-slow metabolism (and thus requiring fewer calories to maintain one's weight), does a person like Cahill *feel* less hungry and so not need to eat as much to feel full as a normal-metabolism counterpart at the same body weight would? In fact, the opposite is true. Immediately following weight loss, hunger levels markedly rise, and even as the years pass, hunger levels may remain considerably higher than they were before that weight loss. Indeed, one study found that losing weight triggers an increase in appetite that is, on average, three times greater than the decrease in food one needs to consume to maintain one's lower weight. In other words, having lost weight, a person needs less food but feels hungrier than before.[9] This is a second key mechanism by which the body fights back against substantial weight loss.

Part of what accounts for how hungry we feel is a hormone called leptin. Leptin is one of several hormones our bodies produce that help regulate our appetites. It contributes to the feeling of fullness we typically get after eating a meal, and a rise in leptin levels post-meal is part of what helps diminish that strong urge to eat that we are apt to feel when we haven't eaten for a while. The *Biggest Loser* contestants all had normal levels of leptin prior to the competition. But just after the competition, their bodies produced virtually no leptin, which would have caused them to continually experience extreme hunger and food cravings. Even six years later, as most of them regained much of the weight they had lost, their leptin levels, on average, rose to only about two-thirds of what they had been at the start of the show.[10]

In addition to the physical symptoms of hunger (e.g., a rumbling stomach) that we're all familiar with, most of us are also well acquainted with the various psychological manifestations of hunger. For instance, in the late morning I sometimes realize I must be getting hungry when I notice that my mind has wandered to the pressing matter of what to have for lunch. Besides hunger prompting us to think about food, it's common to feel irritable when we're really hungry. And if the body's demand to be fed goes unanswered for long, it can be quite difficult for us to give our sustained attention to much else other than the thought of eating. When hunger becomes especially intense, it can feel as if it's consuming us. Our levels of leptin, and of other hunger hormones, seem to strongly influence our tendency to have such thoughts and feelings. The ebb and flow of those hormone levels can explain why, when you are famished, the prospect of eating a huge ice-cream sundae after the pizza you just started eating is tantalizing, and why, after you've eaten a few slices of the pizza and feel full, dessert suddenly doesn't seem so appealing.

That significant weight loss can elicit dramatic changes in people's hunger levels had been noticed by researchers decades earlier. In studying the effects of significant weight loss on two very small groups of obese individuals in the 1960s, Jules Hirsch, who conducted pioneering research on obesity at the Rockefeller University Hospital, stumbled on quite a disturbing finding. He and his collaborators found that obese individuals in a supervised clinical setting who were dieting to facilitate substantial weight loss were exhibiting a host of characteristic psychological and behavioral symptoms of starvation: they were dreaming and fantasizing about food, binge eating, experiencing anxiety and depression, and some were battling suicidal thoughts.[11] This was puzzling to the researchers since none of the subjects had slimmed down to dangerously low levels; indeed, none were anywhere close to being clinically underweight. Yet, on the inside, it appeared that their bodies were driving them to *feel* much like people who were starving to the point of emaciation.

Much of what is known about the effects of starvation was learned from a groundbreaking study conducted toward the end of World War II by Ancel Keys (whose work on the Mediterranean Diet we considered in chapter 3).[12] In this study, known as "The Minnesota Starvation Experiment," 36 healthy, normal-weight men lost 25% of their starting body weights over six months by adhering to a semi-starvation diet and walking 22 miles a week. At the end of that six-month period, the 32 remaining subjects who hadn't strayed from the demanding regime of the study's starvation phase were gaunt, weak, and felt constantly hungry. Following the starvation period, the men went through a two-month rehabilitation phase in which they regained the weight they had lost by gradually increasing the amount they ate, and after that they entered a further phase in which they could eat however they pleased (while being carefully monitored). During the starvation and rehabilitation phases, the men experienced severe mental and emotional distress. They thought of food obsessively. Once the restrictions in their access to food were lifted, some couldn't stop themselves from eating uncontrollably to the point of becoming sick (with one landing himself in the hospital due to excessive consumption).

Although maintaining a large weight loss over a long period of time can be extremely difficult, some people succeed in doing so. Take, for instance, Erinn Egbert, the only one of the 14 *Biggest Loser* former contestants in the study above who didn't regain any of their initially lost weight. Six years after the competition, Egbert had lost and kept off around a hundred pounds from her starting weight. It wasn't that she didn't encounter the difficulties the others faced. Like the others, her metabolism slowed significantly. At that six-year mark, she burned 552 fewer calories than someone her size with a normal metabolism would.[13] Egbert was clear that maintaining her weight loss for years took no small amount of effort, emphasizing that "[y]ou have got to keep at it every single day."[14] For her, staying thin requires "rigid portion control and regular, intense exercise—45 minutes to an hour a day, Monday through Saturday."[15] Testimony from others who sustain significant long-term weight losses, such as those who belong to the National Weight Control Registry, suggests that Egbert's experience is fairly typical. A recurring theme among these folks is that it takes constant vigilance to avoid regaining those lost pounds. Most folks in the National Weight Control Registry, like Egbert, report exercising around an hour each day and carefully monitoring their diets and their weight.[16] One registry member explained that staying thin, as she had done for about five years (after losing 135 pounds), was a full-time effort, "something that has to be focused on every minute."[17] To avoid weight regain, this woman weighs every single thing she eats at home on a kitchen scale to precisely track her calories, and each night, without fail, she religiously documents every morsel she consumed that day and analyzes her dietary choices.

So, it looks like once a person becomes fat, it can be extremely difficult to stop being fat. In particular, based on how substantial weight loss affects people's bodies, it appears to be really hard for most people who lose a lot of weight to avoid regaining much of that lost weight over time. Few manage, and those who do exert a great deal of effort to do so. That fat avoidance proves so difficult for many who are fat seems to hold true, at least, for all the subjects whose weight-loss efforts were documented in the studies surveyed in this section. This raises an important question: What can these studies tell us about whether achieving and maintaining a normal weight would involve comparable difficulties for fat individuals across the board? Of course, fat people aren't all alike. We have looked at relatively small-scale studies of individuals who had to lose large amounts of weight to avoid being fat and who generally attained considerable weight losses, of around hundred pounds. It's not clear to what extent similar hardships might arise for overweight individuals who would have to lose much less weight—say, only 20 or 30 pounds—to avoid being fat.

Even focusing just on those who are obese, and who would thus have to lose considerable weight to avoid being fat, it can't be said with certainty whether most of those individuals would tend to face comparable difficulties in working to avoid being fat as those observed in the subjects of those studies. However, there is good reason to suspect that the trends seen in the studied populations would apply to many, if not most, who have a lot of weight to lose. For one thing, the described trends in those studies, which make maintaining large weight losses very difficult, are ubiquitous. Every obese person in those studies who loses a lot of weight undergoes such changes, getting hit with the cruel combination of a much slower metabolism and a ramped-up hunger drive. Furthermore, these studies are not anomalous. Plenty of other studies reveal similar patterns concerning the difficulties faced by most who attempt to maintain large weight losses. Indeed, having looked through many dozens of studies on this matter, I haven't come across a single one in which most people who started out obese and tried to lose weight didn't find it extremely challenging to maintain a large weight loss over time and thus failed in their efforts. A parallel point holds true of the difficulties observed in the so-regarded "success story" cases: those who sustain large weight losses over time do so only by enduring remarkably similar burdens. There's a final reason for supposing that the tendencies pushing people who have lost a lot of weight toward regain are relatively common. That supposition certainly would go some way toward explaining the extremely low long-term success rates consistently seen in fat people's weight-loss efforts even among those who are highly motivated to not be fat (i.e., the statistic discussed in chapter 3 that upwards of 95% of weight-loss efforts may fail in the long term).

Just as we can't generalize about all fat people being similar with respect to what fat avoidance requires of them, the same holds true of always-been-thin people with respect to what it takes for them to stay thin. Some thin people eat a lot and yet never seem to gain weight; some report having little interest in food and that disposition keeps them thin; and still others regularly exert vigilance to control their weight. Still, it strikes me that many people who have always been thin don't find it really hard to stay thin. As someone who has always been thin myself, I've been thinking about what sort of effort that involves. It's not actually all that simple to figure out. Growing up, I fully and without question embraced the conventional view that it was very important to be thin, and for many years, I deliberately sought to control my weight—dieting and exercising for the express purpose of striving to get my body to look a certain way. I no longer deliberately try to control my weight. Yet, it's hard to say to what extent my current dietary and exercise habits might be conditioned by years of doing just that. As they say, old habits die hard. And sometimes our own motives for behaving in particular ways aren't apparent to us: people tend to be masters of self-deception.

Even if it's a somewhat tricky matter to assess, I can confidently say that staying thin isn't particularly effortful for me. There is no real comparison between what it takes me to be thin and the typical efforts made by the so-called "successful losers" who have maintained substantial weight losses for years. To stay at a normal weight, I have never had to regularly contend with continual hunger pangs or intrusive thoughts of food. If I'm hungry, I eat something. I don't regularly weigh myself. I don't keep track of what I eat or how much I exercise. I don't plan out my meals in advance or avoid eating particular foods for fear of how they might affect my weight. I don't need to exercise (intensively or otherwise) most days to avoid gaining weight. It's not clear to what extent my experiences are representative of the always-been-thin. But plenty of people who have always been thin report much the same.

Overall, there appears to be a vast difference in the effort fat avoidance tends to require for those who have never been fat compared to those who would have to lose a good deal of weight to reach a normal weight. The body of evidence we have on this matter spanning decades paints a bleak picture of how arduous a battle an obese person must fight to keep off large amounts of weight. That evidence makes clear that losing a lot of weight profoundly changes what goes on inside a person's body so as to make weight regain a near inevitability. And when obese individuals lose enough weight to become thin, it seems that they come to resemble people who have always been at a normal weight only in terms of their body size. In terms of what it takes these formerly obese individuals to maintain their new, much lower weights—physically, mentally, and emotionally—their experience is nothing like that of what it takes most always-been-thin individuals to stay thin. Rather, it seems to be much closer to what an underweight person enduring chronic starvation would experience.[18]

If we wish to make a general claim about what it takes for fat people to avoid being fat, we have two competing hypotheses on offer: (1) Many fat individuals are weak-willed, and that's why they fail to become and stay thin; (2) Many fat individuals fail in their fat-avoidance efforts because maintaining a substantial weight loss over time requires extraordinary willpower. The evidence we have examined tells in favor of the latter hypothesis. The charge that most fat people remain fat due to weakness of will gets things wrong in two ways. First, it supposes that fat avoidance requires a similar effort from most who have always been thin and most who are fat. But there's little evidence for that supposition, and plenty of evidence against it. Second, it assumes that fat avoidance isn't *so* difficult for many who are fat, and it just requires them to have normal self-control. Again, available evidence suggests otherwise. For the vast majority who have a lot of weight to lose, fat avoidance tends to be very difficult. The small proportion of individuals who successfully sustain large weight losses in the long term seem to do so only by exerting extraordinary willpower. Those individuals resist temptations that just about everyone equipped with normal self-control would find nearly impossible to resist. If that is so, then to expect most fat individuals to act in a similar way to that small, hyper-vigilant minority—putting forth demanding, draining efforts over time to stay slim—would be to hold them to a patently unreasonable standard.

4. DO PEOPLE GET FAT BECAUSE THEY'RE WEAK-WILLED?

Given the arguments of the last section, one might grant that fat people, in general, shouldn't be regarded as weak-willed for failing to do whatever it takes to become and stay thin. Still, one might argue that weakness of will does explain why many people became fat in the first place and *that* is why it's often blameworthy to be fat. On this line of reasoning, it is posited that the primary reason that some people get fat and others do not comes down to differences in willpower. It is supposed that if only fat people had behaved like those who stay thin do—specifically, exhibiting reasonable self-control in their weight-affecting lifestyle choices—then many, if not most, of them wouldn't have become fat. And so, on this line of reasoning, even if weakness of will doesn't explain why fat people remain fat, it might explain why people who are fat got that way.

This argument for blaming fat individuals for being weak-willed should, like the last one, be rejected. We have no good reason to believe that differences in willpower play a significant role in explaining why some people become fat and others don't. Often, the weight people end up at is greatly influenced by factors that lie outside of their voluntary control (and, thus, isn't a matter of how much willpower they exert). Furthermore, even when different people make different weight-affecting choices, this frequently cannot be attributed to willpower differences. Rather, people's weight-affecting choices are influenced by wide-ranging factors, many of which lie outside their control. As we'll see, what accounts for why some people become fat and others don't is a complex matter in which willpower appears to play a relatively minor role.

To begin with, let's focus on one key assumption of the weakness-of-will charge: that what centrally explains why some people don't ever become fat is the restraint they show in the face of various temptations. This assumption is frequently made by people who have always been thin. They assume that if they didn't actively exert restraint in their daily choices, then they would become fat. Along these lines, a thin person might figure that if she regularly allowed herself to succumb to all those cravings that she's long resisted—chowing down pizza, burgers, fries, milkshakes, and so on to her heart's content—then she would be fat. Plausible as that supposition might seem, it turns out that for some, perhaps many, always-been-thin individuals, getting and staying fat wouldn't prove to be all that easy.

Ethan Sims, a clinical researcher who went on to make pioneering contributions to the scientific understanding of obesity and diabetes, concluded as much based on a series of studies he conducted in the 1960s.[19] In these studies, he set out to investigate what biological changes would occur in people who were induced with "experimental obesity" (obesity that's deliberately produced in non-obese subjects for experimental purposes). Sims wanted to know whether these individuals would develop a risk profile for obesity-related diseases, such as diabetes, similar to that observed in individuals with "spontaneous obesity" (obesity manifested in people who happen to become obese in the real world). The first step was to produce experimental obesity in subjects by getting people who weren't fat to gain considerable weight. Sims and his collaborators initially tried to achieve that outcome with normal-weight college students. But it was a failed effort. The students just couldn't gain enough weight to become fat.

The researchers did succeed in finding a population they could make fat: volunteer inmates at a nearby prison. Working with this population, they carried out several studies in which 19 normal-weight adult men each gained 20–25% of his starting body weight over a four-to-six month period by eating a lot more than usual.[20] At the start of each study, the researchers determined how much the men ate to maintain their usual weights, and they calculated how much each should need to eat to gain the desired amount of weight over the coming months. Then, at the start of the weight-gain stage of the study, the subjects ate 4000 calories a day. Herein came the first surprise to the researchers. For some subjects, despite eating much more than they usually did, their weight gain soon came to a halt. So, these subjects' food intake was progressively increased. To keep gaining weight, some men ended up increasing their daily caloric intake to 10,000 calories, eating, as Sims put it, "impressive amounts of food," (over four times the amount they typically ate!).[21] It wasn't just that these men needed to eat far more than predicted to become fat. Once they had reached their higher target weights, they also had to eat far more to maintain those new weights than the researchers had predicted they would need to eat, based on their projected metabolic rates.

Part of what explained the unexpectedly high caloric intake these men needed to remain fat was that upon gaining so much weight, their metabolisms skyrocketed. At the outset of these experiments, at their usual lower weights, the men had normal metabolisms. But once they gained significant weight, their metabolisms were much higher than is typical for a man of that larger body size. Another study that Sims conducted illustrated this point vividly. In this other study, two spontaneously obese subjects dieted until they lost enough weight to reach a comparable level of fatness to that achieved by some initially thin prisoners post-weight-gain. Despite the men in these two cohorts being comparably fat, the difference in the metabolic rates of the two cohorts was marked. To maintain their new higher weights, the prisoners ate about *twice* the number of calories as the men who had dieted down to reach that same level of fatness.[22] And, unlike the overwhelming majority of those who are spontaneously obese, all the subjects in Sims's study easily returned to their typical, much lower weights following the study's completion.[23]

Numerous studies confirm the finding that people vary significantly in the ease with which they gain weight when they consume more food than usual. In one study, 16 non-obese young adults were "overfed" for eight weeks, consuming

1000 extra calories daily over and above the amount it was calculated that each would need to maintain their initial body weight. At the end of the study, weight gain across the subjects varied over tenfold, from just under .8 of a pound to 9.3 pounds.[24] The authors of this study pinpointed one key mechanism that seemed to account for much of this difference: those who gained the least weight when they ate more were prone to moving around more in small, incidental ways such as pacing around, fidgeting, and standing up more regularly than they ordinarily did. And this ramped-up drive to expend energy in such subtle ways, which was triggered by increased calorie intake for some people but not others, didn't appear to be the product of deliberate choice. It was not as though some consciously decided to pace, fidget, and stand more than they previously had.

The picture that emerges from these studies runs contrary to the popular supposition with which we began. On that supposition, differences in willpower explain why some get fat and some don't. But the science suggests that for those who are naturally thin, getting fat and staying fat seem to be downright effortful. Not effortful in the sense that eating a lot of one's favorite high-calorie treats tends to be onerous or unpleasant. Rather, becoming or remaining fat seems effortful for some individuals in the sense that those outcomes don't tend to arise spontaneously for them, that is, without their actively working to bring them about. It's almost as if their bodies are fighting to keep them thin: doing behind-the-scenes work to prevent them from gaining much weight and driving them to shed pounds easily if their weight does rise much above its typical level—by kicking their metabolism into high gear or prompting them to greatly increase incidental physical activity in response to increased consumption, for instance.

Plainly, these fat-fighting mechanisms don't spring into motion for everyone. For some, substantial weight is put on easily if excess calories are consumed, and upon gaining weight their bodies don't fight back with such compensatory mechanisms to resist further weight gain. Indeed, none of the spontaneously obese subjects in *The Biggest Loser* study had atypically high metabolisms when they were obese. Instead, at their usual high weights, they had normal metabolisms and when their weights decreased, their metabolisms became abnormally low. This suggests that many who are spontaneously obese didn't have to eat a tremendous amount of food to become obese, as the experimentally obese prisoners did. Also, quite unlike the prisoners, we know that spontaneously obese subjects in the aforementioned studies didn't have to eat particularly large amounts of food to remain obese. They eat the amount that would be predicted for a person of that body size with a normal metabolism. When those we might dub the "spontaneously thin"—that is, normal-weight people who haven't ever been fat—become experimentally obese by deliberately gaining large amounts of weight (like the inmates), their experience is, as science writer Gina Kolata aptly puts it, like a "mirror image" of the experience of spontaneously obese people, such as the *Biggest Loser* contestants, when they deliberately lose large amounts of weight.[25] For those in each cohort, their bodies seem to resist deliberate attempts to change their weight by more than a small margin, working hard to push their weights back to their typical level, whether that means nudging them toward being thin or toward being fat.

So, what might account for why some people's bodies seem to drive them toward thinness while others' bodies seem to drive them toward fatness? There's quite compelling evidence that a person's genes significantly influence the weight range that one is pushed toward maintaining. According to the "set-point theory" of weight regulation, each of us has a weight range, usually somewhere between ten and twenty pounds, that we are naturally driven toward, and genetic factors strongly condition what that range is for a given person. Maintaining a weight within that range is relatively easy (as is weight gain or loss within that range), whereas if one's weight shifts above or below it, the body fights hard to get back within it. This theory can explain the well-documented and quite varied ways that different people's bodies respond to deliberate interventions to steer them away from their usual weights—whether through physiological mechanisms that speed or slow their metabolisms, that prompt them to move around more or less, or that manipulate their hunger levels.

In the 1980s, the prominent obesity researcher Albert Stunkard conducted a famous study demonstrating the influence genes exert over the weight that people's bodies gravitate toward.[26] Analysis of data gathered from over 500 Danish adults who had been adopted at a very young age and raised away from their biological parents revealed just how much genes seem to affect our weight. The BMIs of the adoptees in their adult years bore *no* relation whatsoever to the BMIs of their adopted parents who raised them yet were clearly associated with the BMIs of their biological parents. In a later study, Stunkard and collaborators found that identical twins (who, of course, have identical genes) are likely to end up having about the same BMI whether they are raised together or apart, and they're more likely to have similar BMIs to each other than are fraternal twins (who are only as genetically similar to one another as any two biological siblings are).[27]

According to their analysis, "70 percent of the variation in people's weights may be accounted for by inheritance, which means that a tendency toward a certain weight is more strongly inherited than nearly any other tendency, including those that favor the development of mental illness, breast cancer, or heart disease."[28] While other studies have reached more conservative estimates on this matter, suggesting that genes may account for only about 40% of the weight a person ends up at as an adult, scientific experts agree that our genes significantly influence our weight (and that's especially so for those at higher levels of obesity).[29]

Although there seems to be little doubt that some of us are naturally predisposed toward being thin and others fat, it perhaps goes without saying that genes alone don't make us thin or fat. The environment we live in also importantly influences our weight. In an environment of extreme food scarcity, even individuals with a genetic predisposition toward obesity might find it impossible to become obese. Unlike such an environment, the one that obtains in the United States at present is one in which people who are genetically susceptible to obesity find it very easy to become fat. Two factors are usually singled out in explaining what makes the status quo environment "obesogenic."[30] First are technological advances that make it easier than ever before for people to lead sedentary lives; and that so many of us are physically inactive is thought to contribute to the sharp rise in obesity over the past several decades. Second is the ubiquity of cheap, high-calorie, "ultra-processed" foods, or "junk food" for short.[31]

I'll focus on the second factor, which most experts suspect has contributed more to the rise in obesity than the former. To start with, let's clarify what the offending foods are. Most foods that we buy are processed in some way or another (e.g., they may be canned, frozen, dried, or pasteurized). In recent years, the term "ultra-processed" has been introduced to pick out a distinctive sub-category of processed foods that have been linked to health problems and obesity.[32] A hallmark of ultra-processed foods is that they tend to have a long list of ingredients including some things you would never, or only rarely, use in your home kitchen—such as high-fructose corn syrup, emulsifiers, artificial flavors, stabilizers, and food coloring. These foods are generally high in calories, added sugars, saturated fats, and sodium, and they are low in nutritional value (typically, they don't contain much fiber, vitamins, or minerals). This broad category includes soft drinks, donuts, frozen pizza, chicken nuggets, hot dogs, cookies, chips, Twinkies, sugary breakfast cereals, candy bars, and many other mainstays of the standard Western diet. Occasionally eating foods is this category may not be detrimental to our health. However, when ultra-processed foods make up a majority of what we consume on a daily basis—as is currently the case for most people in high-income societies such as the U.S. and the U.K.—*that* is linked to negative long-term health consequences.[33]

In one of several popular books published in recent years documenting how junk food has come to dominate the Western diet, investigative journalist Michael Moss discusses the multitude of forces that conspire in getting a lot of us hooked on junk food.[34] He makes the case that people can, and do, become genuinely *addicted* to junk food. For Moss, what it means for a substance to be addictive is just that some people find it extremely difficult to resist their cravings to indulge in it. So, what makes it the case that some people today are addicted to junk food, in his view? To begin with, he explains how these foods have been deliberately engineered by industry-employed food scientists to make them maximally "craveable." These foods are carefully calibrated to contain a combination of salt, sugar, and fat—a ratio never found in unprocessed foods—that makes consumers want to keep eating more and more of them after that very first bite. Besides the deliberate "hyperpalatability" of their taste, food scientists at these companies also work hard to give these foods textures that we tend to find virtually irresistible. Indeed, there's a whole food science devoted to "sensory texture profile," and companies such as Frito-Lay spend huge sums of money zeroing in on the exact degree of crunch that is optimally pleasing to consumers.[35] Upon taking the first bite of a junk food, a person gets nearly instant gratification, with our brain's pleasure receptors lighting up within seconds, much quicker than it takes us to feel good when drinking an alcoholic beverage or taking the first drag of a cigarette. How quickly the pleasurable feelings arise upon ingesting or otherwise using a substance is a key part of the science of how humans form cravings and become addicted to substances. Adding to our draw toward these foods are enticing packaging and relentless advertising, both of which are intended to get us to associate these foods with positive feelings and warm, fuzzy memories.

In our society, a junk-food habit can be all too easy to start and difficult to kick. Consider, by contrast, the situation of someone who is addicted to an illegal recreational drug. Access to a steady supply to sustain one's addiction may prove a challenge. A person might not have a reliable dealer, getting the drug may require regularly putting oneself in dangerous situations, and maintaining one's habit over time might be financially draining. Someone addicted to junk food typically faces no such barriers. Junk food, frequently packaged in super-sized quantities, is all around us. Usually, it requires little or no preparation and can be eaten on the go. It is often cheaper than more nutritious options. Certainly, this seems true calorie for calorie. Take a person who is strapped for cash and doesn't have the time or the cooking facilities needed to prepare homecooked meals. If such an individual is trying to feed her whole family on a tight budget, purchasing fast food rather than healthier options like fish, whole grains, fruit, and vegetables may be a better bet to ensure that no one goes hungry.

But we might wonder: If these foods are so irresistible, then how come we haven't all become addicted to them and gotten fat as a result? Indeed, it seems clear that many people are able to indulge in junk food in moderation while others manage to mostly, or altogether, refrain. One key reason for this seems to be the marked variance in people's biological susceptibility to becoming hooked on junk food. A recent body of evidence suggests that we don't all experience food cravings in similar ways, and this disparity seems especially pronounced when it comes to cravings for ultra-processed foods. Studies show that for some people, the drive to over-indulge in food (either generally or certain types of foods specifically) can be overwhelming.[36] Researchers using brain scans to gauge different people's responses to various stimuli have found that "food stimulates the brains of chronic over-eaters in just the same way that drugs stimulate the brains of addicts."[37] Even in cases in which food addiction isn't at issue, a number of other internal biological forces lying outside of our control can exert powerful influence over the weight-affecting choices that we make. Studies reveal, for instance, that a person's genes shape which sorts of foods (e.g., high-fat and sugary) one is prone to finding desirable, how satisfied one feels upon eating, how susceptible one is to forming habitual cravings (even if not at the level of addiction), and how greatly one feels driven to eat when not hungry.[38]

In addition to genes influencing the weight ranges that different people's bodies gravitate toward, then, numerous other biological factors play a role in making some of us more predisposed to becoming and staying fat. And the status quo environment is highly conducive to getting some of us hooked on junk food. For some, the urge to eat (some types of) junk food might be nearly impossible to resist. How do these reflections bear on the plausibility of the weakness-of-will charge? The weakness-of-will charge, as we've seen, emphasizes that some of us make better weight-affecting choices than others. Some of us, for example, avoid excess indulgence in junk food and thereby avoid becoming fat, while others don't exert such restraint and thus become fat. Moreover, it is assumed that most fat individuals could have avoided becoming fat had they exerted proper self-control, as most thin people are thought to do. But that reasoning ignores the significant influence that factors lying outside of our control can have on our weight. As evidence surveyed in this section demonstrates, people vary considerably in their susceptibility to gaining weight when they eat more than usual, and this is largely due to factors lying outside their control. For instance, such interpersonal variance can be due to matters such as the speed of one's metabolism or whether eating more than usual prompts a strong drive to fidget—a drive operating below the level of conscious awareness. This suggests that in some cases, two otherwise similar people could make identical choices that produce very different weight outcomes for each of them: making the same choices might lead one person to gain a lot of weight while the other person's weight doesn't budge. In such a case, that one person ends up becoming fat and the other does not isn't explained by their making different choices and thus doesn't plausibly reflect a difference in willpower.

What is more, the picture that emerges from the science is that we're not all on anything like a level playing field when it comes to our respective capacities to make similar weight-affecting choices. Our capacities to make those choices vary quite a bit, as do the environments in which we each make the relevant choices. Different individuals who exhibit a similar degree of self-control might well make very different weight-affecting choices. But these different choices may be a product of each of them responding appropriately to their internal cues that condition their food-seeking behavior in the environment in which they reside. Chalking up people's different weight-affecting choices to differences in willpower, then, misses the point. There is little basis for supposing that fat people and thin people generally differ from one another based on how much willpower they exert. And so, the suggestion that fat people, in general, should be regarded as weak-willed for having allowed themselves to get fat should be rejected.

5. CONCLUSION

Frequently, fat people are deemed blameworthy based on the reasoning that they wouldn't be fat if they weren't weak-willed. I have argued in this chapter that we should reject the widely held belief that, in general, fat people are weak-willed. That belief is at odds with the empirical evidence. Setting the record straight on this issue matters not only because the common supposition that fat people are weak-willed is untrue but also because that supposition has harmful consequences. It contributes to many in society wrongly blaming fat people. In addition, for others to widely regard one as having a certain negative disposition, such as being weak-willed, that is at odds with one's own lived experience, can be alienating and can distort one's sense of self. Such a person can feel deeply misunderstood by others who regard her as weak-willed when she's not. And, over time, being regarded by others as weak-willed can lead a person to believe that she must be weak-willed and even to act as if she were.

1. INTRODUCTION

If fat people are blameworthy for being fat, then fat people would need to be doing something morally wrong. In chapter 4, I argued that, in general, it is not morally wrong to be fat. But even if it were, fat people wouldn't be blameworthy unless their failure to avoid being fat further reflected some moral flaw that could be meaningfully attributed to them. Why think that condition is met? Fat-blamers offer two main reasons. I considered one of those in chapter 5: the claim that fat people are weak-willed. On inspection, I argued, that claim proved to be untenable.

In this chapter I will turn to a different reason that fat people are sometimes thought to be objectionably implicated in being fat. This is the charge that some fat people exhibit *bad values*. On the bad-values charge, a person is criticized for what she does or doesn't care about, or for exhibiting related shortcomings that help explain her failure to do the right thing. The bad-values charge is typically advanced against fat individuals who seem to be just fine with being fat, or, even worse in the eyes of those who blame them, who dare to flaunt their fatness. Those who are criticized on this basis are fat people who are not trying to lose weight and who

DOI: 10.4324/9780367853389-8

have no problem letting others know that. Some of these folks take things a step further and declare that bodies like theirs are perfect as they are. Fat individuals who behave in these ways are condemned by others, often in very public ways, for daring to suggest that there is nothing wrong with being fat—and, indeed, that fatness might even be a positive trait that's worthy of esteem and admiration. On one popular version of the bad-values charge, fat people who promote fat acceptance are accused of irresponsibly serving as poor role models to impressionable others.

In section 2, I will consider this version of the bad-values charge, and I will argue that it tends to be without merit. Based on the arguments of chapters 4 and 5, as well as those I advance in section 2 of this chapter, we will see that in many instances in which fat people are blamed for being fat, that blame is misplaced. Still, I see no reason to deny that *some* fat people might be blameworthy. Certainly, my arguments leave open that possibility. Some fat individuals might be engaged in wrongdoing that pertains to their weight-related lifestyle choices, and some of those individuals might also be objectionably implicated in that wrongdoing. Given this possibility, in section 3, I construct a hypothetical case of a blameworthy fat individual—one that is based on a different popular variant of the bad-values charge than the one considered in the previous section. On this version of the charge, fat people are accused of whole-heartedly embracing a slothful, gluttonous lifestyle in spite of knowing that doing so might harm others. Again, this charge usually misses its mark. Still, I consider what sort of blaming responses might be justified in such a case were the accusation apt. Justified fat-blaming, I argue, would look nothing like most actual fat-blaming that occurs in our society. The chapter concludes by offering some reflections on why fat-blaming is so pervasive when there is little justification for it.

2. BLAMING FAT PEOPLE FOR "GLORIFYING OBESITY"

A frequent target of condemnation on the bad-values charge are fat activists and other fat individuals who publicly express their support of fat acceptance. These are folks who refuse to slim down as society tells them they should, and they are not afraid of letting others know that. Increasingly, there are more and more fat people who publicly profess that their bodies are fine as they are. These individuals make clear that they don't owe anyone else an explanation for their body size. Their critics accuse them of serving as poor role models for others. The problem, as these critics see it, isn't merely that these individuals are fat but moreover that they act in ways that set a bad example for others, making it more likely that others will become or remain fat. In this vein, fat people are variously accused of "glorifying," "celebrating," or "normalizing" obesity. These accusations are commonplace, and, overwhelmingly, their targets are women. Consider a couple of representative illustrations of this charge:

Example 1. In a 2018 opinion piece in The Guardian, a journalist writes: "Fronted by plus-sized models and social media influencers, the fat acceptance movement aims to normalise obesity, letting everyone know that it's fine to be fat. ... suggesting that being a size 30 is just as healthy as being a size 12 isn't a body-positive message ... it's an irresponsible form of denial. ... Whether we want to gorge on 3kg of chocolate, drink until we vomit in the bathtub or line our lungs with carcinogenic tar, informed adults are free to make their own choices. But while your own body is your business, actively encouraging unhealthy lifestyle choices and denying health risks in a public space isn't promoting body positivity." This journalist also bemoans the recent trend of "terms such as 'straight size' and 'fat pride' proliferating."[1]

Example 2. In a 2019 online magazine article, "The Body Positive Movement Is Not Socially Courageous, It's Toxic," the author explains her problem with the very fat model Tess Holliday being featured on the cover of two popular magazines, *Self* and *Cosmopolitan*. She doesn't take issue with Holliday's personal choices or how they affect her own health, but rather with the promotion of "messages in media that manipulate impressionable people on how to live their lives." Responding to a magazine editor who defended putting Holliday on the cover—in part, reasoning that she didn't think that people would respond to seeing the cover by rushing out to get donuts and pile on pounds—the author says, "it is ignorant to say that people won't use this as an excuse to abandon healthy lifestyles because fat is now 'accepted'. It is promoting obesity. People who struggle with binge eating are looking for an excuse to keep binge eating." Finally, she is particularly incensed that Holliday told her fans that, although she intended to start eating healthier, she's "still going to eat Cheetos and all of that." As the author sees it, that sort of message reflects a serious problem with the fat-acceptance movement at large: "The movement should be about self-love, self-care, compassion, but instead it's about eating Cheetos as a way to say, 'fuck you' to beauty standards."[2]

So, people like Tess Holliday are criticized for spreading a dangerous message. Through their words and actions, such fat activists are thought to be conveying to others that it's absolutely fine to be fat, which, in turn, leads others (most worrisomely, perhaps, the impressionable youth) to follow in their footsteps—embracing unhealthy, Cheetos-munching lifestyles and being fat. But, as their critics see it, it's not just that folks like Holliday cause such harm. Furthermore, they are thought to be *acting in bad faith* in causing such harm: they are accused of knowingly promoting unhealthy lifestyle choices, downplaying the risks of being fat, and glamorizing fatness.

This criticism of fat-acceptance advocates should be rejected. It relies on empirical falsehoods, a misunderstanding (or, perhaps, a mischaracterization) of the aims and probable consequences of the efforts of fat activists, and offensive stereotypes and generalizations about fat people.

Let's begin with that last issue. Those who blame fat people on this basis seem to assume that being fat necessarily indicates that one makes unhealthy lifestyle choices. As they see it, being accepting of fatness is tantamount to being accepting of, if not outright encouraging, binge eating and eating lots of "bad" foods. But being fat doesn't in itself tell us anything about a specific individual's lifestyle choices. Not all fat people binge eat or eat much, if any, junk food. We know that people can eat nutritious diets and exercise and still be fat. Fat acceptance isn't about signaling support for the sorts of unhealthy lifestyle choices that critics raise concern about. Rather, it is neutral on the matter of how people ought to eat.

However, one might respond, isn't it Tess Holliday who explicitly mentions that she has no plans to stop eating Cheetos? Yes. But notice that critics of fat activists accuse them of encouraging others to engage in "binge eating" and not just of eating some chocolate but of "gorg[ing] on 3kg" of it. Some individuals, fat or not, no doubt do these things. On what basis, though, do these critics presume that these fat individuals in particular must be eating copious amounts of Cheetos or chocolate, or that they are encouraging others to do so? Why can't fat people just eat some Cheetos or chocolate without that being regarded as a sure sign of their having dysfunctional eating habits more generally?

By contrast, consider how junk-food eating is often regarded when it's engaged in by thin people. In her highly offensive documentary *My Fat Story*, fat-hating British pundit Katie Hopkins embarks on a self-described mission to prove to fat people that they have no excuse for being that way. She tries to accomplish this by gaining a bunch of weight over three months—adding over 40 pounds to her very slim build—and then spending the next three months losing most of that weight. Hopkins repeatedly emphasizes that she'll lose weight only by using widely accessible, commonsense tactics (to drive home the point, of course, that fat people *have no excuse*). For her, this means no fad diets, no fancy gym or personal trainer; just eating "normal" foods when she's hungry and exercising regularly. A typical lunch in her weight-loss phase involves a good-sized serving of potato chips alongside a sandwich. She really wants her audience to understand that one can regularly eat chips and still be healthy and thin. This sentiment reflects a fairly common double standard. For the most part, when thin people eat junk food, they're commended for striking the right balance in being neither overly restrictive nor overly indulgent. But fat people like Tess Holliday? Well, if *they're* eating Cheetos, they must be shoveling them into their mouths all day long, and, to boot, encouraging others to do the same.

So, besides making problematic and unwarranted generalizations about fat people eating unhealthily, these critics of fat activists also seem to hold fat people to a different, and a much more stringent, standard than thin people: apparently, only the thin have a right to eat any junk food. (Of course, Hopkins entirely ignores the fact that some naturally thin people find it relatively effortless to lose weight they temporarily gain—due to their weight gain triggering changes in their metabolism, appetite, and drive to move around that are favorable to weight reduction—while others find weight loss anything but easy.)

Let's turn to the concern that the positive representation of very fat people's physical appearance—for instance, reflected in a glamorously made-up Tess Holliday on the cover of a mainstream magazine—signals to readers that it is acceptable for them too to be really fat. Challenging the conventional anti-fat narrative, featuring Holliday on a magazine cover suggests that fat people too can be attractive, fashionable, sexy, confident, and happy. Might some folks see Holliday on the cover of Cosmopolitan (alongside other positive representations of fat individuals) and, as a result, end up fatter (and let us grant, for the sake of argument, unhealthier) than they would otherwise be? Sure, that's possible. However, the question we should be asking is whether it's likely that someone like Holliday is doing net harm in her capacity as a role model. To answer that question, we need to consider the big picture.

On the one hand, consider the harm that fat activists might do. It doesn't seem plausible that the fat-positivity message upheld by Holliday and others would cause a great many people to drastically change their lifestyle habits in ways that would make them much heavier or much less healthy than they would otherwise be. For one thing, to suppose otherwise flies in the face of what we currently know about how weight and choice tend to interact. For the most part, people do not simply decide that they are fine with becoming fat (or decide to stop caring about being thin) and then go on to easily gain a whole bunch of weight. Similarly, it doesn't seem that many people who are already fat would stay fat just because, thanks to Holliday and others, they have now decided that it's OK to be fat. That is because we know that the overwhelming majority of fat people who *don't* make that decision are also likely to remain fat. For another thing, the message of fat positivity doesn't occur in a vacuum. Rather, it occurs against the backdrop of pervasive anti-fat sentiment. Consequently, whatever fat activists say or do, there is still immense social pressure on people to *not* be fat. That gives us further reason to doubt that fat activists have the profound influence their critics suppose that they do in making droves of people fat.

On the other hand, we need to consider who stands to benefit from the message of fat acceptance and how. It is a plain fact that many people are going to be fat quite apart from what any fat activists say or do. As plenty of evidence indicates, most fat individuals who have tried repeatedly to become thin don't succeed in keeping off much weight for very long. Frequently, such people are harshly criticized by others and beat themselves up for these "failures." Exposure to the message of fat acceptance might go some way toward helping such individuals, most of whom are going to be fat anyway, make peace with their bodies. It might help them let go of the shame and self-hatred society has long taught them to feel about their bodies. These individuals stand to benefit enormously from the message of fat acceptance, in terms of improved mental and physical health and overall well-being. In recent years, numerous people attest to being positively influenced by fat activism in just these ways. So, against the status quo backdrop of widespread anti-fat sentiment, it seems unlikely that the message of fat acceptance is going to make all that many of the otherwise-would-be-thin get, or stay, fat, and it might well benefit a lot of people who would be fat anyway.

Those who accuse fat activists (and other advocates of fat positivity) of irresponsibly "glorifying obesity" do so based on an uncharitable construal of the motives of fat activists (and these others). Holliday's critics suppose that she is actively encouraging people to be fat (e.g., "Hey folks, look how wonderful my body is, you should jump on the bandwagon and get fat too!"). But no one is being actively encouraged to become or stay fat. There's quite an important difference between actively encouraging fatness in those who wouldn't otherwise likely be fat and encouraging acceptance of fatness in people who are, and will likely remain, fat. People aren't told to become or stay fat; they are told they don't have to desperately try to stop being fat unless that's something they personally choose for themselves and for their own reasons. Crucially, fat activists strive to promote fat acceptance *against a backdrop of fat stigma*. They set out to counter fat-hatred, which, again, is not the same as actively encouraging fatness. The core message of fat acceptance, then, is along these lines: "Hey, if you are fat, and have been unsuccessfully trying not to be fat because society tells you to do that, you may stop. You don't need to hate yourself because you're fat. Indeed, you have the right to go through life feeling good about yourself whatever your body size."

This isn't to say that fat acceptance is merely about contesting the notion that *fat is bad*. Advocates of fat acceptance also sometimes promote *fat positivity*: casting fatness as a trait worthy of celebration in its own right. On this count too, it's important not to ignore the backdrop against which this message is conveyed. *Fat pride* is akin to *gay pride* or *disability pride*, or to the message *Black is beautiful*.[3] It is about according proper social esteem to a trait that dominant social norms have long cast as deviant and inferior. Fat acceptance, or fat pride, is about affirming that which society frequently denies: that people who are fat are just as deserving of living good lives, of enjoying a secure sense of self-worth, and of being treated with dignity and respect as anyone else is. Understanding the aims of fat activism in this way also suggests that the accusation that fat activists wantonly push others toward unhealthy lifestyles is baseless. Fat activists aren't acting with reprehensible, self-serving motives. Quite the opposite. Proponents of fat acceptance often have commendable motives for acting in those ways that others take issue with. Frequently at considerable personal cost—enduring not just mean-spirited criticism but relentless trolling, harassment, and threats to their own safety—fat activists work to combat weight stigma and to promote the health and well-being of many people.

But what of the accusation that fat activists contribute to the spread of misinformation by denying or downplaying the health risks of being fat? Some critics attack folks like Tess Holliday because they suppose that she is outright lying to the public when she states that she is in good health and is fit.[4] This is a troubling accusation. In general, we should assume that people are being truthful unless we have credible evidence of their dishonesty. A different accusation is that someone like Holliday sends the public a misleading message about the health risks of being fat. Even if she is healthy and fit now, when Holliday is featured in a fitness magazine like *Self* or posts details of her intensive workouts on social media, this might lead people to conclude that it's not unhealthy to be fat when her critics allege it, in fact, is.

However, a person *can* be fat and healthy. As we saw in chapter 3, the relationship between weight and health admits of considerable nuance. Should the nuance be ignored? Should we instead promote the false public health message that being fat is always a serious health risk and that all fat people ought to follow the standard lifestyle advice to try to become thin? No. Here too, we need to consider the context in which fat-acceptance messaging occurs. Given that the claim that it's unhealthy to be fat is endlessly rehearsed, it would be quite remarkable if seeing Tess Holliday and Lizzo on a handful of magazine covers would lead people to conclude that there aren't any health risks associated with being really fat. We should give people more credit than that. And again, it's a complicated matter: being really fat is associated with certain health risks, we are pretty clueless about what fat people are supposed to do to stop being fat, various lifestyle habits are linked to better health regardless of people's weight, and making fat people feel ashamed of their bodies is doing them serious harm. Although few fully understand all that, most understand enough not to let the occasional fat-acceptance messages they see lead them to conclude that being very fat tends to carry no health risks.

So, the bad-values charge typically misses its mark. Frequently, those who blame fat people on this basis rely on unsubstantiated, offensive generalizations about fat people. Further, they fail to undermine the reasoning that actually motivates fat-acceptance messaging. Indeed, they often fail to even engage with that reasoning at all.

3. HOW TO RESPOND WHEN BLAME IS FITTING?

Blaming fat people, as so many regularly do, tends to be unjustified because there's no good reason to conclude that most, or even many, fat individuals are blameworthy in connection to their being fat. For a person to be blameworthy for being fat, as we have seen, it would need to be morally wrong to be fat and one would need to be objectionably implicated in their wrongdoing (e.g., via their values, attitudes, or dispositions). Yet, I have argued, it is doubtful that either, let alone both, of these conditions are satisfied by all that many fat people. Still, some individuals may be blameworthy for being fat. What sorts of blaming reactions—that is, means of expressing protest toward the blameworthy—might be justified in such cases? In this section, I seek to answer this question, and I do so in service of the broader aim of assessing much actual fat-blaming that occurs in the status quo. I argue that even for fat individuals who are blameworthy, there would be no warrant for blaming them in most of the typical ways that fat people are blamed at present.

Let's construct a hypothetical case of a blameworthy fat person, based on popular anti-fat stereotypes, tropes, and assumptions. By no means do I endorse the unrealistic and offensive caricature of a villainous fat person that follows. When Marcy is in her late twenties, she decides to embrace a hedonistic way of life and begins to treat herself to generous portions of rich desserts every day. Over the next few years, she becomes very fat owing to this lifestyle change, and that, in turn, causes her a host of health problems. She harms others. Largely footing the bill of Marcy's considerable medical expenses imposes a serious burden on her employer, a small company struggling to stay financially afloat. Eventually, her poor health forces her to stop working, and she begins to collect government disability benefits. Her health issues prevent her from carrying out childcare and other household duties that she and her partner used to evenly divide. Understandably, her family is devastated about the sudden decline in her health. They love her and want her to be healthier. Overall, her health problems place an immense emotional and financial toll on her partner and children.

Marcy is well aware of how her poor health harms others. And she knows how she could stop causing these harms. Her doctor tells her she would very likely cease to experience these medical problems were she to revert to her former, healthier lifestyle and lay off the excessive dessert. But she simply doesn't want to do so. It's not that she would find it difficult or burdensome to give up dessert. She really loves eating lots of dessert, and she selfishly cares more about experiencing the pleasure she derives from that habit than she does about alleviating the burdens she imposes on others. Indeed, she unabashedly defends her dessert-loving ways to anyone who will listen. She even tries to get her children to adopt a similar lifestyle, regularly coaxing them to have extra helpings of dessert.

It strikes me as plausible that Marcy is blameworthy.[5] In any case, let us assume that she is. If Marcy is blameworthy, then might some others be justified in blaming her—that is, might some others be justified in expressing to her their disapproval of her transgressions? Let's consider what sort of blaming reactions might be aptly directed toward Marcy and by whom. It might seem appropriate for Marcy's family members to reproach her for failing to demonstrate proper concern for the suffering she causes them. However, it isn't obvious that anyone else would have the right to blame her. That's because for someone to be warranted in blaming another person, one would need to have a sound basis for judging that person blameworthy. This is an epistemic requirement: you need to know enough about relevant matters to judge a person blameworthy for a given transgression. To reasonably judge Marcy blameworthy, one would need to know much about her health, her lifestyle choices, her weight, and the interaction between those things; about how she harms others via her weight-related lifestyle choices; about her ability to change her weight and improve her health; and about her knowledge and attitudes about all those matters. That is quite a bit! Typically, except for perhaps those who are closest to a person, no one would have access to such wide-ranging, in-depth information about someone.

These reflections about who would be justified in blaming Marcy generalize to other like cases that involve individuals who are blameworthy for being fat. In those cases too, epistemic obstacles likely significantly restrict the scope of those who could appropriately blame such individuals for being fat. Usually, at most, that scope would be limited to those who are intimately acquainted with an individual (one's family members, close friends, and the like). In our society, however, a great deal of fat-blaming is carried out by people who aren't even remotely well acquainted with those whom they blame. People frequently blame complete strangers or passing acquaintances for being fat. This observation alone suggests that much actual fat-blaming that occurs in our society is unjustified: even if it targets fat individuals who are, in fact, blameworthy, those who do the fat-blaming lack the proper epistemic standing to do so.

But consider that Marcy doesn't just wrong her loved ones but that she wrongs others as well. For instance, one might think that she wronged her former employer and that she now wrongs her fellow citizens by collecting government benefits when it's her own fault that she can't work. Let us suppose, for the sake of argument, that Marcy does, in fact, commit wrongdoing in these ways (and is objectionably implicated in that wrongdoing). Granting, then, that Marcy is blameworthy for wronging those others but also granting that those others wouldn't typically satisfy the epistemic requirement to establish her blameworthiness, one might think that it would be a good thing to facilitate certain others gaining access to the relevant information they would need to establish her blameworthiness and to thus hold her accountable. Consider what that might entail, practically speaking. We might adopt policies that would license government agencies and employers to gather quite detailed and extensive information about citizens' and workers' health, weight, lifestyle choices, and much else.

We have compelling reasons to oppose such policies. For one thing, such policies would likely do serious harm to those whose weight and lifestyle choices would be subjected to scrutiny. Consider how they might harm many fat people who aren't blameworthy—which, of course, is *most* fat people. Having to prove to others that one is not blameworthy for one's weight or related health issues might be an emotionally draining, humiliating, or demoralizing exercise. For instance, to prove one's innocence, one might have to reveal to a total stranger that her struggles with compulsive overeating were spawned by childhood trauma. Individuals might be forced to reckon with deeply uncomfortable personal matters that they otherwise wouldn't have to, which, in turn, might make them feel ashamed or otherwise bad about themselves. Having to reckon with and disclose such information about oneself would seem to be odds with the mandate that people be treated with respect and dignity by state-sanctioned policies.

Such policies would likely harm many fat individuals in other ways too. We already live in a society that excessively monitors fat people, with those around them often keenly attuned to fluctuations in their weight and regularly policing their lifestyle choices. These practices have profoundly damaging effects. On a near-daily basis, the message is conveyed to fat people that they aren't trustworthy (surely, they must be eating more than they admit!), and that's why others take it upon themselves to keep a careful eye on each morsel they put in their mouths. Across the United States, in thousands of schools, parents receive "BMI report cards," alerting them if their kids weigh too much (a practice which, not surprisingly, appears to have no positive effects on children's health and may harm them).[6]

What is more, an ever-present threat of facing various social sanctions can encourage fat individuals to behave in ways that greatly compromise their emotional and mental well-being. Here, it's helpful to consider a phenomenon that fat studies scholars draw attention to, which is our society's problematic tendency to categorize fat people as either "good fatties" or "bad fatties."[7] In the court of public opinion, being deemed a bad fatty (for being perceived as someone who isn't trying to lose weight or otherwise behave healthily) invites harsh repercussions. To qualify as a good fatty, one must conspicuously perform their compliance with stringent social expectations—for instance, eating minimally and healthfully when in front of others (certainly, never eating "bad" foods such as Cheetos), regularly exercising, demonstrating that one is working hard to slim down, and apologizing for one's body and for taking up as much space as one does. It's not just that doing these things all the time can be exhausting. But there is also the added psychological toll of always worrying about whether one is doing enough to show others that one isn't a bad fatty. *No one* deserves to be treated in these ways: to be presumed untrustworthy and to be made to continually prove to others that one is acting in "all the right ways." Especially, it is an affront to one's dignity to be treated in these ways when a fat person owes no one an explanation for her weight or related lifestyle choices, and when the exacting standards fat people are expected to comply with are patently unreasonable. So, we have ample reason to be wary of policies seeking to distinguish fat individuals who are blameworthy from those who aren't. Those policies would likely treat many people in morally objectionable ways.

Reflecting on the Marcy case reveals a further point that is worth underscoring. That is the observation that even when fat-blaming might be justified, what we would be blaming a fat person for has little to do with one's being fat. Although Marcy is blameworthy *in connection to being fat*, that is a very loose connection. As stipulated in that case, her being fat contributes to her poor health and thus to her harming others. But her blameworthiness is more fundamentally explained by her values, her attitudes, her abilities, and so on; not by her being fat. Consider an example of a thin person who might be blameworthy in connection to her weight and related choices. Roxy has long been unhealthily obsessed with having a very thin, toned physique, and to that end she excessively exercises and engages in extreme dieting. This lifestyle takes a serious toll on her health and on her loved ones. But because Roxy is so singularly focused on being thin, she is unmoved by her family's pleas to change her ways. Plausibly, if we judge Marcy as blameworthy, we should judge Roxy as blameworthy by appeal to similar reasoning.

As by now is clear, much real-life fat-blaming is directed at fat people merely because they are fat. Based on fat individuals being fat, those who blame them spin a story to explain why they must be blameworthy—a story that, as we've seen, is rarely backed by solid empirical evidence or plausible moral reasoning. Now, we are further positioned to observe that even when a fat person is, in fact, blameworthy, there doesn't seem to be a particularly tight connection between a person's being fat and a person's being blameworthy. Obviously, just because some thin people behave like Roxy, we shouldn't engage in thin-blaming, i.e., blaming thin people for being that way. And just because some fat people might behave like Marcy, that doesn't give us a reason to engage in fat-blaming.

So, even though *some* individuals may be blameworthy for being fat, most of the actual ways that fat people are blamed prove unjustified, and so too does the general practice of fat-blaming.

4. CONCLUSION

Why is our society so quick to blame fat people? Plainly, it's not because there are compelling arguments for doing so. Indeed, as I have shown, the arguments for fat-blaming rely on dubious factual suppositions and unsound moral reasoning. A more plausible explanation for why we blame fat people is that anti-fat prejudice is deeply ingrained in all of us. Prejudice conditions our emotional responses to stimuli. Fatness offends people's aesthetic sensibilities and stirs in many a sense of repulsion. Plenty of us experience a visceral discomfort or unease when confronted with fatness in the flesh, both in ourselves and in others: this is not something we want to see or touch. This aversion that we feel toward fatness, in turn, makes us susceptible to constructing, as well as accepting, rationalizations of why, intellectually, we should oppose fatness and, by extension, fat people. Social scientists studying prejudice call these rationalizations "legitimizing myths."[8] Legitimizing myths take the form of dominant cultural narratives that provide a justification for regarding and treating some social groups as inferior. They serve a useful function in that they help us achieve greater harmony between our emotions and beliefs. On a gut level, we don't like fatness, and, owing to anti-fat legitimizing myths, we take ourselves to have a good reason for that aversion.

Often, the brute dislike and aversion so many individuals feel toward fat people is on naked display, e.g., when the airline passenger seated between fat passengers goes on about the prospect of being "squished" between "pigs" (in the example discussed in chapter 4). But in other cases, it can take some more work to spot the ways that anti-fat prejudice shapes how we think about and talk about fatness. Take, for instance, Peter Singer's ethical assessment of obesity that was considered in chapter 4. Singer seeks to provide his reader with an unbiased, rational case for why it's wrong to be fat. Yet, consider how anti-fat prejudice seems to color his analysis. At the outset of his piece, Singer remarks that "it has become commonplace to see people so fat that *they waddle rather than walk*."[9] And he explains that some people are now so large that hospitals must install "extra-large toilets" and "extra-large refrigerators in their morgues."[10]

Let's think about what's conveyed by his use of those particular words and examples. Fat people are cast in a patently undignified light. We are invited to view them as something of a spectacle. Waddling? The implication is that *that's* not how human beings should move about (shouldn't we leave the waddling to penguins and ducks?). Furthermore, the imagery of the waddling individual may bring to mind several negative stereotypes about fat people—depicting them as moving about like non-human animals encourages us to regard them as irrational, unintelligent, clumsy, and oafish. Then, there's the matter of Singer getting us to think about toilets and corpses. For many of us, doing so is likely to stir up a sense of disgust. Disgust is a primitive emotion that is already frequently elicited in individuals when they think about fatness. Singer could have chosen any number of other examples of what is required to properly accommodate larger bodies (like the need for appropriately sized desks and seats in classrooms and offices) that don't have any obvious connection with disgust. But by using these particular examples, Singer primes his reader to feel disgust, part and parcel of anti-fat sentiment, as we process the moral arguments he offers for why it's wrong to be fat.

In discussing these examples, my aim is neither to speculate about Singer's motives (i.e., whether he is deliberately appealing to these baser dimensions of anti-fat sentiment to bolster his case) nor to draw any inference about how he truly feels about fat people. Rather, my aim is to bring attention to the insidious nature of anti-fat prejudice, to notice how stealthily it might appear and nudge us toward accepting bad arguments for blaming fat people. Anti-fat prejudice is pervasive, and it affects each and every one of us, influencing how we regard our own bodies and those of others. We have all been raised with this prejudice. From early childhood on, it's been ingrained in us that fatness is unseemly, a moral failing, and deviant. This social conditioning is reinforced in popular culture, with fat individuals being woefully underrepresented in fashion magazines as well as on television and in movies. And in its frequent alarmist coverage of the obesity epidemic, the mainstream media is fond of using images of "headless fatties" (photos or videos of fat bodies without faces), a tactic that strips fat people of their agency and humanity.[11] We have been taught to view fat individuals through the lens of negative stereotypes, particularly ones that ascribe to them deficient characters and that are key to fat-blaming narratives we have examined—they're being weak-willed, ignorant, selfish, greedy, lazy, and irresponsible. These and other popular negative representations of fat people can make it very hard for us to not regard being fat as a bad thing, in one way or another. Adding to all this, as we have seen in earlier chapters, anti-fat bias intersects with sexism, classism, and racism, thereby augmenting our predisposition to harbor biases against those who are fat.

That we have been so thoroughly culturally conditioned to harbor negative feelings and attitudes toward fat people makes us all the more likely to accept specious moral arguments that fat people are to blame for various social problems and to cling to false beliefs (e.g., about fat people's lack of willpower) despite their being scientifically questionable. As we have seen in chapter 4, we cherry-pick in condemning fat people for (supposedly) ruining the healthcare system and for destroying the earth while not blaming others who seem to act in similarly harmful ways. Anti-fat prejudice helps us make sense of why we single out fat people for blame in these ways. Our biases lead us to *moralize* and treat being fat as a moral issue when it's not one. It is important for us to be clear-eyed about the background social context that we inhabit. We do *not* approach the issue of fat-blaming from an impartial perspective. We bring with us the baggage of deeply ingrained anti-fat feelings and attitudes, and thus we approach this matter through the lens of those biases. Because of this, we must recognize that arguments that call for blaming fat people might seem more convincing than they in fact are.

Part III

Reconceiving Fatness

Part III

7

1. INTRODUCTION

Previous chapters have argued that the standard ways our society responds to fatness are problematic. We shouldn't reproach fat people based on health concerns. We shouldn't blame people for being fat. In this chapter, I offer an account of how we should instead think and talk about fatness. First and foremost, I argue, we should regard our society's treatment of fat people as a social injustice. Specifically, we ought to view fat people as *oppressed*. Oppression is a distinctive type of social injustice. To be oppressed involves systematically enduring, or being at risk of systematically enduring, wide-ranging, unjust harms because one belongs to a given social group. Oppression isn't something that incidentally happens to members of an oppressed group, but rather it is perpetuated through social arrangements—through institutions, practices, and norms that shape our day-to-day lives.[1]

The idea that fat people are oppressed is deeply at odds with how we are accustomed to thinking about what it means to be fat. As I have argued in previous chapters, those conventional ways of thinking are misguided. Still, that fat individuals are oppressed isn't obvious. In this chapter, I advance a step-by-step case for why we should view fat people as oppressed,

DOI: 10.4324/9780367853389-10

and I explain how this way of seeing things can help us better understand the injustices that fat people endure.

2. FAT PEOPLE ARE OPPRESSED

2.1 What does it mean to be oppressed?

Oppression is a group-based harm. Oppressed individuals are harmed in virtue of belonging to some group or another. In this vein, as the feminist philosopher Marilyn Frye puts it, "Women are oppressed, *as women*."[2] Similarly, *Blacks* are oppressed as *Blacks*. Before considering whether, and if so on what basis, fat individuals might be oppressed in virtue of being fat, it will be helpful to take up a question that we don't usually think to ask: What does it even mean to be fat? It would seem that we need a basic sense of what the defining features of being fat are, so that we can determine who belongs to this group.

One helpful way of understanding what it is to be fat is as follows. Being fat is a matter of belonging to a social category—a category that we, in our society, make relevant for those we place in it. In part, being fat concerns physical characteristics of one's body, in terms of its size, shape, and other such properties. But moreover, it is a matter of the social significance that is attributed to one's body size. In the status quo, as per dominant cultural standards, to be fat is to have a body that is deemed too large. And being ascribed the status of having a too-large body has implications for how one is treated.[3]

Let us now return to the claim that fat people are *oppressed*.[4] Enduring oppression is about being unjustly and systematically socially disadvantaged (such that one faces wide-ranging disadvantages with respect to what one is able to have, do, or be) in a particular context, and this occurs because one belongs to a particular group. This rough account of what it means to be oppressed is advanced by Sally Haslanger in *Resisting Reality*.[5] On Haslanger's account, being oppressed is a matter of the social position that one occupies (e.g., being a woman, being Black, or being gay), and oppressed social positions are enmeshed in a wider network of unequal social relations. Specifically, belonging to an oppressed group entails occupying a social position that is, all things considered, subordinate to some other social position occupied by members of a privileged group. So, for example, women are oppressed relative to men, Blacks are oppressed relative to Whites (or relative to other racial groups depending on the context), and so on.

Oppressive social hierarchies are *durable*. That is, they persist over time and tend to be quite resistant to change. Part of what makes these hierarchies durable is that they are sustained by numerous interrelated and mutually reinforcing mechanisms. Also key to the ongoing reproduction of oppressive relations is that dominant ideology that operates in a context serves to rationalize those unequal relations. Such ideology is a matter of widely held beliefs, attitudes, and norms that give voice to the relevance of people being a certain way (or being perceived as being a certain way) that is the basis for their belonging to an oppressed group. Belonging to an oppressed group involves being "marked," on a society's dominant ideology, as an appropriate target for oppressive treatment— as someone who, as Haslanger puts it, "*ought to* occupy certain kinds of social position that are in fact subordinate."[6] Conversely, oppressive ideology serves to rationalize the view that those who belong to a privileged group, in relation to the oppressed, should enjoy their privilege.

Another feature of oppressive systems that contributes to their durability has to do with the fact that the unequal social relations they involve are typically reinforced in numerous, exceedingly subtle ways (usually, in addition to more overt ways). Oppressive structures are baked into the mundane, into the quotidian.[7] Because the fabric of our everyday lives is so pervasively inflected with norms, habits, beliefs, practices, and much else that together uphold oppressive relations, it can be easy enough for it to go largely unnoticed that oppressive forces exist at all. In this way, the workings of an oppressive system frequently hide in plain sight—from those who are complicit in oppression, from those who benefit from oppression, and even from those who are oppressed. So, although oppressive forces profoundly harm people, that they do so is often invisible to us.[8]

Equipped with this understanding of what oppression is, let us now consider what it would mean for fat people to be oppressed in virtue of being fat. Fat individuals would qualify as oppressed if, and only if, the following conditions obtain:

- It is widely supposed that it is a bad thing to be fat and that those who are fat thus ought to occupy a socially subordinate position.
- Social disadvantages are systematically imposed on fat individuals in virtue of their being fat, and consequently they tend to be materially worse off than thin individuals.
- It is an injustice that fat individuals are disadvantaged in the preceding ways—i.e., that they are systematically regarded and treated badly in virtue of being fat.

- The size-based hierarchy that relegates fat individuals to a socially subordinate position is durable.

Are all of these conditions satisfied when it comes to how our society regards and treats fat people? In what follows, I will demonstrate that they are.

2.2 Are fat individuals systematically socially disadvantaged?

To start with, we will consider whether fat individuals endure systematic, social disadvantages in virtue of being fat.[9] In previous chapters, we surveyed some of the various ways in which being fat is regarded as a bad thing and how fat people are treated badly because of that. Here, we can recall some of the basic facts. Fat people are subject to damaging stereotypes according to which they "are lazy, weak-willed, unsuccessful, unintelligent, lack self-discipline, have poor willpower, and are noncompliant with weight-loss treatment."[10] Fat children are frequently bullied and teased. Fat adults face pervasive workforce discrimination. Prevalent in our society are both explicit anti-fat bias, which concerns consciously held and endorsed negative attitudes about fat people, and implicit anti-fat bias, which refers to a disposition to subconsciously regard fat people less favorably. And widely held explicit and implicit weight bias both appear to play a significant role in explaining why fat people fare worse in the domains of education, employment, and healthcare, among others.

Now, it is becoming more commonplace in our society for people to take issue with some of the more blatant and egregious ways in which fat individuals are harmed. Increasingly, it seems, we do not think it's OK for fat people to be bullied, harassed, teased, shamed, or insulted for being fat. Still, in understanding how fat people are harmed by the system of size-based oppression, or *sizeism*, that persists in the status quo, it is important to appreciate the ubiquity of cases that involve overt and often downright cruel mistreatment of fat individuals. Yet, these cases, as I will illustrate, only scratch the surface of the far-reaching ways in which fat people are harmed by sizeism. Indeed, there are plenty of other, more subtle ways in which the status quo system of sizeist oppression harms fat individuals—harms that usually do not receive as much attention in public discourse as those more overt harms.[11] These are cases in which we may altogether fail to even recognize that fat people fare worse than others due to an oppressive system that penalizes them for being fat. It is cases of this sort, involving less obviously oppressive harms endured by fat people, to which we will now turn. Let's consider an example.

Anna. Anna, a fat woman in her thirties, has not had a routine wellness visit with a healthcare provider for several years, and she rarely exercises. As a result, her health suffers. Anna is well aware that she should do these things for the sake of her health. She genuinely wants to do them, and she forms the intention to do them. She even takes concrete steps toward fulfilling that intention. Yet, time and time again, she doesn't follow through. For the past five years, each January, she schedules an annual check-up with a physician, but each time as the appointment nears, she cancels it. Years ago, Anna joined a neighborhood gym that she passes on her daily commute to the office. Many days, she vows to herself that she'll go to the gym after work and even packs her gym bag. But then, at the very last minute, she changes her mind and doesn't go.

On the account set out above, if fat people are oppressed for being fat, then they are disadvantaged based on how they are generally regarded and treated in virtue of being fat. So, to work out whether Anna is the victim of size-based oppression, here are the sorts of questions we need to answer. Do social forces play a key role in causing Anna to suffer poorer health (based on her acting in the described ways)? In particular, are social forces implicated in making Anna worse off based on how we, in our society, tend to regard and treat fat people? On the face of it, it might not seem that Anna has been harmed by an oppressive system under which she is generally regarded and treated badly due to her fatness. Crucial to this judgment is the reasoning that Anna's poor health is a consequence of her own freely made choices. She could avoid the relevant poor health outcomes by making better choices, and so it might not seem plausible to suppose that she has been harmed by a sizeist system.

However, the reasoning leading to that verdict moves too quickly. It's true that Anna could have made different choices and likely would have been healthier if she had. But it doesn't follow that her being worse off in this respect is not, at least in part, due to her subjection to a system of sizeist oppression. Consider why Anna makes these choices that aren't conducive to promoting her health. For one thing, suppose that the primary reason for Anna repeatedly failing to go in for an annual check-up is that she dreads how such an appointment will go. In the past, numerous interactions with medical professionals left her feeling really bad about herself. On a typical visit, she notices a nurse's raised eyebrow or slight grimace upon seeing the high number on the scale when she is weighed at the start of her appointment. Usually, that is followed by a doctor lecturing her at length about the dangers of her weight and on the importance of eating a healthier diet. When Anna tries to explain that she *does* eat quite healthfully and that she has tried countless diets that never seem to help her lose much weight, she is cut off and informed in a somewhat exasperated tone that she must not be trying hard enough. She frequently leaves these appointments with a sense of frustration that doctors seem more interested in discussing her weight rather than other medical concerns unrelated to her weight that she had wanted to be the focal point of the appointment.

Similarly, suppose Anna's reluctance to go to the gym has to do with it being a space in which she doesn't feel welcome. Anytime she has been there, she has felt incredibly self-conscious, and because of this the very prospect of returning there is anxiety-inducing. Based on past experiences, she worries that other patrons will rudely stare or laugh at her on account of her body size and her low level of fitness. She suspects that even if these folks don't say anything, they must be silently judging her—e.g., for how horrible she looks in workout clothes or based on how quickly she tires during exercise. Last time she went to the gym, a friendly employee congratulated her on starting her fitness journey and assured her that she would soon be well on her way toward meeting her weight-loss goals. Anna feels mortified wondering what that employee would think of her now that she hasn't returned in months and hasn't lost any weight.

The sorts of concerns Anna has about going to the doctor or to the gym are ones that many fat people in our society have. For instance, obese patients often report that healthcare providers treat them disrespectfully, make upsetting comments about their weight, and do not take seriously how much they struggle to lose weight.[12] Several studies also suggest that having these types of negative experiences helps explain why fat individuals are less likely than normal-weight individuals to seek preventative healthcare.[13] As for exercising in public spaces, nearly one-half of 141 obese Australian adults who were interviewed in a qualitative study said they "were unwilling to participate in exercise" based on their expectations that others would "laugh at," "ridicule," "stare at," or "abuse" them.[14] A different study revealed that individuals who had experienced weight discrimination were more likely to avoid exercising in public.[15] Consider Roxane Gay's description in her memoir *Hunger*:

> When I go to the gym on my own, I always feel like all eyes are on me. ... My self-consciousness magnifies at the gym. ... And there is, of course, the self-doubt, the nagging sense that I shouldn't even bother, that I don't belong in the gym, that any attempt toward fitness is pathetic and delusional.[16]

It seems quite plausible to suppose that many fat people engage in behaviors like those exhibited by Anna due, in part, to their concerns about negative encounters in healthcare settings and gyms (and like venues).

Importantly, that many fat individuals have such concerns shouldn't be chalked up to their self-conceived, paranoid imaginings—imaginings that are not borne out by how they are, in fact, regarded and treated in such domains. Quite the opposite. They *are* frequently treated badly in those (and in plenty of other) settings. Moreover, such mistreatment itself is the product of how we are taught to view fat people. Indeed, against the backdrop of widespread anti-fat ideology, we should expect negative stereotypes about fat people—that they are lazy, undisciplined, and noncompliant—to influence how doctors view and respond to their fat patients. This plausibly explains why a fat patient like Anna's weight-loss efforts would be quickly dismissed on the grounds that she must not be trying hard enough. Doctors and nurses, just like the rest of us, are conditioned by our anti-fat culture, which tells us that fat individuals have only themselves to blame for being fat. Evidence suggests that medical practitioners exhibit high levels of anti-fat bias and endorsement of negative stereotypes about fat people that are on a par with the population at large.[17]

That oppressive social forces help cause Anna's behavior and the subsequent disadvantages that she suffers does not require that explicit anti-fat animus be a factor. For instance, suppose that Anna's doctor doesn't endorse anti-fat bias. She genuinely cares about the health and well-being of her fat patients. She lectures them on the importance of weight loss and the need for them to be vigilant about their lifestyle choices only because she wants to help them become healthier. Even so, it would be reasonable for a fat patient like Anna who has such an interaction to feel that she is mistreated for her weight in that setting. Anna's being lectured by a doctor about her "weight problem" for the umpteenth time, while not having the health concerns she wishes to discuss adequately attended to, makes for a frustrating medical encounter. So too might Anna reasonably feel disrespected when she gets the sense that her doctor doesn't believe her when she insists that the weight just won't come off even when she has tried very hard to slim down by dieting. And, again, this is so even if Anna can see that her doctor acts out of concern rather than dislike for her fat patients.

Similarly, in a culture in which we're all taught to value and pursue thinness, it's no surprise that a well-meaning personal trainer would assume that a fat person like Anna is exercising to facilitate weight loss and thus offer words of encouragement based on that assumption. But intentions aside, it is reasonable for Anna to hear precisely the message that she does from such a comment: "You should be trying to slim down, and if you're not working out regularly that just goes to show that you are lazy, undisciplined, and it's your own fault for remaining so large." Widely held negative stereotypes about fat people can, and frequently do, influence how fat people see themselves. And so, even if the trainer doesn't mean to convey anything like that harsh message to Anna with his comment, it wouldn't be unreasonable for her to interpret it that way.[18]

Even if Anna weren't likely to experience the sorts of negative reactions she anticipates, that wouldn't make her concerns unreasonable. To see this, suppose that were Anna to go in for a routine check-up this year, her doctor wouldn't bring up her weight unless Anna wished to talk about it, and in that case the doctor would respectfully engage with her on that matter. Similarly, imagine that part of Anna's worry about being mocked by others at the gym (which feeds into her broader fears about being negatively judged in that space) is grounded in a misinterpretation of a previous encounter. The last time she was at the gym, she felt sure that two fit, thin women were pointing at her and laughing—no doubt in connection with her weight, Anna figured. However, as it happens, those women were laughing at a ridiculous advertisement on the television just behind Anna. That Anna was wrong about that one instance doesn't imply that her worries about how she might be perceived by others at the gym are, in general, unreasonable. On the contrary, it is perfectly reasonable for Anna, and for other fat people, to anticipate facing hostile or otherwise unwelcome treatment at gyms and at doctors' offices (as well as in a host of other settings).

Now we are well positioned to appreciate one important way that a fat person like Anna can be harmed by a sizeist system even when the relevant disadvantages that she suffers are traceable to her own choices. By acting in various health-promoting ways such as going in for an annual check-up or exercising in public, fat people can reasonably expect to endure non-trivial social penalties, penalties that are not imposed on thin people who choose to act in those same ways. Society makes it harder for fat individuals to act in such health-promoting ways. Specifically, due to how members of our society are taught to view fat people, through the lens of numerous damaging stereotypes, fat people are constrained in their ability to act in certain ways that they might well want to act and that would tend to benefit them if they did.

The harms that Anna suffers can be usefully theorized about by drawing on a concept from the field of social psychology called "social identity threat."[19] Here the term "social identity" refers to a person's belonging to a social category, such as that of "being fat," and their awareness of so belonging. So, for instance, for a person like Anna to have the social identity of being fat would mean that most others regard her as fat and that she is aware of that fact. Social identity threat is a phenomenon that can arise, specifically, in individuals who have a social identity that is culturally devalued. The "threat" at issue refers to a psychological state that can be activated in a person with a devalued identity when they become highly attuned to the prospect of "being devalued, judged negatively, or rejected based on their social identity."[20] When a person experiences social identity threat, their keen awareness of the risk of being devalued in virtue of their identity triggers an excessive preoccupation with that risk—say, of confirming others' negative judgments or stereotypes, or of being mistreated—and that, in turn, can flood them with negative emotions, such as anxiety and fear.

Anna is plausibly understood as experiencing weight-based social identity threat when she entertains the prospect of going to the gym, a setting that she has good reason to regard as weight-stigmatizing. Imagining herself at the gym makes Anna acutely aware of how society negatively judges her for being fat—as lazy, unhealthy, unfit, weak-willed, unattractive, and so on. One behavioral response that social identity threat is well known to elicit in individuals is "stigma avoidance," which refers to individuals consciously choosing to avoid domains in which they fear being stigmatized.[21] Stigma avoidance seems an apt description of what is going on when Anna acts in ways she knows are detrimental to her health, such as not going to the gym and cancelling doctor's appointments. Plausibly, she behaves in these ways due, in part, to her awareness of having a socially devalued identity.

An emerging body of evidence suggests that social identity threat likely harms fat individuals in other ways too. Several studies found that exposing women who were fat, or who identified as fat, to weight-stigmatizing content was linked to their eating more. For instance, in one study, among women who identified as overweight, those who read a news article about weight discrimination ate more high-calorie snack foods and felt less capable of exerting self-control over their eating than those who read a non-weight-stigmatizing art-icle.[22] In another study, overweight individuals who were made aware of negative weight-related stereotypes just before placing an online meal order, ordered meals that were much higher in calories than overweight individuals for whom those stereotypes were not activated.[23] And in a different study, overweight women ate a much greater quantity of snack foods after watching a video compilation of weight-stigmatizing content (when compared both to overweight women who watched a neutral video and to normal-weight women who watched the weight-stigmatizing video).[24]

Jeffrey Hunger, a social psychologist who studies weight-based social identity threat, proposes an explanation for what might cause the behaviors observed in the just-discussed studies. Surveying wide-ranging evidence on the impacts of weight stigma, he and co-authors write:

> Coping with the stress generated by weight-based social identity threat undermines overweight individ-uals' executive functioning and impairs their subse-quent capacity for self-control over eating. Regulating the stress, negative emotions, intrusive thoughts, and interpersonal anxieties triggered by weight stigma is effortful.[25]

In general, it is hypothesized that experiencing social iden-tity threat can compromise one's "executive functioning," a catch-all term encompassing the crucial cognitive capacities (e.g., employing working memory, focusing, and ignoring distractions) that enable a person to do well in planning, reasoning, and problem-solving tasks. This harmful effect of social identity threat has been studied not just in the case of weight, but additionally (and much more extensively at that) in cases involving other groups who face the prospect of social identity devaluation.

Numerous studies indicate that when individuals experience social identity threat and suffer compromised executive functioning, that, in turn, can negatively affect their ability to perform well on various tasks—in particular, cognitively demanding tasks. In one experiment, fat women were paired with a thin partner to play a collaborative word game.[26] Half of these fat women were paired with someone they were made to believe held anti-fat attitudes (which, plausibly, would activate social identity threat in them). Among those women, the more they worried about facing social rejection from their partners, the greater their likelihood of underperforming at the word game. Additionally, the fat women who thought they were paired with an anti-fat partner reported experiencing more negative emotions and anxious thoughts as well as having tried harder to be likable to their partners. Other studies too suggest that when individuals who perceive themselves as fat experience weight-based social identity threat—by having their conscious awareness of others' anti-fat attitudes triggered—they are at higher risk of enduring a slew of detrimental psychological effects, including feeling stress and anxiety and exhibiting higher levels of concern about social rejection.[27]

To be clear, we don't yet know to what extent or in which specific ways fat people might be harmed by weight-based social identity threat *in the real world*. To date, the research on weight-based social identity threat (including the findings just surveyed) has been conducted in lab-based experimental settings. And whether findings involving subjects who typically partake in a study for a few hours would translate into similarly detrimental consequences being experienced by fat individuals in the real world isn't known for sure. But still, based on those findings, it's quite reasonable to suppose that fat people stand to be harmed in the real world by experiencing weight-based social identity threat. In particular, we have good reason to suppose that making fat individuals consciously aware of their devalued social identity might well, in the real world, impose a hefty mental and emotional toll on them: increasing stress and anxiety; causing intrusive negative thoughts and feelings; increasing vigilance about the prospect of others' negative judgments; and worsening self-image. It seems plausible that experiencing those psychological harms of weight-based social identity threat might cause many fat people to experience deficits in valuable cognitive resources (resources that are in limited supply for all of us within a given time period). And that, in turn, might help explain why many fat individuals would tend to perform less well than they are capable of, potentially in a variety of domains.

This naturally raises a question: In which real-world domains might fat people be susceptible to being harmed by social identity threat? In part, the answer depends on the particular ways that fat people are negatively judged or stereotyped and how that relates to their ability to perform well in particular domains. The negative judgments and stereotypes ascribed to fat people are sweeping in their scope. Because they are fat, their physical and mental abilities are judged inferior. Fat individuals are seen as stupid, unattractive, unhealthy, unfit, and clumsy. Their moral characters are maligned too. They are seen as lazy, undisciplined, and greedy. Society's condemnation of fat people's perceived health status, appearance, and character, in turn, leads many to judge them as disgusting.

Consequently, it seems reasonable to suppose that fat people experiencing social identity threat are likely to be penalized not just in a few domains but quite pervasively—for instance, in the classroom, in the workforce, as well as in forming romantic partnerships and friendships. Indeed, evidence from experimental settings suggests that when fat individuals are engaged in activities, or are in social contexts, in which they are particularly prone to being negatively judged for their body size, they may be especially likely to experience social-identity-threat-induced harms. One study suggests that such harms are faced by fat women in the realm of dating.[28] Another study found that overweight and obese individuals who feel negatively stereotyped for their weight in the workplace tend to judge themselves as being less capable of performing their jobs than those who don't feel that way.[29] And, to recall from previous chapters, numerous studies find that fat individuals fare worse than thin individuals in these and other ways too.[30]

If weight-based social identity threat causes fat individuals to underperform or to behave in other ways that do them harm, how would this bear on our broader inquiry into whether fat people are oppressed? To help answer this question, let's turn to another example.

Betsy. Betsy is a fat woman who has worked at an accounting firm for the past decade. Her performance at work suffers due to her deep-seated anxieties about how others might regard her for being fat. In meetings, she finds herself excessively preoccupied with concerns about clients critically judging her appearance or assuming that she isn't as bright as her thin colleagues, and because of this she doesn't come up with nearly as many good ideas on the spot as her thin colleagues do—and which she would if she weren't so pre-occupied. Even when she does have good ideas in meetings, she hesitates to raise them. That's because she is embarrassed about drawing attention to herself and having all eyes in the room on her. She sometimes finds it hard to focus because she feels bad about herself, wondering, for instance, if she can't even manage to lose and keep off twenty pounds, does she really have what it takes to succeed in the demanding line of work she's chosen to pursue? Owing to all this, Betsy's job performance suffers, and that explains why she is regularly passed up for promotions and raises.

Initially, one might be tempted to conclude that Betsy isn't made worse off by a sizeist system (as might also have seemed initially plausible in the Anna case). After all, Betsy's lack of career advancement isn't due to, say, a fat-hating boss who favors equally qualified thin employees over her. Rather, it's explained by her performing less well at her job than her co-workers who are promoted. So, one might infer that it is no one's fault but Betsy's that she isn't more successful at her job.

However, against initial appearances to the contrary, the social identity threat framework can plausibly help explain why Betsy suffers *social* disadvantages and, moreover, why she is harmed by *systematic* social forces. It is true that Betsy is held back by her own anxieties and low self-esteem. But these features of her psychology don't occur in a vacuum. Instead, her propensity to experiencing those and other related forms of psychological distress is aptly understood as the product of a confluence of social forces that ascribe to her a devalued social identity on account of her body size. How our society views Betsy gets in her head in ways that predictably compromise her ability to flourish at her job. People do not voluntarily choose to succumb to the pernicious effects of social identity threat. Rather, social identity threat is a consequence of their social environment. It is imposed on those who experience it against their will. Yet it harms its victims in ways that makes it seem like it is a disadvantaged person's own fault for becoming so disadvantaged. It operates by hijacking a person's psychology, making someone like Betsy prone to having certain negative thoughts, feelings, and concerns that render one susceptible to underperformance.

As in the Anna case, available evidence supports the contention that the sorts of harms suffered by Betsy affect many fat people in our society.[31] On the face of it, there's good reason to suppose that many fat individuals may experience weight-based social identity threat with some frequency and potentially with wide-ranging detrimental effects. Those harms, I have argued, are plausibly understood as a product of a system of sizeist oppression that pervasively penalizes fat individuals for being fat.

2.3 Are fat individuals unjustly disadvantaged?

I have discussed cases like Anna's and Betsy's—cases involving harms that may seem, in a sense, self-inflicted—to draw attention to the more subtle ways that a sizeist system penalizes fat individuals for being fat. Such cases are ones in which it might initially seem less plausible that sizeist forces are in play. Yet, even in those cases, sizeism is in play. In more straightforward cases, it is easier to see that sizeism causes harm (e.g., when fat people face overt workplace discrimination). There are plenty of other subtle ways that sizeism harms fat people that I won't discuss in detail. But, we might further wonder, are individuals like Anna and Betsy victims of injustice? To recall from the outset of the section, for fat people to qualify as oppressed, they must be systematically subject to unjust social disadvantages in virtue of being fat. In what follows, I will argue that fat people are unjustly disadvantaged, and I will explain on what grounds that is so. This is a matter of identifying what is morally wrong with fat people being socially disadvantaged in the ways that they are.

In our society at present, fat people are deprived of equal standing. They are made to occupy a subordinate social position. This is the fundamental injustice that fat individuals endure. Enjoying standing as a social equal is something that fat individuals, and, indeed, all of us who belong to a society, are owed. Specifically, equal standing is something that each of us owes to others with whom we share a society: we owe it to one another to ensure that the collective social arrangements that we each play a role in upholding do not avoidably deprive entire groups of people of the ongoing ability to meaningfully stand in relations of equality with their fellow members of society. These are the core tenets of a relational egalitarian theory of justice.[32]

But what does having equal standing, or being deprived of the same, involve? That we enjoy equal standing is a mandate that has two key components. First, all members of society must be able to participate in, and benefit from, the gains of our social system on terms of equality. One important dimension of lesser standing is characterized by material deprivation—having or being able to do less than others. As we've seen, fat individuals, as a group, are so deprived. Owing to socially imposed disadvantages, fat people are not on a par with others when it comes to such things as enjoying decent healthcare or economic advancement. These are deprivations analogous to those that other oppressed groups have long sought to remedy. Indeed, if we look to social movements fighting other forms of oppression—such as racism, sexism, and ableism—we see that oppressed groups in those cases work to dismantle social barriers that limit their inclusion, as equals, in important domains of social, political, and economic interaction. These groups demand enjoyment of valuable goods and opportunities, such as a decent education, employment, political participation, and dignified accommodation in public spaces, *on a par with others in society*.

Equal standing, however, isn't just about enjoying valuable goods and opportunities on a par with others. This brings us to the second key component of the mandate of equal standing. We are each entitled to social conditions that enable us to enjoy *recognition* as equals. Enjoying equal recognition is about how individuals express their mutual regard for one another—through everyday interactions, through informal social norms and practices that shape attitudes and guide behaviors, and through institutions and policies. Someone might be deprived of equal recognition if it's regularly communicated to her via cultural practices that people like her crucially matter less than others. As the philosopher Nancy Fraser puts it, to be unjustly misrecognized is "to be denied the status of a full partner in social interaction, as a consequence of institutionalized patterns of cultural value that constitute one as comparatively unworthy of respect or esteem."[33] A lack of equal recognition can, in turn, profoundly shape the character of social relations. Social relations may be organized hierarchically in ways that prevent people from relating as equals. Such hierarchies might, for instance, reflect significant disparities in power or social esteem. That individuals deserve recognition as equals supposes that, cutting across interpersonal differences (e.g., in our talents, abilities, or social identities), we are each foundationally worthy of equal respect and moral consideration. On relational egalitarianism, justice requires the social arrangements that collectively regulate our lives to enable us all to interact as equals, on terms that express a commitment to our equal standing.

A call for equal recognition too has been a key demand of oppressed groups. Consider long-standing struggles to advance gay rights in the United States. A core aim of this movement has been to combat the stigma imposed on gay and lesbian individuals—for instance, by demanding that the American Psychiatric Association stop classifying homosexuality a mental disorder (as it did until 1973) and by protesting the "Don't-Ask-Don't-Tell" policy (repealed in 2010) requiring gays and lesbians to remain closeted if they wished to serve in the military and enjoy the full benefits of doing so. A demand for equal recognition also underlies gay rights advocates' fight for inclusion in the institution of marriage (over and above having the right to enter into same-sex civil unions, even if the material benefits of civil unions were on a par with those of marriage). Appeal to the value of equal recognition can explain why civil unions won't do. Offering gay and lesbian couples an arrangement that closely resembles marriage but isn't granted the same label naturally invites the question of "Why call it something different if, for all intents and purposes, it's the same?" Against a backdrop in which being gay has long been cast as deviant and shameful, being granted civil unions instead of marriage can be reasonably interpreted as conveying to gays and lesbians that they are, on some fundamental level, inferior to heterosexuals.

Unequal standing isn't merely a matter of suffering isolated or occasional incidents that involve being unfairly treated or regarded based on group membership. Take Jake, who is blue-eyed. Once, he didn't get a job because the company's boss detests blue-eyed people. Sometimes, his parents and siblings tease him for being the only blue-eyed person in the family, and this hurts his feelings. Jake isn't oppressed in light of these facts. In general, our society doesn't make having blue eyes a bad thing. The injustice of unequal standing is a matter of someone being both pervasively treated as lesser *and* pervasively regarded as lesser in virtue of their group membership in a given context. My claim is that this is the fundamental injustice that fat people endure. As we have seen above, an interplay of social forces marks as inferior those who are deemed fat and prevents fat individuals from enjoying cooperative gains of society on a par with others. No one should be treated that way.

With this account of egalitarian justice set out, let's now revisit the Anna case. Consider what might be unjust about the typical interactions Anna experiences in healthcare settings. In those settings, she is frequently treated by medical professionals in ways that make her feel bad about herself. But has she been wronged, and if so, precisely how has she been wronged? Focusing on just one aspect of those interactions, we can recall that on several past occasions Anna simply isn't believed when she tells a doctor that she has tried hard before to lose weight. The philosopher Miranda Fricker introduces the concept of "testimonial injustice," which can help make sense of what happens in those instances.[34] A testimonial injustice occurs when a speaker's testimony is given less credibility by hearers due to prejudice.

Specifically, on Fricker's framework, members of a group facing systematic prejudice are prone to suffering what she calls an "identity-prejudicial credibility deficit," which is a matter of these individuals' devalued identity causing others to discount their testimony.[35] Indeed, based on Anna's devalued identity as a fat person, her relationship with her doctor is marked by a troubling asymmetry. At least when it comes to her weight and lifestyle choices, she is regularly presumed by others to be dishonest or as lacking in credibility to attest to her own experiences. Another way that Anna may suffer a loss of credibility is by others supposing that because she is fat, she must also be ignorant. For example, at the doctor's office or at the gym, others may wrongly presume that she must not know what a healthy diet or exercise routine consists of. It's commonplace for fat people to be subjected to condescending lectures from thin people who tediously rehearse to them widely believed (though often misguided) maxims about nutrition, fitness, and weight loss.[36] Parallel to "mansplaining," we might categorize such behavior (whereby a privileged thin person supposes that she has greater insight into a fat person's body than the latter herself does) as "thinsplaining."[37]

At least when it comes to what fat individuals have to say about their weight-related behaviors, plenty of anecdotal evidence suggests that they are frequently presumed to be dishonest or ignorant. If a fat person claims that she doesn't eat what most others would consider an excessive amount, all too often it's assumed that she is lying. Ditto with exercising. Fat people, it's commonly supposed, must be lying when they say they don't eat huge amounts or that they regularly exercise since, after all, if they actually did those things, they wouldn't remain fat. It is possible that the credibility deficits that fat people suffer with respect to those matters negatively affect how their testimony is received by others more generally. That is, they may be regarded as less honest or as less knowledgeable when they speak up about matters unrelated to their weight. But even if their credibility were diminished only in this one domain, that would be no small thing. That's because it's an exceedingly common experience for fat individuals to have their weight and related lifestyle choices continually scrutinized by others (e.g., being carefully watched during meals by family or friends who express concern for their health or being asked by total strangers if they've heard about some diet trend). So, fat individuals may be regularly denied epistemic authority to credibly speak to their own experiences.

What is more, being treated this way over time might well make a person susceptible to facing other epistemic harms as well. Someone who becomes accustomed to not being believed or to not being taken seriously might not speak up when she otherwise would have. For instance, Anna might refrain from setting the record straight when her doctor tells her (without any sound evidence to support the accusation) that she must not have tried very hard to lose weight in the past. Anna might remain silent having resigned herself to the frustrating social reality that any protests she makes would likely fall on deaf ears. The philosopher Kristie Dotson has coined the term "testimonial smothering" to refer to this particular way in which someone can be unjustly silenced.[38] A person subject to this injustice, like Anna, chooses to censor oneself. But it is an instance of what Dotson describes as "coerced silencing": one silences oneself because she has a reasonable expectation that her perspective won't be understood or that speaking freely might invite hostile or other unwelcome reactions.[39]

Enduring either of these types of epistemic injustice (an identity-prejudicial credibility deficit or testimonial smothering) might cause one to suffer distinct though interrelated harms. To begin with, when a person is regularly deprived of a meaningful voice in social exchanges, one is likely to fare worse as a direct consequence. When a person isn't really heard by those around her—either because others uncharitably interpret what she says or because she silences herself in anticipation of how her perspective may be received—one's ability to advance one's interests is thereby compromised. For instance, Anna's health might suffer because her doctor fails to explore a plausible medical diagnosis, a failure that might have been avoided had the doctor really heard and taken seriously what her patient was trying to tell her. Being the victim of such epistemic harms can also cause one to experience psychological distress. It is extremely frustrating to not be heard by others or to feel that there's little point in speaking up. Being regularly treated in those ways understandably can make a person feel upset, angry, or helpless.

But even if Anna isn't made worse off in either of those ways, she's harmed by such interactions in a different way. Being treated as she is conveys to her a demeaning and deeply insulting message. In such exchanges, she suffers a *recognitional* harm: she is made to feel lesser because her perspective isn't afforded the recognition that it deserves, namely, the recognition that is given to others who are like Anna in all respects except that they aren't fat. In virtue of her devalued identity, Anna fails to be regarded by others as she deserves to be. It is disrespectful to treat someone as if she doesn't know what she is talking about without a sound basis for supposing that. Anna deserves to be heard just as anyone else does, and her body size has no bearing on that being so.

Let us now turn to another dimension of our society's size-based hierarchy. Doing so will help us better understand its unjust nature. This other dimension concerns how body size is a trait that has come to be an especially important source of social (dis)esteem. Thinness is a highly esteemed trait and fatness a highly disesteemed one. Based on this esteem hierarchy, our perception of people's body sizes greatly conditions how we rank one another. In general, being thin earns you a higher social status, while being fat diminishes your social status. Currently, this practice of granting or withholding social esteem based on body size threatens to seriously compromise fat people's ability to enjoy equal standing. Now, it is not the case that all esteem hierarchies that obtain in our society are incompatible with people's enjoyment of equal standing. All manner of traits, behaviors, and accomplishments merit social esteem. And, at least on the face of it, not all esteeming practices—e.g., publicly recognizing and rewarding certain displays of academic achievement, athletic excellence, and creative talent—are a basis for morally troubling social hierarchies. So, we should ask: What, if anything, might make our esteeming practices surrounding body size relevantly different from these other cases?

Let's focus on one concrete case of a highly esteemed accomplishment: excelling at sports. No doubt, our society cares a great deal about athletic achievement. Now, I'm pretty bad at all sports. But it's not an injustice that some folks, like me, who aren't good at sports might be deprived of social esteem on this basis. On reflection, a few considerations seem to make this case relevantly different from that of body size.[40] To begin with, the prescriptive standard *people shouldn't be fat* is widely endorsed and taken to apply to everyone. That is, just about everyone in our society believes that it's really bad to be fat and that it's really bad for anyone at all to be fat. Furthermore, we accord a great deal of esteem to people for being thin. People's body sizes and related lifestyle choices (both our own and those of others) are topics that most people don't tire of raising on a day-to-day basis. We are always talking about our diets and workout regimes and our physiques. How one does on this count, then, seems to be a matter of great concern. In addition, with respect to what a low ranking implies about a person, anti-fat judgments run deep. This is a point about the substantive judgments that concern how a person ranks based on their body size. To know that others find my body *disgusting* and feel *contempt* for me because they suppose I utterly lack willpower and am greedy and lazy isn't something that can be taken lightly by most.[41] These are scathing indictments. No wonder, then, that the particularities of how our society disesteems fatness are a basis for inflicting profound harms on fat people, threatening to undermine their status as social equals. Nothing similar applies in the case of someone being bad at sports.

Furthermore, the esteem hierarchy tracking body size likely helps cause or reinforce other harms that fat people suffer. That fat individuals are regularly judged so harshly is, plausibly, a key factor in explaining much overt mistreatment that they endure, e.g., as when a boss who looks down on heavier workers discriminates against them. Our disesteeming of fatness also may play a role in causing some of the more subtle harms discussed above. For instance, when an individual, like Betsy, is acutely aware of personally falling short of standards that others hold her to, that can greatly compromise one's ability to succeed in the workforce (and in other domains).

But the status-harms that track this esteem hierarchy are more far-reaching still. Even a fat person who isn't harmed at work and who fares well in their social relations, despite knowing that others look down on them for their weight, may be seriously harmed by this hierarchy. Take Carl, who is a terrific father and husband as well as a successful lawyer. He knows that he is well loved by his family and that he excels at his job—and reflecting on what gives his life meaning reveals that he cares most about his family and career. So, unlike Betsy, having the disesteemed trait of fatness doesn't harm Carl's job performance (nor does it harm his close relationships). What is more, Carl doesn't *want* to care about his weight: when he rationally reflects on what really matters, he truly believes that thinness isn't something that he should care about attaining. Yet, try as he might, he can't shake the feeling that because he is really fat, there's a sense in which he is a loser. His being fat, for him, is a persistent source of shame, and it overshadows those other accomplishments, accomplishments to which he himself accords greater value. Anti-fat norms have such a hold over us precisely because they are so widely endorsed and because they are taken to matter so much by most people. This means that one cannot easily escape their force simply by trying not to be bothered by the fact that one's body doesn't conform to social norms.

Let's return to the disanalogy between being fat and being bad at sports. My standing as an equal in society is not diminished by my (serious) shortcomings in this area. The admiration our society reserves for the athletically skilled doesn't negatively affect my self-conception or how others, in general, regard me. I don't care that I'm bad at sports. Folks around me do not judge me as lesser for being bad at sports, if that's something that they even know about me. So, it's just not a big deal. There are other things that matter a lot more to me (e.g., raising a happy pug and advancing social justice causes). Now, for folks like Betsy and Carl too, plenty of other things besides their weight matter to them. But because of how significantly our society esteems thinness and disesteems fatness, how these individuals stack up in other ways threatens to be undermined to some degree, if not wholly eclipsed, by their weight. Moreover, Betsy's and Carl's fatness function as a highly visible badge of demerit nearly everywhere they go. In the workplace, at restaurants, on the streets, our bodies are there for all others to lay eyes on and pass judgment. The inferiority a fat person is branded with affects how they are regarded in wide-ranging social domains. I can avoid joining my friends for a soccer game and thus be spared the potential embarrassment of my shoddy abilities being on display to all those on the recreational field. Betsy and Carl have no such luxury: unless they avoid being around people entirely, there is no escape from others judging them as deficient for their size.

Despite all this, some fat people might manage not to be tangibly harmed by how others negatively view them. Take Dina, a body-positive fat person whose fatness is esteemed by her fellow members of a tight-knit fat activist community. She rejects anti-fat norms and has no desire to be thin. She is also unusually resilient and isn't bothered in the least by how others in society regard her body. On the account I've sketched, even a confident, thick-skinned individual like Dina is unjustly harmed by society's size-based esteem hierarchy. This is because the particular ways that fatness is disesteemed deprive fat individuals, in general, of recognition as social equals. A person is demeaned when she is regularly judged by others as fundamentally inferior and is accorded lower social standing in virtue of some aspect of her identity, such as her body size. When that happens, one suffers a recognitional harm. There is no warrant for someone being widely perceived by others in that way, even if a person's healthy sense of self-confidence enables her to ignore those reactions or to altogether fail to notice them. By analogy, a Black person who maintains a strong sense of self-respect and self-esteem in the face of continual racist disparagement is nevertheless recognitionally harmed by racism. The unjust harm at issue concerns such individuals being deprived of a secure basis for enjoying, and knowing that they enjoy, equal standing with others, and this is something to which all in society are entitled.

Let's return to the query with which we began: What, if anything, is the wrong-making feature that might account for why fat people are unjustly disadvantaged? To explain the nature of the injustice that fat people endure, I have appealed to a relational egalitarian theory of justice, a theory on which all individuals are entitled to equal standing. Fat individuals, I have argued, are unjustly deprived of equal standing. The primary injustice these individuals suffer isn't about their occasionally enduring some social harm or another in virtue of being fat. That is, the primary injustice they suffer isn't reducible to any particular discrete weight-related social disadvantage that they experience: for instance, Anna's long-term health suffering due to her reasonably choosing to avoid clinical settings or her doctor's disrespectful dismissal of her perspective; Betsy's continual worries about her fatness negatively affecting her job performance; the low self-esteem that Anna, Betsy, and Carl all struggle with; or Dina's subjection to anti-fat practices and norms that insultingly convey to her that she's less worthy of respect and esteem than thin individuals are (regardless of her tangibly faring no worse as a result). Rather, the primary injustice these individuals suffer concerns how these and other harms they encounter fit together as a whole. These harms are part of a broader structure that keeps fat people in a subordinate position over time. Fat individuals are deprived of a meaningful ability to relate to others on terms of equality. All the different ways that someone like Anna (and each of the others) is prone to being mistreated and misrecognized in virtue of being fat constitute and reflect one's lower standing, a lower standing that one is made to bear for being a fat person living in an anti-fat society.

One might wonder whether we have good reason to embrace a relational egalitarian theory of justice. I have offered only a brief sketch of this theory. Whether we should accept this theory, and just how its main commitments should be understood, are matters of ongoing debate.[42] Although I cannot offer a more robust defense of this theory here, it is worth underscoring its considerable intuitive appeal. Relational equality does well in capturing the fundamental injustice involved in paradigm cases of oppression, such as racism, sexism, and homophobia. As with racism, sexism, homophobia, and other forms of oppression, the central injustice of sizeism is the social creation and perpetuation of a hierarchical system that relegates an entire group of people to an inferior class. We make it a bad thing for people to be Black and gay and fat, and we make it the case that people with those traits tend to suffer a multitude of serious harms. Doing that, according to this theory, is a grievous wrong.

2.4 Is the size-based hierarchy imposed on fat people durable?

Thus far, we have established that three of the four necessary and jointly sufficient conditions for fat people to count as oppressed are satisfied: it is widely seen as a bad thing to be fat; fat people are systematically socially disadvantaged (and that they are is often rationalized); and the interrelated ways in which fat people are regarded and treated badly is an injustice. Now, we will turn to the fourth condition, which concerns whether the size-based hierarchy imposed on fat individuals is *durable*. This condition too, I will argue, is met.

To recall, that a social hierarchy is *durable* implies that once in place, that hierarchy tends to be self-perpetuating. Put simply, over time, oppressive systems keep the subordinated in an inferior position (and the privileged in a superior position). These hierarchies are maintained by numerous, mutually supporting mechanisms, which work together to reproduce the subordination of some and the privilege of others. Furthermore, the persistence of oppressive hierarchies tends to be due, in part, to oppressive forces that operate insidiously. Many people may fail to recognize that a given form of oppression occurs around them when it does. That oppressive systems, either wholesale or partially, can be invisible in this way, in turn, is sometimes explained by a tendency for unjust disadvantages suffered by the oppressed to be subject to popular rationalization, and thus, not to be seen as injustices at all.

Let's consider how sizeism is durable. To see how sizeism is a self-perpetuating system, we can return to the two main examples discussed in section 2.2. Imposing on fat individuals, like Anna and Betsy, a devalued identity frequently proves to be a self-fulfilling prophesy. By perceiving being fat as bad, we *make* being fat bad. Based on widely held negative attitudes and beliefs about fat individuals, our society makes folks like Anna feel disrespected or uncomfortable in healthcare settings and gyms. When that predictably causes some such individuals to avoid routine check-ups or regular exercise and become unhealthier as a result, this leads doctors and nurses to find confirmation of their negative suppositions about fat patients. Their fat patients exhibiting such behavior just proves that they are lazy, imprudent, and undisciplined, as the medical professionals already suspected. With such harmful stereotypes so reinforced, these medical professionals are even more likely to act in precisely those ways that cause fat patients to feel disrespected and mistreated in medical settings, which, in turn, only reinforces the desires of those fat patients to avoid stigmatizing encounters of this sort by limiting such interactions.[43] This negative feedback loop is one example of a mechanism that helps perpetuate sizeism over time.

A vicious cycle occurs in a case like Betsy's too. We make fat people well aware that society views them negatively. And, as the social identity threat literature indicates, when a person is made to feel that most others think badly of her, this can get in one's head and can make one behave in ways that she doesn't want to—behavior that she would likely avoid if not for that hyper-awareness of others' negative judgments. On this basis, a fat individual like Betsy may eat more than she wants to because she's made to feel she has less self-control, or she might underachieve in the classroom or workplace having internalized the belief that she's less capable. When these things happen, in addition to fat individuals being directly, tangibly harmed, many in our society are apt to find further confirmation yet of prevalent anti-fat stereotypes (*"Hey look, just as predicted, fat people have no willpower and aren't as smart or as competent as thin people!"*). So, in this case too, treating fat people as if they were deficient in some respect might well contribute to making them so.

When widespread anti-fat stereotypes are further strengthened in these ways, that also provides fodder for rationalizing various unjust disadvantages that fat people suffer. This happens in cases like Anna's and Betsy's, where many in our society embrace explanations of what makes those individuals worse off that are taken to support the conclusion that no injustice is involved. So, for example, it is commonly supposed that the disadvantages that fat individuals like Anna and Betsy experience (worse health and worse job performance) result from their personal choices (choosing not to exercise and choosing not to be more assertive) and, accordingly, that it's these individuals' own fault for being worse off. Those explanations aren't completely wrong. Those choices *are* a causal factor in producing the relevant outcomes. But the fact that such choices are a causal factor doesn't imply that these cases don't involve injustice. As we've seen, these popular explanations are overly simple. For instance, this explanation of why Anna acts as she does and ends up in poorer health focuses exclusively on individualistic factors (i.e., Anna's choices), while ignoring entirely the influence that social-structural factors have on those choices (i.e., Anna's avoiding the gym to shield herself from stigmatizing experiences she's apt to endure there due to widespread anti-fat bias). Here, it's helpful to think of individuals acting with "socially embedded agency," which, as Haslanger explains, is a matter of socially imposed constraints on individuals' behavior (and on much else): "The terms of our action and interaction are not up to us as individuals. What is valuable, what is acceptable, even what we do, and want, and think, depend on cultural frameworks of meaning."[44]

Only if we are willing to seek out and be receptive to these more sophisticated, social-structural explanations of individual behavior—which, I've argued, are explanations that enable us to perceive things more accurately—can we see the serious injustices these cases involve. In the status quo, however, it's hard for many people to move beyond the simpler individualistic explanations. We are drawn to those simpler explanations because dominant anti-fat ideology—comprised, in key part, by negative stereotypes—significantly influences how we both perceive and interpret what happens around us. When we have been culturally conditioned to suppose that fat people are lazy, undisciplined, and so on, it's to be expected that many will be drawn to those more superficial explanations of the observed phenomena in the cases under discussion. Those explanations fit better with our preexisting beliefs. Yet by favoring those simpler explanations over the more complicated (and accurate!) ones, we fail to see the serious injustice occurring in such cases.

In sum, sizeism undoubtedly qualifies as a durable social hierarchy. Anti-fat cultural beliefs and attitudes profoundly shape how fat people view themselves, how fat people are viewed by others, and fat people's awareness of how they are viewed by others. Those cultural beliefs and attitudes affect how all those parties behave, producing predictable patterns of behavior that over time make fat people worse off in tangible ways. That fat people are made worse off in those ways (i.e., owing to the anti-fat cultural lens through which we all view the world) is an outcome that we are prone to grossly misunderstand. We suppose that it's a fat person's own fault for becoming worse off in those ways, and, consequently, we conclude that both the negative cultural attitudes at issue and the material harms that fat people endure are justified. So, as with other forms of oppression, it is the nature of sizeism that the imposition of social disadvantage begets further social disadvantage for the oppressed.

3. CONCLUSION

In general, we fail to grasp what it truly means to be fat. We can't get past the ways we are so used to seeing it: it's unhealthy, it's unattractive, it's gross, it's a sign of weakness, and so on. But "fat" doesn't refer to some way that people's bodies just happen to be independently of how we judge those bodies. Fatness is a trait that we collectively define, and it is a trait that we collectively make into a bad thing. Fat people, then, are those whom we judge as being too large and, on that basis, for whom we make life much worse than it would otherwise be. From a social justice standpoint, this is troubling. It's troubling that we assign an entire group of people to an inferior social position and then keep them there through durable structures.

Even when we acknowledge that society makes fat people badly off, we seldom appreciate the extent or the severity of the harms that this involves. Fat people are systematically mistreated, and the unjust harms that they suffer are severe and wide-ranging. To be fat in our society is to be subject to a hierarchy that is so seamlessly interwoven into our everyday existence that we hardly notice its effects: the countless subtle ways in which it operates to reproduce patterns of social inequality. It is on this basis, I contend, that it is apt to see fat people as oppressed.   ·

To defend this claim—that fat people are oppressed for being fat—takes considerable work. It requires us to zoom out, so to speak, and to approach sizeism as a system. Upon doing so, we can see just how far-reaching the influence of this oppressive system is: we can see how social-structural forces, steeped as they are in anti-fat ideology, condition fat individuals' choices, behaviors, and preferences in ways that disadvantage them and that can make it appear to be their own fault for ending up badly off. To draw those connections, in turn, can require investigation of complex social-scientific matters, such as examining how social identity threat harms those who experience it. It can also require broadening our conceptual toolkit in ways that facilitate a more sophisticated understanding of the interconnections between distinctive harms produced by an oppressive system, e.g., appreciating how fat individuals, as targets of oppression, may be deprived of epistemic authority via testimonial smothering.

I have tried to do some of that work here. I have, in particular, sought to make manifest dimensions of sizeist oppression that are often obscured. In doing so, I have drawn on parallel projects engaged in by scholars theorizing about other forms of oppression, such as racism and sexism. Indeed, in approaching fatness via a framework of oppression, we see some of the striking similarities between the workings of sizeism and other forms of oppression. Once we consider relevant empirical evidence and these parallels with other forms of oppression, the claim that fat people are oppressed becomes highly plausible. Still, I expect my conclusion that fat people are oppressed to be met with skepticism, if not outright rejection, by many. The anti-fat cultural forces that condition us to firmly believe that fatness is something we should oppose are powerful—so powerful as to motivate significant resistance to the conclusions that I have defended here. But, if I am right, such resistance would be ultimately rooted in unwarranted bias, not in reason.

8

1. TAKING STOCK

Here is what this book has argued. Being fat isn't what we're used to thinking it is. To be fat is not to be unhealthy. Nor is it a reflection of some internal deficiency such as a lack of willpower or objectionable values. It is not morally wrong to be fat. To be fat is, however, something that we in our society have made into a very bad thing. It is a social identity we have constructed. Collectively, we have decided what counts as an acceptable body size, and that is a social norm that we impose on one another. Transgressors of this norm are treated harshly. They are not recognized as social equals. We, as a society, uphold a system that oppresses an entire group of people in virtue of their body size. This needs to end.

We can summarize all those points into two main claims. The first concerns how we *should not* regard fat people: We should reject the dominant social narratives that currently define how fat people are generally regarded. The second concerns how we *should* regard fat people: We *should* regard fat people as oppressed.

We are all complicit in upholding this system of sizeist oppression. Thus, working to end it is a burden we all share. Unfortunately, many are ambivalent about fat acceptance. And

DOI: 10.4324/9780367853389-11

as I mentioned in chapter 1, in my experience, such ambivalence is common even among those who are whole-heartedly committed to fighting racism, sexism, classism, homophobia, transphobia, ableism, and other structural injustices. These are folks who are inclined to agree with much of what I have argued in previous chapters. In particular, they agree that we shouldn't presume that all fat people are unhealthy or that all fat people could avoid being fat if they just made reasonable lifestyle changes. They also agree that we must bring an end to the cruel ways that we currently treat so many fat people. Still, they can't quite shake the feeling that, at some fundamental level, there is something bad about being fat that goes beyond how our society regards and treats fat people. On this view, being fat is sometimes unhealthy, and it's thought that quite a few fat people wouldn't find it especially difficult to avoid being fat by making reasonable lifestyle changes. And so, being *fat* strikes such folks as relevantly different from being those other ways that they readily agree are oppressed. For instance, they point out, there is nothing bad about being *gay* or *Black*, and those aren't typically traits that people can change through voluntary effort. If being fat differs from these other traits in these two respects then, the line of reasoning continues, we shouldn't be fully accepting of fatness.

Suppose for a moment that it is bad for people to be fat quite apart from society's role in making that so. Would that imply that fat people couldn't qualify as oppressed? No, it would not. Even if it were bad to be fat independently of what society does to fat people, for our society to regard and treat fat people as we currently do on top of that would qualify as oppressive. That is because, as we've seen, we, as a society, do a great deal to make it really bad to be fat— unjustly depriving fat people of basic respect and dignity as well as of equitable access to valuable social goods and opportunities. Importantly, even if it were unhealthy to be fat and even if fat avoidance were meaningfully achievable for most, still that wouldn't warrant *oppressing* fat people because they are fat. Oppression is never deserved. No one, regardless of their health status or whether they have a meaningful ability to avoid certain poor health outcomes, deserves to be oppressed. And so, the moral imperative to bring *that* to an end—that is, to stop oppressing fat people—would still obtain. We should never make any class of people into social inferiors who are trapped in a vicious cycle of ongoing disadvantage based on their group membership.

That last point has implications for the relationship between the book's two main claims. Specifically, the truth of the second claim—that we should view fat people as oppressed—does not depend on the truth of the first claim—that we should reject the conventional narratives that define how our society typically views fat people (namely, that it is unhealthy to be fat and that it is fat people's own fault for being fat). I have argued at length that those narratives are damaging, false, and misleading. But even if they were true, fat people would still be oppressed if our society regarded and treated them as it does in the status quo: depriving them of the equal standing that they are owed.

Still, the above-described ambivalence about approaching fatness via the framework of sizeism raises a question. If fatness is an oppressed trait, what follows for how accepting of fatness we should strive to be? For instance, must we strive toward viewing fatness as an entirely neutral trait, one that reflects just another way in which individuals differ from one another and that is not a legitimate basis for hierarchically ordering them, as is widely taken to be the appropriate response when it comes to differences in race or sexual orientation?

The idea that fatness should be seen as being on a par with thinness sits uneasily with lots of people. And if that is a claim implied by fat acceptance, then it is supposed that fat acceptance is something that we should reject. Here's a typical way that this resistance to fully fledged fat acceptance is expressed:

> Obviously, we shouldn't be mean to fat people or make them feel ashamed about their bodies. That needs to change. But I worry that we'd be throwing the baby out with the bathwater were we to conclude that it's OK to be fat, full stop. After all, some of us can easily enough avoid being fat and thus be much healthier. So, are advocates of fat acceptance telling me that I shouldn't actively try to stay at a weight at which I feel my best? Or that I should be totally fine with letting my own children get fat because they mostly eat junk food and never move around, when I could instill in them better habits that would enable them to avoid being fat? Undoubtedly, as a society, we must adopt a more compassionate stance toward fat individuals. Still, given legitimate health concerns, we should also strive for a future in which not so many people are fat, for instance, by working to change the harmful "obesogenic" environment that we live in.

There are some reasonable claims in the vicinity of these concerns. However, these claims are compatible with being wholly accepting of fatness. Fully fledged fat acceptance entails that fat individuals are equally deserving of moral consideration and respect as anyone else, and that they should be recognized and treated as such. Fat acceptance, so understood, is a non-negotiable social justice imperative. It demands that we bring an end to the oppression that fat people endure in virtue of being fat. Having clarified what fat acceptance requires, let's turn to the first concern that fat acceptance implies that one cannot strive to be thin themselves or encourage their own children to make certain weight-related lifestyle choices. In fact, it isn't incompatible with the social justice imperative of fat acceptance that some individuals might have good reasons to become, or to stay, thin. Recognizing the urgent need to dismantle sizeist structures that harm fat people doesn't imply that it would be wrong for any particular individuals to make particular choices concerning their own weight. Nor does it preclude parents from encouraging their kids to forge healthy habits. So, this basis for ambivalence about fat acceptance is predicated on a misunderstanding of what is entailed by recognizing that we live in a sizeist society and that we must work to change that. One can have a sound basis for striving to not be fat oneself while being fully on board with the cause of fat acceptance.

That being said, we must pay heed to the feminist slogan *the personal is political*. Sizeist structures aren't something that exist "out there," disconnected from our day-to-day lives. Appreciating that we are all part of an oppressive system, ideally, should prompt us to be self-reflective in examining how living in a sizeist society has shaped our own attitudes, preferences, and choices. Might our personal attitudes and experiences (such as "feeling best" at a particular weight) be influenced by what society tells us a healthy body looks like? Furthermore, we might think critically about matters such as how to strike the right balance in encouraging our children to eat veggies and move around without instilling in them anti-fat attitudes about their own or others' bodies.

Still, some folks seem to embrace fat acceptance with a caveat: "I'm on board with fat acceptance for other people but not for myself (or my close ones)." What might be behind this exceptionalism, this resistance to accepting one's own fatness (or that of a few select others)? It sounds a bit like a White person professing a commitment to racial justice yet being opposed to their own child having a Black partner, or someone claiming to be fully accepting of gay rights but being uncomfortable with the prospect of a family member being gay. We all have deeply internalized fatphobia, so it's not surprising that many bristle at the prospect of they themselves, or their loved ones, being fat. But even if one has a strong personal desire to be thin, a desire that is largely conditioned by sizeist norms, one can still recognize that one should fully embrace fat acceptance. And the hope is that in embracing this cause, one might become curious about interrogating one's own anti-fat attitudes and even work to change how one personally feels about one's own body size.

Let's turn to the second concern raised above by those who are ambivalent about fat acceptance. This is the line of reasoning that we shouldn't mistreat people who are fat now but that our society should work toward the goal of eliminating, or at least greatly reducing, the incidence of fatness in our population. Is that view compatible with fat acceptance of the sort that we should embrace? To answer that question, there are a few things to consider. To begin with, we need to clarify the envisioned goal. If the goal is the adoption of infrastructural changes that can be reasonably expected to produce meaningful net health benefits for society, then that would seem, all else equal, a worthy pursuit. Here, it's important to acknowledge that there may be legitimate social pursuits in the vicinity of problematic attempts to fight obesity, e.g., a campaign providing people with meaningful access to nutritious food and better opportunities for engaging in physical activity, improving people's access to decent healthcare, or addressing food insecurity issues.

But suppose that the goal is explicitly weight focused. Take, for instance, a social initiative aimed at significantly reducing rates of overweight and obesity. In that case, an immediate problem that arises, as discussed at length in chapters 2 and 3, is that we simply don't know at present how to realistically achieve that goal or whether attempts to make most fat people thin would even be health-promoting. Suppose, however, that our evidence on these matters drastically shifts and we're able to identify an initiative that would both help many people substantially slim down and would equitably produce meaningful net health improvements across the population. If our evidence so changes (a very big if!), then we would have one compelling reason for adopting such an initiative. Still, in that case, we would need to consider how adopting the given initiative might contribute to reinforcing or even worsening fat stigma (and other social inequalities). If such health-promoting efforts were in tension with the urgent demand to address sizeism, then figuring out how to proceed would require careful assessment of the projected outcomes and of the competing moral considerations at play. Here, there is a parallel with policies aimed at addressing the medical needs of disabled individuals against a backdrop of ableism: namely, that there are serious structural injustices concerning how disabled people are treated in the status quo doesn't imply that there aren't, or couldn't be, legitimate pursuits aimed at reducing the mental or physical suffering associated with some disabilities.

Still, in light of recent advances in weight-loss drugs and surgery (discussed in chapter 3), one might press: Shouldn't social efforts focus on eliminating fatness through these methods rather than on promoting fat acceptance? Unequivocally, the answer is no. Even though some fat people may be able to substantially reduce their weight in the long term via drugs or surgery, these methods don't produce that result for everyone. But let's imagine for a moment that these methods were so effective that they would enable all fat individuals to become and stay thin. Even if that were so, no fat person's claim to being treated as a social equal should be made contingent on their electing to either take drugs for the rest of their life or have major surgery that would profoundly alter their digestive system (to say nothing of the risks of suffering a host of adverse side effects and dangers associated with both methods). Choosing to take weight-loss drugs indefinitely or to have bariatric surgery are significant personal decisions. Fat people shouldn't be pressured to undergo these weight-loss methods, either by those around them or by an anti-fat cultural environment more generally. Nevertheless, we can reasonably expect many fat people to want to pursue these options, and that is their right. Looking forward, then, there will be a fine line to walk between, on the one hand, working to improve the safety, efficacy, and accessibility of these drugs and surgeries for fat individuals who want them, and, on the other hand, avoiding making things worse for fat individuals who don't.

Consider a different reason one might reject the claim that sizeist oppression exists. One might think that sizeism isn't an oppressive system in its own right but rather is entirely reducible to other forms of oppression. For instance, it might be supposed that anti-fat attitudes and treatment are fully explained by society's sexism, classism, racism, ableism, and/

or other extant structural inequalities. Certainly, as we've seen in earlier chapters, just how sizeism affects different people crucially intersects with other aspects of their identities. Women tend to be treated much more punitively than men for not being thin. The pressure to be thin may be even greater yet and experienced in quite different ways for folks who are gay, trans, or gender non-conforming, and there are important interactions between identifying as fat and as queer.[1] There is also significant variance in how sizeism is experienced by individuals within the wide-ranging category of being fat. Being very fat makes a person the target of much harsher social penalties than are experienced by those who aren't nearly as fat. In addition, being fat may compound disadvantages faced by individuals who are marginalized in other ways too, such as for being disabled or belonging to a racial or ethnic minority.[2] So, in light of the gendered, racialized, classist, and ableist dimensions of sizeism, one might reason that there's no standalone social injustice, sizeism, that exists independently of these (and perhaps other) systemic inequalities.

There might be something to this. Still, to my mind, the question of whether it makes sense to approach sizeism as a distinct form of oppression—one that isn't subsumed by these other forms of oppression—should be resolved, at least in part, with an eye to pragmatic concerns. That is, we should consider whether there is a sufficiently unified social phenomenon at issue that if investigated in its own right can help us better understand and fight an injustice. I believe that there is. Anti-fat ideology isn't just a matter of ideologies of, say, sexism or ableism or racism, though those ideologies plausibly help constitute it. One version of the objection that sizeism is reducible to another form of oppression is that because weight-based harms disproportionately affect girls and women, we should approach anti-fat bias as a feminist issue rather than conceiving of sizeist oppression harming all fat people regardless of gender. However, boys, men, and gender non-conforming individuals too are profoundly harmed by sizeism. And so, we shouldn't approach sizeism merely as a feminist issue.[3] A different version of the objection is that we should regard fatness as a type of disability by way of a social model of disability.[4] Although in many respects, fatness can be usefully approached via a social model of disability, there are distinctive aspects of anti-fat ideology that aren't well suited to that framework. For example, consider the widespread belief that fat people are weak-willed. This does not neatly fit into the framework of regarding fatness as a disability.

Sizeism plausibly involves relevantly distinct harms from the harms associated with other forms of oppression. That being said, the trajectory and workings of sizeism cannot be adequately understood without an analysis of the classist, sexist, racist, and ableist structures in which they are embedded. In theorizing about sizeism, we must pay attention to how anti-fat attitudes and practices are rooted in and interact with those other social inequalities and ideologies. Indeed, we should embrace a genuinely intersectional analysis that explores how the oppressive harms experienced by, say, a fat Black woman are not merely reducible to the additive harms that person might face in virtue of being fat, in virtue of being Black, and in virtue of being a woman. Rather, we must investigate how an individual may be susceptible to facing distinctive harms in virtue of being a fat Black woman.[5] What is more, we cannot fight sizeism without also fighting these other forms of oppression to which it is inextricably tied.

2. REMEDIES

In what follows, I will say a bit about some concrete measures that might be adopted to help address sizeism. I won't offer a detailed account. For one thing, I am a philosopher, not a social scientist. For another, there are limits to the progress that can be made in trying to identify remedies from a purely academic standpoint. Here, the slogan popularized by the disability rights movement *Nothing about us without us* is instructive. What should be done to fight this injustice must be crucially informed by the perspectives of fat individuals themselves. Also, there's only so far we can get with devising remedies in the abstract. The true test concerns how that which seems justified in theory actually works when put into practice.

Still, with those caveats in place, drawing on insights from relevant scholars and fat activists, I want to discuss a few remedies whose adoption would seem to mark a step in the right direction. Here, my main aim is to demonstrate how understanding the unjust nature of sizeism can help us identify the sorts of remedies that might be called for. First, there is a compelling case for adding "weight" to the list of traits that society recognizes as *protected classes*—such as race, religion, national origin, and sex. Doing so would make weight-based discrimination illegal at least in the workforce and potentially in other domains as well. Adopting such legislation would make it illegal for employers to discriminate against fat individuals in hiring, promotion, and termination decisions, unless body size could be credibly demonstrated to impede one's ability to competently perform job duties.

Second, addressing sizeism would seem to call for recognizing larger individuals as having a legal entitlement to *reasonable accommodation* in public spaces, including in the workplace.

This might require a reconfiguration of workspaces to enable larger employees to carry out their jobs without difficulty—for instance, by creating wider aisles and providing armless desk chairs—and requiring similar provisions in hospitals, schools, and other venues. Third, it's hard to see how we can meaningfully address sizeism without reconceiving the central role that body weight currently plays in public health policy and clinical practice. Increasingly, more researchers who study fat stigma call for replacing the dominant "weight-centric approach" to promoting public health and crafting health policy with "a weight-inclusive approach."[6] On a weight-inclusive approach, health practitioners and policymakers would abandon the status quo practice of informing all fat individuals that they should strive for a normal weight; they would recognize the reduction of fat stigma as a significant health initiative in its own right and would work to change procedures accordingly; and, they would seek to equitably promote the health of all individuals *regardless of their weight*.

Why should society adopt such measures? The rationale for doing so is grounded in the nature of the injustice that fat people endure. The primary injustice of sizeism, I've argued, is that fat people are deprived of equal standing: they aren't regarded and treated as equals, and their inferior social status is perpetuated and reinforced by numerous interrelated structural mechanisms. Dismantling sizeism, then, requires nothing short of overturning a massive, multifaceted system that subordinates fat people and that frequently does so in such subtle and deeply ingrained ways that many fail to even notice that this happens. This will be no simple task.

Consider the basis for making weight a legally protected trait. Take the case of Jennifer Portnick, a highly capable aerobics instructor, who happened to be fat. Initially, she wasn't hired by Jazzercise to teach fitness classes because she didn't meet the company standard that an instructor "look fit," which, as they understood it, included being thin.[7] It is unfair for a capable fitness instructor to be denied employment due to widespread anti-fat bias—bias that leads many to suppose that Portnick's larger body size is an indication of her lack of fitness. However, the rationale for adding weight to the list of characteristics protected by anti-discrimination law isn't just about combating the unfair disadvantages that someone like Portnick faces. Rather, the call for this remedy is motivated more broadly by the need for society to address the *systematic* injustices that such cases involve. As we have seen, fat individuals are caught in a durable cycle of disadvantage (e.g., negative stereotypes imposed on them make them materially worse off, and that, in turn, helps reinforce those stereotypes). Protecting fat people from workforce discrimination is about rectifying their unjustly diminished economic prospects. It's also about challenging pernicious stereotypes. It can do so by providing direct counterevidence, that is, by demonstrating that people who look like Portnick can be very fit. Changing laws can, moreover, help change social attitudes. By banning weight-based discrimination, the government would signal to the public that it's wrong to treat people differently based on their body size. Over time, more folks in society might thereby come to accept that view. Also, some evidence suggests that such laws might instill in fat individuals a greater sense of empowerment and belonging while making them less likely to internalize anti-fat bias.[8]

What our society owes fat people isn't merely about combatting disadvantages they endure that result from explicit anti-fat bias. Take, for instance, the call for legally mandating reasonable accommodation of larger bodies. Such accommodation is justified regardless of whether anti-fat animus played any role in the spatial design of public venues that fail to comfortably accommodate larger bodies. Perhaps too-small seating and hospital equipment are a vestige of decades-old design policies adopted at a time when people were, on average, smaller than they are today. However, in working out what we should do about this matter now, it is beside the point that no one intended to exclude larger people from social spaces. Rather, what matters is that, at present and going forward, it is up to us as a society to decide how we configure social spaces. We should make those decisions knowing full well that some spatial designs will privilege the interests of some individuals over others and will effectively deny some people from meaningful access to those spaces.[9]

Parallel reasoning has been at the forefront of long-standing disability rights advocacy. The disability rights movement has drawn attention to how certain spatial designs (e.g., high curbs on sidewalks that aren't accompanied by ramps, or multi-story buildings without elevators) exclude individuals who use wheelchairs. The demand for disabled people to enjoy meaningful social inclusion has shaped key provisions of the 1990 Americans with Disabilities Act (ADA), which requires the reasonable accommodation of disabled individuals in places of employment and schools, on public transportation, and in wide-ranging privately owned operations that are "generally open to the public" including restaurants, movie theaters, recreational facilities, medical facilities, and hotels.[10] We should similarly work to dismantle spatial barriers preventing larger individuals from enjoying meaningful inclusion in civil society on terms of equality with their fellow citizens. Remedies to address sizeism are informed by the same principles embodied in the civil rights tradition.

They are called for to extend the scope of civil rights protection to the trait of body size, and specifically to work toward the goal of enabling fat individuals to enjoy recognition and treatment as equals.

In working out the domains in which the imperative to accommodate larger bodies applies, we need to reflect on the social meaning of various policies, norms, and practices that reproduce weight-based disadvantages. Consider the matter of too-small seating on airplanes—an issue that in recent years has attracted regular media coverage, perhaps because of the volatile emotional reactions it has elicited in quite a few passengers. Some fat passengers have spoken out publicly about the humiliation they have endured when flying, and they protest the shameful indignity of flying in seats far too small for their bodies.[11] The immediate seatmates of larger passengers fume over others encroaching on their space. Frequently, these outraged thinner passengers argue that anyone too big for a standard economy seat should be required to buy two seats (as, increasingly, numerous airlines make larger passengers do). Meanwhile, airlines have exacerbated the problem by making seats in economy considerably smaller over the years.[12] To make matters worse, the Federal Aviation Administration has made clear that it doesn't intend to intervene to address this problem (indeed, it denies that there is any such problem, despite credible concerns having been raised not just about passenger comfort but about safety in emergency situations).[13]

From a social justice standpoint, this is unacceptable. Airlines should accommodate larger passengers. It is not unreasonable to demand that commercial aircrafts be designed with an eye toward what actual people's bodies are like—e.g., that some folks need extra legroom, some need wider seats and aisles, and so on. In the meantime, airlines should grant larger passengers an extra seat without charging them more for that. Some airlines, like Southwest, already do this, but that practice appears to be the exception rather than the norm.[14] The moral imperative for doing so is straightforward. It's about granting fat people that to which they are entitled. It's no good for airlines to make fat individuals flying economy pay the full price of two airline tickets. Doing so would effectively prohibit many larger people from air travel, since flying is already so expensive. We should not be looking for ways to further the social exclusion fat people face. Moreover, airlines shouldn't charge fat passengers more for seating that comfortably accommodates their bodies on the grounds that those individuals deserve to be accommodated in a manner that doesn't reinforce the weight stigma they already suffer. Presumably, airlines' motivation for charging fat passengers added fees is to maximize profits rather than to punish fat people for being fat. But that is irrelevant. Such a policy could be reasonably interpreted by fat people as a reflection of anti-fat bias. And it would thereby serve to reinforce the stigma that those individuals have long faced in this domain.

Some wonder whether this mandate would be fair to airlines based on the costs it would imply for them. In response, we might consider that prior to the passage of the ADA, the business community strenuously objected on parallel grounds to the ADA provision that would require them to adopt reasonable accommodations for disabled customers. But now, several decades later, we no longer seriously debate whether disabled individuals are entitled to such accommodations. We accept that they are. And rightly so. We see the progress we have made as a society in removing at least some key barriers that impeded disabled individuals from meaningfully participating in civil society. Indeed, airlines have long been legally required to accommodate disabled passengers, granting them available airplane seating that meets their needs as well as special assistance without charging them more. By appeal to parallel reasoning—that no group of people should be denied equal standing in society—fat individuals are owed the same consideration. Besides treating fat passengers as they deserve to be treated, adopting this policy would also have expressive value. It would affirm to fat people their status as equals, and it would publicly communicate the message to all that social spaces ought to equitably include individuals across the body-size spectrum.

The call for embracing weight-inclusive public health policies and clinical practices is also a social justice imperative that would serve distinct but interrelated moral ends. As earlier chapters have discussed, there is overwhelming evidence that the current weight-centric ethos of health policy and practice harms fat individuals: their physical and mental health suffers; they feel disrespected and unheard; they feel bad about themselves for being fat and for failing to lose weight; and they are more susceptible to acting in ways that worsen their health. Furthermore, available evidence suggests that making public health policies and broader social practices more weight-inclusive and reducing fat stigma could meaningfully improve the health and well-being of many fat people.[15]

A paradigm shift in public health messaging and clinical practices surrounding weight might also, over time, help change people's views about fatness. Specifically, it might lead more people to question widely held assumptions about being fat that, as I've argued, are both misleading and harmful: crucially, that weighing too much (as per BMI standards) is always really bad for one's health and that the goal of long-term fat avoidance is meaningfully accessible to most fat people if only they tried harder. By adopting a weight-inclusive approach, we might make some progress as a society toward viewing and treating fat people as they deserve. Doing so might lead more people to come to regard fat individuals as worthy of equal respect and as having due epistemic authority to attest to their experiences. There's also some evidence to suggest that a more weight-inclusive, less weight-stigmatizing social environment might help reduce fat people's internalization of anti-fat bias and thereby offer some protection from the associated harms of low self-esteem and low self-worth.[16]

Sometimes, fat acceptance is understood as an imperative that falls on fat individuals themselves. It is thought that fat acceptance is about fat individuals cultivating fat-positive attitudes; working to accept their bodies just as they are; celebrating and even proudly showing off their bodies, regardless of their size and shape; viewing themselves as beautiful or handsome and worthy of love; and coming to believe that shrinking their bodies isn't a prerequisite to living a happy, healthy, and flourishing life. These ideas closely align with the body-positivity movement, which, as discussed in chapter 1, is centrally about encouraging people to feel good about their bodies even when they don't conform to conventional standards of attractiveness. When it comes to what victims of sizeist oppression should do, as a matter of navigating an anti-fat social environment, these prescriptions can be helpful ones for some to embrace.

But a focus on such individual prescriptions shouldn't distract us from the significant work to be done on a social-structural level. Fundamentally, we must fight the unjust sizeist structures that make it hard for fat individuals to feel good about their bodies in the first place. Fat acceptance is about so much more than fat individuals changing how they feel about themselves.[17] For the most part I have drawn attention to structural remedies to sizeism. Legal and institutional remedies are crucial. However, we shouldn't lose sight of the fact that sizeism is a deeply embedded cultural problem. Fighting sizeism isn't merely about changing laws and institutional practices. Just as importantly, it requires changing cultural norms, habits, beliefs, and attitudes that are heavily steeped in anti-fat ideology. So, there is a great deal of work to be done at many different levels.[18]

Without doubt, fighting injustice is always hard work. But social revolution isn't all drudgery and doom; there is joy, hope, and beauty to be found in these efforts. On this count, fat activism is no exception. Increasingly, more and more fat people are engaging in extraordinary activist, artistic, and educational projects to challenge sizeism. On podcasts, social media, and elsewhere, and through fashion, art, food, fitness, acts of personal resistance, and much else, many fat people are pushing back against sizeism in dazzling, inspiring, and powerful ways.

3. WE MUST RESIST SIZEISM

So, is it OK to be fat? I have argued "Yes." It is OK to be fat because there's nothing wrong with being fat. There's nothing wrong with being fat, of course, except for all that our society does to make it bad to be fat: oppressing fat people for their body size by imposing on them the gross injustice of sizeism. Dismantling this system of oppression won't be easy. There is little doubt, however, about the urgency of engaging in such efforts. As this book has argued, doing so is a pressing moral imperative that we should no longer be ambivalent about. We must work together to end sizeism.

Acknowledgments

I am indebted to Torin Alter and Russell Daw for generously providing me with detailed and tremendously helpful feedback on the full manuscript. I am grateful to anonymous referees for Routledge who made valuable suggestions on both the manuscript and the original book proposal. I owe thanks to my editor Andrew Beck for his support for this project and his great patience in seeing it through.

The project benefitted from helpful conversations and exchanges that I had with Sam Bruton, Holly Kantin, David Spewak, Louise Williams, my colleagues at the University of Alabama, and my fellow summer residents at the National Humanities Center. I received useful feedback on portions of the work from audiences at the University of Mississippi, the University of Southern Mississippi, the Alabama Philosophical Society, and the University of Alabama at Birmingham. I owe a special thanks to the enthusiastic and talented students enrolled in my Social Philosophy and Philosophy of Oppression courses who so thoughtfully engaged with earlier versions of these chapters. Finally, I am grateful to Alexa Tullett and Jeffrey Hunger for helping me navigate unfamiliar terrain in the social psychology literature.

Additional Online Material

This book has an online supplement that can be found at rekhanath.net. There I elaborate on empirical evidence concerning weight and health (ch. 3), weight loss and weight gain (ch. 5), and social identity threat and related social-scientific phenomena (ch. 7). I discuss further philosophical dimensions of blame (chs. 4–6). I address issues raised by fat scholars and activists including the following: critiques of body positivity; debate over the term "fatphobia"; and problems raised about "junk food" and related terms. I consider a different objection to stigmatizing fat people, that it's inherently inhumane (ch. 2). I critically engage with two further fat-blaming arguments raised in popular discourse: the accusation that fat people exhibit culpable ignorance and that fat people selfishly embrace hedonistic lifestyles (chs. 4–6). I discuss formidable obstacles we currently face in working to fight sizeist oppression: vested financial interests, as well as psychological, aesthetic, and epistemic grounds for resisting fat acceptance (ch. 8). In the online materials, the interested reader will also find additional footnotes, further references, and a list of popular resources on fat acceptance and related topics.

SOCIAL ATTITUDES ABOUT FATNESS

1 Here and in what follows, the "we" to whom I refer is most people in Western societies. Most of us, fat and thin alike, take issue with being fat—whether that trait is exhibited in ourselves or in others. Throughout the book, when I describe and refer to this widely held aversion to fatness, I shouldn't be read as endorsing it or personally identifying with it. My interest is in critically examining it.
2 LaRosa 2022.
3 Cramer and Steinwert 1998.
4 Ambwani et al. 2014, 368.
5 Schwartz et al. 2006.
6 Brewis et al. 2011.
7 Popenoe 2005.
8 Saguy 2013, 56.
9 Pollock 1995.
10 Lupton 2013, 51–52; Farrell 2011; Forth 2019.
11 Wann 2009.
12 Wann 2009, xii.
13 Gordon 2023, xix.
14 Fryar, Carroll, and Afful 2020.
15 Parikh et al. 2007.
16 Brewis et al. 2011.
17 Puhl and Latner 2007; Kolata 2016c.
18 Ibid.
19 Rimm and Rimm 2004; Thompson et al. 2020.
20 Thompson et al. 2020.
21 Major, Tomiyama, and Hunger 2017.
22 Puhl and Latner 2007; Crandall 1995.
23 Puhl and Heuer 2009; Roehling, Roehling, and Pichler 2007.
24 Personnel Today 2005.
25 Zee 2017.

26 Pausé 2017.
27 Gray 2012.
28 Abu-Odeh 2014, 247–248.
29 Puhl and Heuer 2009.
30 King 2013.
31 Nittle 2019.
32 Gay 2018, 153.
33 Glass 2016.
34 Gay 2018, 210.
35 Rosa 2018.
36 https://www.merriam-webster.com/dictionary/fat-shaming.
37 Martin, Martin, and Martin 2021.
38 Gordon 2023, 88–97.
39 Greenberg et al. 2003; Baker 2015, 55–58; Gordon 2020, 122–136.
40 "Pool," Season 1, Episode 4, aired March 15, 2019.
41 Brodesser-Akner 2017.
42 Tiffany 2019.
43 Wischhover 2018.
44 Bacon 2010.
45 I take "traditional dieting" to refer to the practice of restricting the amount or type of food one eats for the purpose of losing weight. For further discussion of the points in this paragraph, see Harrison (2019, ch. 2).
46 *Real Time with Bill Maher*, Season 17, Episode 26, aired September 6, 2019. In a 2022 episode, Maher devotes another segment of his show to this theme.
47 Esmonde 2020.
48 See, e.g., Cooper 1998; Campos 2004; LeBesco 2004; Kirkland 2008; Rothblum and Solovay 2009; Farrell 2011; Saguy 2013; Brown 2016; Strings 2019.
49 A few exceptions include: Abu-Odeh 2014; Eller 2014; Eaton 2016; Leboeuf 2019; Reiheld 2020; Davidson and Gruver 2022; Frazier 2023.
50 That being the case, I take especially seriously the imperative articulated by fat studies scholars (e.g., Pausé 2020) that anyone theorizing about fatness should pay attention to the perspectives of fat people. Throughout the book, I aim to do so.
51 At times, though, a preoccupation with such proposals can be elitist, out of touch with the needs of intended beneficiaries, or downright patronizing. See Kirkland (2011).
52 For a helpful overview of different conceptions of "ideology," see Shelby (2003). Here, I rely on the definition defended by Haslanger (2017).
53 Shelby 2003.

54 Haslanger 2012, 19.
55 Haslanger 2017.

AGAINST FAT STIGMA

1 Mokdad et al. 2004.
2 Caffrey 2017.
3 Fryar, Carroll, and Afful 2020.
4 Centers for Disease Control and Prevention 2021.
5 Statistics Canada 2019; Baker 2023; Australian Institute of Health and Welfare 2020; Ministry of Health NZ 2022.
6 To remind the reader, I use the term "excess weight" to refer to any weight a person carries that puts them above a normal-weight BMI (and I do so without endorsing current BMI standards or the notion that carrying excess weight so defined is necessarily a bad thing).
7 Baker 2023.
8 World Health Organization 2021.
9 World Health Organization 2024.
10 World Health Organization 2018.
11 Callahan 2013b, 40.
12 Ibid., 39.
13 Callahan 2013a, 792.
14 Centers for Disease Control and Prevention 2019.
15 Callahan 2013b, 38.
16 Goffman 1986.
17 Sutin and Terracciano 2013.
18 Puhl and Heuer 2010.
19 Zabinski et al. 2003.
20 Major et al. 2014.
21 Simmonds et al. 2016.
22 Anderson, Butcher, and Schanzenbach 2019.
23 Puhl and Heuer 2010, 1024.
24 Ibid.
25 Ibid.
26 Conversely, if we thought that structural factors rather than individual factors were key to making people fat, then why would we find it appropriate to shame people at all, or to expect doing so to be helpful?
27 Whether adopting such structural measures would help meaningfully reduce obesity rates, and if so to what extent, is at this point anyone's guess. Still, it seems plausible that such measures offer the best chance of meaningfully reducing obesity rates and that weight stigma makes their adoption less likely.

28 Sutin, Stephan, and Terracciano 2015.

29 Puhl and Heuer 2009.

30 Hatzenbuehler, Keyes, and Hasin 2009.

31 Tomiyama 2014.

32 Wilkinson and Pickett 2011, 95 and 101; Marmot 2004, 119.

33 Muennig 2008.

34 Puhl and Heuer 2010; Pascoe and Richman 2009.

35 This paragraph surveys evidence discussed by Puhl and Heuer (2010).

36 Flint et al. 2021.

37 Kolata 2016b; Schapiro 2021.

38 Puhl and Heuer 2009; Major, Tomiyama, and Hunger 2017; Baum and Ford 2004.

39 Cawley 2004; Judge and Cable 2011.

40 Marmot 2004; Wilkinson and Pickett 2011, 75–77.

41 Greenhalgh 2017.

42 Unless otherwise noted, all statistics discussed in the next couple paragraphs are from Ogden et al. (2010).

43 These categories correspond to the following income groupings employed by Ogden et al. (2010): a family of four is classified as "high-income" if its annual household income is above $77,000, as "middle-income" with household earnings between $29,000 and $77,000, and as "low-income" if its household income is below $29,000.

44 In describing these findings, I use the terms "Whites" and "Blacks" to respectively refer to "non-Hispanic Whites" and "non-Hispanic Blacks."

45 In 2017–2018, 17% of Asian-American adults were obese, whereas for every other racial or ethnic adult cohort the obesity rate was at least 42%. Fryar, Carroll, and Afful 2020.

46 Goldberg 2012.

47 Bell et al. 2010.

48 Here, I focus on how racism inflects much contemporary anti-fat rhetoric. In addition, as the sociologist Sabrina Strings (2019) argues, there is a long history of anti-fat attitudes in Western societies being steeped in racism, and specifically in anti-Black racism.

49 Critser 2000. Quoted in Campos (2004, 64).

50 Ogden et al. 2010.

51 Saguy 2013, 98–100.

52 See also LeBesco 2004, 112–114.

53 Fikkan and Rothblum 2012. Most of the evidence discussed in this paragraph reveals a correlation between being fat and being socially disadvantaged for women. Do we know that anti-fat bias toward women causes these disadvantages? No. But in light of wide-ranging evidence on this matter, that seems a reasonable conclusion to draw.

54 Roehling et al. 2009.
55 Fikkan and Rothblum 2012.
56 Ibid.
57 Gogoi 2023.
58 Fikkan and Rothblum 2012.
59 Brownstein 2019.
60 Greenwald and Krieger 2006.
61 Charlesworth and Banaji 2019a.
62 Charlesworth and Banaji 2019b.
63 Teachman and Brownell 2001.
64 Ibid.; Schwartz et al. 2003.
65 Walls et al. 2011; Gill and Boylan 2012.

WEIGHT AS A PUBLIC HEALTH ISSUE

1 Field et al. 2001.
2 Kenchaiah et al. 2002.
3 National Cancer Institute at the National Institute of Health 2022.
4 Division of Cancer Prevention and Control, Centers for Disease Control and Prevention 2022.
5 Flegal et al. 2013.
6 Prospective Studies Collaboration 2009.
7 Kitahara et al. 2014.
8 Ibid.
9 Ibid.
10 Cleary and Grossmann 2009.
11 Gastaldelli, Gaggini, and DeFronzo 2017.
12 Wang and Nakayama 2010.
13 Berg and Scherer 2005.
14 Deng et al. 2016.
15 Keys et al. 1986.
16 Ros et al. 2014.
17 Ibid.
18 Salas-Salvadó et al. 2011.
19 Dwyer et al. 2007; Duncan 2010.
20 Ekelund et al. 2015.
21 Barry et al. 2014.
22 Fogelholm 2010.
23 Contrary to the just-discussed findings, some studies (e.g., Christou et al. 2005) suggest that fatness is a better predictor of cardiovascular health than fitness.
24 Myers et al. 2015.
25 Gaesser, Angadi, and Sawyer 2011.
26 Wildman et al. 2008.

27 "Lean body mass" refers to the total weight of everything in the body besides fat—including muscles, skin, bones, organs, and fluids.

28 Manolopoulos, Karpe, and Frayn 2010.

29 Janssen, Katzmarzyk, and Ross 2004.

30 Taylor and Holman 2015.

31 Blüher 2020.

32 Levine and Crimmins 2016; Jha 2020.

33 Ryan and Yockey 2017.

34 Flegal et al. 2013.

35 Hales et al. 2020.

36 For helpful discussion, see, e.g., Burgard (2009).

37 Harrington, Gibson, and Cottrell 2009.

38 The Look AHEAD Research Group 2014.

39 The Look AHEAD Research Group 2013.

40 Ibid.

41 Wing et al. 2020.

42 Wing and Hill 2001.

43 Ibid.

44 Fildes et al. 2015.

45 Franz et al. 2007.

46 Mann et al. 2007.

47 Ibid., 221.

48 Wing and Hill 2001.

49 Exceptions include individuals with relatively rare medical conditions (such as lipedema, Cushing's syndrome, and some thyroid disorders), for whom lifestyle changes may not produce sufficient weight loss.

50 Pi-Sunyer 2014.

51 Hamman et al. 2006.

52 Cosslett 2018; Cohen 2014.

53 Dalle Grave et al. 2015.

54 Mann et al. 2007, 228.

55 Ibid., 224.

56 Brownell and Rodin 1994.

57 Mehta et al. 2014.

58 For an overview of different types of bariatric procedures, see: https://asmbs.org/patients/bariatric-surgery-procedures.

59 Maciejewski et al. 2016.

60 Cadena-Obando et al. 2020.

61 Adams et al. 2015; Carlsson et al. 2020.

62 Chang et al. 2018.

63 Raves et al. 2016.

64 Lupoli et al. 2017.

65 Wilding et al. 2021.

66 Garvey et al. 2022.

67 Rubino et al. 2021.

Notes

68 Garvey et al. 2022.
69 Blum 2023.

IS IT WRONG TO BE FAT?

1 In the philosophical literature, there's much debate about what blaming involves. In what follows, I rely on a conception of blame defended by Smith (2013).
2 Ibid., 39.
3 One can do wrong by an action (doing something) or by an omission (*not* doing something). So, I might do wrong by failing to help a friend when I'd promised that I would.
4 Wootson 2019.
5 Harris 2015.
6 Platell 2017.
7 Another somewhat less popular basis for accusing fat people of being objectionably implicated in being fat is to charge them with culpable ignorance in connection to their lifestyle choices. I address this charge in the online supplement.
8 Singer 2012. All quotations attributed to Singer in this section are from this piece, which was later reprinted in a 2016 collection of his essays, *Ethics in the Real World: 82 Brief Essays on Things That Matter*.
9 Magkos et al. 2020.
10 Whipple 2019.
11 Finkelstein, Fiebelkorn, and Wang 2003; Cawley et al. 2015. These estimates are based on the American healthcare context.
12 Musich et al. 2016.
13 van Baal et al. 2008.
14 For further discussion, see Nath (2024).
15 Mayes 2015, 219.
16 Here I draw on reasoning advanced by Wikler (1987).
17 For further discussion, see Ibid., 19–21.
18 Buyx 2008; Davies and Savulescu 2019.
19 Davies and Savulescu 2019.
20 Ibid., 137.
21 Ibid., 136.
22 Ibid., 137.
23 Ibid., 138.
24 Ibid., 133.
25 Fully one-half of global emissions can be attributed to the world's richest 10%. Gore 2020.
26 Ibid. See also Wiedmann et al. (2020).

27 Crippa et al. 2021.

28 U.S. Department of Agriculture 2022.

29 Jaglo, Kenny, and Stephenson 2021.

30 Riley 2017.

WEAKNESS OF WILL

1 Here I rely on Watson's (1977) account of what weakness of will entails.

2 This verdict reflects a specific view on the relationship between blameworthiness and wrongdoing. On this sort of view, see Kelly (2013).

3 My understanding of these issues is greatly informed by Gina Kolata's body of work, especially her *Rethinking Thin* (2007).

4 Fothergill et al. 2016.

5 Ibid.

6 Ibid.

7 Kolata 2016a.

8 Ibid.

9 Polidori et al. 2016.

10 Fothergill et al. 2016.

11 Glucksman and Hirsch 1968; Glucksman et al. 1968; Kolata 2007, 115.

12 Keys et al. 1950.

13 Kolata 2016a.

14 Kolata 2017.

15 Ibid.

16 Parker-Pope 2011.

17 Ibid.

18 Kolata 2007, 114.

19 For an excellent survey of Sims's work, which I draw on in the next few paragraphs, see Kolata (2007, ch. 5).

20 Sims et al. 1973.

21 Sims 1976, 383.

22 Ibid., 384.

23 Sims et al. 1973, 488.

24 Levine, Eberhardt, and Jensen 1999.

25 Kolata 2007, 118.

26 Stunkard et al. 1986.

27 Stunkard et al. 1990.

28 Kolata 2007, 123.

29 Bouchard 2021.

30 Swinburn and Egger 2002.

31 Some people avoid using the term "junk food" on the grounds that it might demonize certain foods and those who eat them. This is an important concern that I discuss in the online supplement. Still,

because of the prominent role this colloquial term plays in anti-obesity discourse, I use it in what follows.

32 Monteiro et al. 2019; Piore 2021.

33 Ibid.

34 Moss 2021.

35 Beggs 2020.

36 Kessler 2009, 137–177.

37 Wilkinson and Pickett 2011, 96.

38 Kessler 2009.

FAT PRIDE, GLUTTONY, AND SELFISHNESS

1 Cernik 2018.

2 Glover 2019.

3 For an excellent treatment of disability pride, see Barnes (2016, ch. 6).

4 Docherty 2020.

5 For further discussion of this verdict and of related cases, see the online supplement.

6 Madsen et al. 2021.

7 Gibson 2022.

8 Pratto et al. 1994.

9 Singer 2012 (my emphasis).

10 Ibid.

11 The term "headless fatty" was coined by fat scholar and activist Charlotte Cooper (2007).

SIZEIST OPPRESSION

1 Cudd 2006.

2 In her seminal essay "Oppression" in *The Politics of Reality* (Frye 1983, 16).

3 In Nath (n.d.), I elaborate on and defend this understanding of what it is to be fat, which I more or less stipulate here.

4 For defense of this claim along similar lines to that advanced here, see Eller (2014).

5 Haslanger 2012 (see, especially, chs. 7 and 11). Other key works on oppression that inform my discussion include: Frye (1983); Bartky (1990); Young (1990); Cudd (2006).

6 Haslanger 2012, 234 (my emphasis).

7 Young 1990, 41.

8 Frye 1983.

9 In what follows, I'll sometimes omit the qualifier that fat people are harmed or oppressed "in virtue of being fat." But it should be taken to apply throughout.

10 Puhl and Heuer 2010, 1019.

11 In talking about anti-fat oppression, I use the terms "sizeist" and "sizeism" rather than the terms "fatphobic" and "fatphobia" used by many (though not all, e.g., Gordon 2021) fat studies scholars and fat activists in discussing the same. As a thin person, I accept that it is not my place to legislate these terms, and I use the ones I have settled on advisedly.

12 Puhl and Heuer 2009.

13 Alberga et al. 2019.

14 Lewis et al. 2011, 1354.

15 Major, Tomiyama, and Hunger 2017, 509; Thedinga, Zehl, and Thiel 2021.

16 Gay 2018, 164.

17 Major, Tomiyama, and Hunger 2017; FitzGerald and Hurst 2017.

18 Here, I draw on Haslanger (2015) on the importance of considering how members of marginalized groups might reasonably interpret the meaning of various social interactions.

19 Steele, Spencer, and Aronson 2002, sec. VII.

20 Hunger et al. 2018, 148.

21 Major, Tomiyama, and Hunger 2017.

22 Major et al. 2014.

23 Brochu and Dovidio 2014.

24 Schvey, Puhl, and Brownell 2011.

25 Hunger et al. 2015, 259

26 Hunger et al. 2018.

27 Blodorn et al. 2016; Major, Tomiyama, and Hunger 2017.

28 Major, Eliezer, and Rieck 2012.

29 Zacher and von Hippel 2022.

30 Major, Tomiyama, and Hunger 2017.

31 One recent study found that over one-half of obese American adults internalize high levels of anti-fat bias. Puhl, Himmelstein, and Quinn 2018.

32 For a classic defense of this theory, see Anderson (1999).

33 Fraser 2008, 135.

34 Fricker 2007.

35 Ibid., 28.

36 Chastain 2022; Gordon 2023, 32–34.

37 This term has been used in the fat activist community for some time now (e.g., in a 2012 blog post "Thinsplaining?" by ArteToLife).

38 Dotson 2011.

39 Ibid., 244.

40 On esteem hierarchies, see Anderson (2012); Fourie (2015).

41 Conversely, we excessively praise and moralize thinness. In the eyes of many, being thin implies that a person is healthy, flourishing, rational, virtuous, and disciplined.

42 For further discussion of relational egalitarianism, see Nath (2020).

43 A growing body of evidence suggests that healthcare providers' weight bias is linked to fat patients receiving lower-quality medical care. Phelan et al. 2015.

44 Haslanger 2014, 20.

WHAT DOES FAT ACCEPTANCE ENTAIL?

1 Braziel and LeBesco 2001; Pausé, Wykes, and Murray 2016; Harrison 2021.

2 Mollow 2017; Harrison 2021.

3 Eller 2014, 236–237.

4 Mollow (2015) proposes doing so. For a defense of a social model of disability, see Howard and Aas (2018).

5 Crenshaw 1989.

6 Hunger, Smith, and Tomiyama 2020.

7 Kirkland 2008, 39–40.

8 Pearl, Puhl, and Dovidio 2017.

9 Kirkland 2008, 45–46, 133.

10 For the full text of the legislation, see https://www.ada.gov/law-and-regs/ada.

11 Gibbs 2022.

12 Elliott 2022.

13 Schaper 2018.

14 Elliott 2022.

15 Tylka et al. 2014; Hunger, Smith, and Tomiyama 2020.

16 Hunger, Smith, and Tomiyama 2020.

17 Gordon 2020, ch. 8.

18 On the diverse aims and methods of fat activism, see Cooper (2016, ch. 3).

Abu-Odeh, Desiree. 2014. Fat Stigma and Public Health: A Theoretical Framework and Ethical Analysis. *Kennedy Institute of Ethics Journal* 24 (3): 247–265.

Adams, Ted, Tapan Mehta, Lance Davidson, and Steven Hunt. 2015. All-Cause and Cause-Specific Mortality Associated with Bariatric Surgery: A Review. *Current Atherosclerosis Reports* 17 (12): 74.

Alberga, Angela, Iyoma Edache, Mary Forhan, and Shelly Russell-Mayhew. 2019. Weight Bias and Health Care Utilization: A Scoping Review. *Primary Health Care Research & Development* 20: e116.

Ambwani, Suman, Katherine Thomas, Christopher Hopwood, Sara Moss, and Carlos Grilo. 2014. Obesity Stigmatization as the Status Quo: Structural Considerations and Prevalence Among Young Adults in the U.S. *Eating Behaviors* 15 (3): 366–370.

Anderson, Elizabeth. 1999. What Is the Point of Equality? *Ethics* 109 (2): 287–337.

Anderson, Elizabeth. 2012. Equality: A Distributive Principle or an Ideal of Social Relations? In *The Oxford Handbook of Political Philosophy*, edited by David Estlund, 40–57. New York: Oxford University Press.

Anderson, Patricia, Kristin Butcher, and Diane Whitmore Schanzenbach. 2019. Understanding Recent Trends in Childhood Obesity in the United States. *Economics & Human Biology* 34: 16–25.

ArteToLife. 2012. Thinsplaining? This is Thin Privilege. Tumblr. <https://thisisthinprivilege.tumblr.com/post/25654225442/thinsplaining>.

Australian Institute of Health and Welfare. 2020. *Overweight and Obesity.* <https://www.aihw.gov.au/reports/australias-health/overweight-and-obesity>.

Bacon, Lindo. 2010. *Health at Every Size: The Surprising Truth About Your Weight*. Rev. & Updated. Dallas, TX: BenBella Books.

Baker, Carl. 2023. Obesity Statistics. *House of Commons Library*. <https://researchbriefings.files.parliament.uk/documents/SN03336/SN03336.pdf>.

Baker, Jes. 2015. *Things No One Will Tell Fat Girls: A Handbook for Unapologetic Living*. Berkeley, CA: Seal Press.

Barnes, Elizabeth. 2016. *The Minority Body: A Theory of Disability*. Oxford: Oxford University Press.

Barry, Vaughn, Meghan Baruth, Michael Beets, J. Larry Durstine, Jihong Liu, and Steven Blair. 2014. Fitness vs. Fatness on All-Cause Mortality: A Meta-Analysis. *Progress in Cardiovascular Diseases* 56 (4): 382–390.

Bartky, Sandra Lee. 1990. *Femininity and Domination: Studies in the Phenomenology of Oppression*. New York: Routledge.

Baum, Charles, and William Ford. 2004. The Wage Effects of Obesity: A Longitudinal Study. *Health Economics* 13 (9): 885–899.

Beggs, Alex. 2020. There's an Entire Industry Dedicated to Making Foods Crispy, and It Is WILD. *Bon Appétit*. <https://www.bonappetit.com/story/crispy>.

Bell, Kirsten, Amy Salmon, Michele Bowers, Jennifer Bell, and Lucy McCullough. 2010. Smoking, Stigma and Tobacco 'Denormalization': Further Reflections on the Use of Stigma as a Public Health Tool. *Social Science & Medicine* 70 (6): 795–799.

Berg, Anders, and Philipp Scherer. 2005. Adipose Tissue, Inflammation, and Cardiovascular Disease. *Circulation Research* 96 (9): 939–949.

Blodorn, Alison, Brenda Major, Jeffrey Hunger, and Carol Miller. 2016. Unpacking the Psychological Weight of Weight Stigma: A Rejection-Expectation Pathway. *Journal of Experimental Social Psychology* 63: 69–76.

Blüher, Matthias. 2020. Metabolically Healthy Obesity. *Endocrine Reviews* 41 (3): 69–76.

Blum, Dani. 2023. Ozempic Can Cause Major Weight Loss. What Happens if You Stop Taking It? *The New York Times*. <https://www.nytimes.com/2023/02/03/well/live/ozempic-wegovy-weight-loss.html>.

Bouchard, Claude. 2021. Genetics of Obesity: What We Have Learned Over Decades of Research. *Obesity* 29 (5): 802–820.

Braziel, Jana Evans, and Kathleen LeBesco, eds. 2001. *Bodies out of Bounds: Fatness and Transgression*. Berkeley: University of California Press.

Brewis, Alexandra, Amber Wutich, Ashlan Falletta-Cowden, and Isa Rodriguez-Soto. 2011. Body Norms and Fat Stigma in Global Perspective. *Current Anthropology* 52 (2): 269–276.

Brochu, Paula, and John Dovidio. 2014. Would You Like Fries (380 Calories) with That? Menu Labeling Mitigates the Impact of Weight-Based Stereotype Threat on Food Choice. *Social Psychological and Personality Science* 5 (4): 414–421.

Brodesser-Akner, Taffy. 2017. Losing It in the Anti-Dieting Age. *The New York Times*. <https://www.nytimes.com/2017/08/02/magazine/weight-watchers-oprah-losing-it-in-the-anti-dieting-age.html>.

Brown, Harriet. 2016. *Body of Truth: How Science, History, and Culture Drive Our Obsession with Weight—And What We Can Do About It*. First Da Capo Press paperback edition. Boston, MA: Da Capo Lifelong.

Brownell, K.D., and J. Rodin. 1994. Medical, Metabolic, and Psychological Effects of Weight Cycling. *Archives of Internal Medicine* 154 (12): 1325–1330.

Brownstein, Michael. 2019. Implicit Bias. In *The Stanford Encyclopedia of Philosophy*, edited by Edward N. Zalta. Stanford University. <https://plato.stanford.edu/archives/fall2019/entries/implicit-bias/>.

Burgard, Deb. 2009. What is "Health at Every Size"? In *The Fat Studies Reader*, edited by Esther D. Rothblum and Sondra Solovay, 42–53. New York: New York University Press.

Buyx, A.M. 2008. Personal Responsibility for Health as a Rationing Criterion: Why We Don't Like It and Why Maybe We Should. *Journal of Medical Ethics* 34 (12): 871–874.

Cadena-Obando, Diego, Claudia Ramírez-Rentería, Aldo Ferreira-Hermosillo, Alejandra Albarrán-Sanchez, Ernesto Sosa-Eroza, Mario Molina-Ayala, and Etual Espinosa-Cárdenas. 2020. Are There Really Any Predictive Factors for a Successful Weight Loss After Bariatric Surgery? *BMC Endocrine Disorders* 20 (1): 20.

Caffrey, Mary. 2017. Obesity Tops List of Causes for Lost Years of Life, Beating Tobacco. *The American Journal of Managed Care*. <https://www.ajmc.com/view/obesity-tops-list-of-causes-for-lost-years-of-life-beating-tobacco>.

Callahan, Daniel. 2013a. Children, Stigma, and Obesity. *JAMA Pediatrics* 167 (9): 791–792.

Callahan, Daniel. 2013b. Obesity: Chasing an Elusive Epidemic. *Hastings Center Report* 43 (1): 34–40.

Campos, Paul. 2004. *The Obesity Myth: Why America's Obsession with Weight Is Hazardous to Your Health*. New York: Gotham Books.

Carlsson, Lena, Kajsa Sjöholm, Peter Jacobson, Johanna Andersson-Assarsson, Per-Arne Svensson, Magdalena Taube, Björn Carlsson, and Markku Peltonen. 2020. Life Expectancy After Bariatric Surgery in the Swedish Obese Subjects Study. *New England Journal of Medicine* 383 (16): 1535–1543.

Cawley, John. 2004. The Impact of Obesity on Wages. *The Journal of Human Resources* 39 (2): 451–474.

Cawley, John, Chad Meyerhoefer, Adam Biener, Mette Hammer, and Neil Wintfeld. 2015. Savings in Medical Expenditures Associated with Reductions in Body Mass Index Among US Adults with Obesity, by Diabetes Status. *PharmacoEconomics* 33 (7): 707–722.

Centers for Disease Control and Prevention. 2019. Cigarette Smoking Among U.S. Adults Hits All-Time Low. *CDC Newsroom*. <https://www.cdc.gov/media/releases/2019/p1114-smoking-low.html>.

Centers for Disease Control and Prevention. 2021. *Childhood Obesity Facts*. <https://www.cdc.gov/obesity/data/childhood.html>.

Cernik, Lizzie. 2018. It's Not Fine to Be Fat. Celebrating Obesity Is Irresponsible. *The Guardian*. <https://www.theguardian.com/commentisfree/2018/apr/10/fat-pride-obesity-public-health-warnings-dangerous-weight-levels>.

Chang, S.-H., N.L.B. Freeman, J.A. Lee, C.R.T. Stoll, A.J. Calhoun, J.C. Eagon, and G.A. Colditz. 2018. Early Major Complications After Bariatric Surgery in the USA, 2003–2014: A Systematic Review and Meta-Analysis. *Obesity Reviews* 19 (4): 529–537.

Charlesworth, Tessa, and Mahzarin Banaji. 2019a. Patterns of Implicit and Explicit Attitudes: I. Long-Term Change and Stability from 2007 to 2016. *Psychological Science* 30 (2): 174–192.

Charlesworth, Tessa, and Mahzarin Banaji. 2019b. Research: How Americans' Biases Are Changing (or Not) Over Time. *Harvard Business Review*. <https://hbr.org/2019/08/research-on-many-issues-americans-biases-are-decreasing>.

Chastain, Ragen. 2022. If You're Thinking About Offering Advice to a Fat Person About Their Health... Substack Newsletter. *Weight and Healthcare*. <https://weightandhealthcare.substack.com/p/if-youre-thinking-about-offering>.

Christou, Demetra, Christopher Gentile, Christopher DeSouza, Douglas Seals, and Phillip Gates. 2005. Fatness Is a Better Predictor of Cardiovascular Disease Risk Factor Profile than Aerobic Fitness in Healthy Men. *Circulation* 111 (15): 1904–1914.

Cleary, Margot, and Michael Grossmann. 2009. Obesity and Breast Cancer: The Estrogen Connection. *Endocrinology* 150 (6): 2537–2542.

Cohen, Pieter. 2014. Hazards of Hindsight—Monitoring the Safety of Nutritional Supplements. *New England Journal of Medicine* 370 (14): 1277–1280.

Cooper, Charlotte. 1998. *Fat and Proud: The Politics of Size*. London: Women's Press.

Cooper, Charlotte. 2007. *Headless Fatties*. <http://charlottecooper.net/fat/headless-fatties-01-07/>.

Cooper, Charlotte. 2016. *Fat Activism: A Radical Social Movement*. Bristol: HammerOn Press.

Cosslett, Rhiannon Lucy. 2018. 'I Thought It Was a Miracle. Then I Started Shaking': The Danger of Buying Diet Pills Online. *The Guardian*. <https://www.theguardian.com/lifeandstyle/2018/nov/03/diet-pills-danger-sweat-heart-attack-weight-loss-rhiannon-lucy-cosslett>.

Cramer, Phebe, and Tiffany Steinwert. 1998. Thin Is Good, Fat Is Bad: How Early Does It Begin? *Journal of Applied Developmental Psychology* 19 (3): 429–451.

Crandall, Christian. 1995. Do Parents Discriminate Against Their Heavyweight Daughters? *Personality and Social Psychology Bulletin* 21 (7): 724–735.

Crenshaw, Kimberlé. 1989. Demarginalizing the Intersection of Race and Sex: A Black Feminist Critique of Antidiscrimination Doctrine, Feminist Theory, and Antiracist Politics. *University of Chicago Legal Forum* 8 (1): 139–167.

Crippa, M., E. Solazzo, D. Guizzardi, F. Monforti-Ferrario, F.N. Tubiello, and A. Leip. 2021. Food Systems Are Responsible for a Third of Global Anthropogenic GHG Emissions. *Nature Food* 2 (3): 198–209.

Critser, Greg. 2000. Let Them Eat Fat: The Heavy Truths About American Obesity. *Harper's Magazine*. <https://harpers.org/archive/2000/03/let-them-eat-fat/>.

Cudd, Ann E. 2006. *Analyzing Oppression*. Studies in Feminist Philosophy. New York: Oxford University Press.

Dalle Grave, Riccardo, Simona Calugi, Angelo Compare, Marwan El Ghoch, Maria Letizia Petroni, Franco Tomasi, Gloria Mazzali, and Giulio Marchesini. 2015. Weight Loss Expectations and Attrition in Treatment-Seeking Obese Women. *Obesity Facts* 8 (5): 311–318.

Davidson, Lacey J., and Melissa D. Gruver. 2022. Public Philosophy and Fat Activism. In *A Companion to Public Philosophy*, edited by Lee McIntyre, Nancy McHugh, and Ian Olasov, 154–165. Hoboken, NJ: John Wiley & Sons.

Davies, Ben, and Julian Savulescu. 2019. Solidarity and Responsibility in Health Care. *Public Health Ethics* 12 (2): 133–144.

Deng, Tuo, Christopher Lyon, Stephen Bergin, Michael Caligiuri, and Willa Hsueh. 2016. Obesity, Inflammation, and Cancer. *Annual Review of Pathology: Mechanisms of Disease* 11: 421–449.

Division of Cancer Prevention and Control, Centers for Disease Control and Prevention. 2022. *What Are the Risk Factors for Lung Cancer?* <https://www.cdc.gov/cancer/lung/basic_info/risk_factors.htm>.

Docherty, Kiana. 2020. *The Toxic World of Tess Holliday and Fat Activism | Politics, Lies ... and Health?* <https://www.youtube.com/watch?v=hlkkG6mKTCk>.

Dotson, Kristie. 2011. Tracking Epistemic Violence, Tracking Practices of Silencing. *Hypatia* 26 (2): 236–257.

Duncan, Glen. 2010. The 'Fit but Fat' Concept Revisited: Population-Based Estimates Using NHANES. *International Journal of Behavioral Nutrition and Physical Activity* 7 (1): 47.

Dwyer, T., D. Hosmer, T. Hosmer, et al. 2007. The Inverse Relationship Between Number of Steps Per Day and Obesity in a Population-Based Sample: The AusDiab Study. *International Journal of Obesity* 31 (5): 797–804.

Eaton, A. W. 2016. Taste in Bodies and Fat Oppression. In *Body Aesthetics*, edited by Sherri Irvin, 37–59. Oxford: Oxford University Press.

Ekelund, Ulf, Heather Ward, Teresa Norat, et al. 2015. Physical Activity and All-Cause Mortality Across Levels of Overall and Abdominal Adiposity in European Men and Women: The European Prospective Investigation into Cancer and Nutrition Study (EPIC). *The American Journal of Clinical Nutrition* 101 (3): 613–621.

Eller, G.M. 2014. On Fat Oppression. *Kennedy Institute of Ethics Journal* 24 (3): 219–245.

Elliott, Christopher. 2022. Passengers of Size Present a Challenge for Seatmates and Airlines. *Elliott Report*. <https://www.elliott.org/blog/passengers-of-size-problems/>.

Esmonde, Katelyn. 2020. What Celeb Trainer Jillian Michaels Got Wrong About Lizzo and Body Positivity. *Vox*. <https://www.vox.com/culture/2020/1/15/21060692/lizzo-jillian-michaels-body-positivity-backlash>.

Farrell, Amy Erdman. 2011. *Fat Shame: Stigma and the Fat Body in American Culture*. New York: New York University Press.

Field, Alison, Eugenie Coakley, Aviva Must, Jennifer Spadano, Nan Laird, William Dietz, Eric Rimm, and Graham Colditz. 2001. Impact of Overweight on the Risk of Developing Common Chronic Diseases During a 10-Year Period. *Archives of Internal Medicine* 161 (13): 1581–1586.

Fikkan, Janna L., and Esther D. Rothblum. 2012. Is Fat a Feminist Issue? Exploring the Gendered Nature of Weight Bias. *Sex Roles* 66 (9–10): 575–592.

Fildes, Alison, Judith Charlton, Caroline Rudisill, Peter Littlejohns, A. Toby Prevost, and Martin C. Gulliford. 2015. Probability of an Obese Person Attaining Normal Body Weight: Cohort Study Using Electronic Health Records. *American Journal of Public Health* 105 (9): e54–e59.

Finkelstein, Eric A., Ian C. Fiebelkorn, and Guijing Wang. 2003. National Medical Spending Attributable to Overweight and Obesity: How Much, and Who's Paying? *Health Affairs* 22 (Suppl1): 219–226.

FitzGerald, Chloë, and Samia Hurst. 2017. Implicit Bias in Healthcare Professionals: A Systematic Review. *BMC Medical Ethics* 18 (1): 19.

Flegal, Katherine M., Brian Kit, Heather Orpana, and Barry Graubard. 2013. Association of All-Cause Mortality with Overweight and Obesity Using Standard Body Mass Index Categories: A Systematic Review and Meta-Analysis. *JAMA* 309 (1): 71–82.

Flint, Stuart W., Meghan Leaver, Alex Griffiths, and Mohammad Kaykanloo. 2021. Disparate Healthcare Experiences of People Living with Overweight or Obesity in England. *eClinicalMedicine* 41.

Fogelholm, M. 2010. Physical Activity, Fitness and Fatness: Relations to Mortality, Morbidity and Disease Risk Factors. A Systematic Review. *Obesity*

Reviews: An Official Journal of the International Association for the Study of Obesity 11 (3): 202–221.

Forth, Christopher E. 2019. *Fat: A Cultural History of the Stuff of Life*. London, UK: Reaktion Books.

Fothergill, Erin, Juen Guo, Lilian Howard, et al. 2016. Persistent Metabolic Adaptation 6 Years After "The Biggest Loser" Competition. *Obesity* 24 (8): 1612–1619.

Fourie, Carina. 2015. To Praise and to Scorn: The Problem of Inequalities of Esteem for Social Egalitarianism. In *Social Equality: On What It Means to Be Equals*, edited by Carina Fourie, Fabian Schuppert, and Ivo Wallimann-Helmer, 87–106. Oxford; New York: Oxford University Press.

Franz, Marion, Jeffrey VanWormer, A. Lauren Crain, Jackie Boucher, Trina Histon, William Caplan, Jill Bowman, and Nicolas Pronk. 2007. Weight-Loss Outcomes: A Systematic Review and Meta-Analysis of Weight-Loss Clinical Trials with a Minimum 1-Year Follow-Up. *Journal of the American Dietetic Association* 107 (10): 1755–1767.

Fraser, Nancy. 2008. *Adding Insult to Injury: Nancy Fraser Debates Her Critics*. Edited by Kevin Olson. London: Verso.

Frazier, Cheryl. 2023. Beauty Labor as a Tool to Resist Antifatness. *Hypatia* 38 (2): 231–250.

Fricker, Miranda. 2007. *Epistemic Injustice: Power and the Ethics of Knowing*. Oxford: Oxford University Press.

Fryar, Cheryl D., Margaret D. Carroll, and Joseph Afful. 2020. Prevalence of Overweight, Obesity, and Severe Obesity Among Adults Aged 20 and Over: United States, 1960–1962 through 2017–2018. *NCHS Health E-Stats*. Division of Health and Nutrition Examination Surveys. <https://www.cdc.gov/nchs/data/hestat/obesity-adult-17-18/obesity-adult.htm>.

Frye, Marilyn. 1983. *The Politics of Reality: Essays in Feminist Theory*. Trumansburg, NY: Crossing Press.

Gaesser, Glenn, Siddhartha Angadi, and Brandon Sawyer. 2011. Exercise and Diet, Independent of Weight Loss, Improve Cardiometabolic Risk Profile in Overweight and Obese Individuals. *The Physician and Sportsmedicine* 39 (2): 87–97.

Garvey, W. Timothy, Rachel L. Batterham, Meena Bhatta, et al. 2022. Two-Year Effects of Semaglutide in Adults with Overweight or Obesity: The STEP 5 Trial. *Nature Medicine* 28 (10): 2083–2091.

Gastaldelli, Amalia, Melania Gaggini, and Ralph DeFronzo. 2017. Role of Adipose Tissue Insulin Resistance in the Natural History of Type 2 Diabetes: Results from the San Antonio Metabolism Study. *Diabetes* 66 (4): 815–822.

Gay, Roxane. 2018. *Hunger: A Memoir of (My) Body*. New York: Harper Perennial.

Gibbs, Alice. 2022. Plus-Size Woman Defends Not Buying 2 Seats on Airplane: 'Why Should I?' *Newsweek*. <https://www.newsweek.com/plus-size-woman-defends-not-buying-2-seats-airplane-1754743>.

Gibson, Gemma. 2022. Health(ism) at Every Size: The Duties of the "Good Fatty." *Fat Studies* 11 (1): 22–35.

Gill, Timothy, and Sinead Boylan. 2012. Public Health Messages: Why Are They Ineffective and What… Can Be Done? *Current Obesity Reports* 1 (1): 50–58.

Glass, Ira. "Tell Me I'm Fat." *This American Life*. Podcast. June 17, 2016. <https://www.thisamericanlife.org/589/transcript>.

Glover, Ciara Louise. 2019. The Body Positive Movement Is Not Socially Courageous, It's Toxic. *Women UK*. <https://womenuk.co.uk/health/the-body-positive-movement-is-not-socially-courageous-its-toxic/>.

Glucksman, M.L., J. Hirsch, R.S. McCully, B.A. Barron, and J.L. Knittle. 1968. The Response of Obese Patients to Weight Reduction. II. A Quantitative Evaluation of Behavior. *Psychosomatic Medicine* 30 (4): 359–373.

Glucksman, Myron L., and Jules Hirsch. 1968. The Response of Obese Patients to Weight Reduction: A Clinical Evaluation of Behavior. *Psychosomatic Medicine* 30 (1): 1.

Goffman, Erving. 1986. *Stigma: Notes on the Management of Spoiled Identity*. New York: Simon & Schuster.

Gogoi, Pallavi. 2023. The Weight Bias Against Women in the Workforce Is Real—And It's Only Getting Worse. *NPR*. <https://www.npr.org/2023/04/29/1171593736/women-weight-bias-wages-workplace-wage-gap>.

Goldberg, Daniel S. 2012. Social Justice, Health Inequalities and Methodological Individualism in US Health Promotion. *Public Health Ethics* 5 (2): 104–115.

Gordon, Aubrey. 2020. *What We Don't Talk About When We Talk About Fat*. Boston: Beacon Press.

Gordon, Aubrey. 2021. I'm a Fat Activist. I Don't Use the Word 'Fatphobia.' Here's Why. *Self*. <https://www.self.com/story/fat-activist-fatphobia>.

Gordon, Aubrey. 2023. *'You Just Need to Lose Weight': And 19 Other Myths About Fat People*. Boston: Beacon Press.

Gore, Tim. 2020. *Confronting Carbon Inequality: Putting Climate Justice at the Heart of the COVID-19 Recovery*. Oxfam Media Briefing.

Gray, Emma. 2012. Georgia Anti-Obesity Ads Say 'Stop Sugarcoating' Childhood Obesity. *Huffington Post*. <https://www.huffpost.com/entry/georgia-anti-obesity-ads-stop-sugarcoating_n_1182023>.

Greenberg, Bradley, Matthew Eastin, Linda Hofschire, Ken Lachlan, and Kelly Brownell. 2003. Portrayals of Overweight and Obese Individuals on Commercial Television. *American Journal of Public Health* 93 (8): 1342–1348.

Greenhalgh, Susan. 2017. *Fat-Talk Nation: The Human Costs of America's War on Fat.* Ithaca, NY: Cornell University Press.

Greenwald, Anthony, and Linda Hamilton Krieger. 2006. Implicit Bias: Scientific Foundations. *California Law Review* 94 (4): 945–967.

Hales, Craig, Margaret Carroll, Cheryl Fryar, and Cynthia Ogden. 2020. *Prevalence of Obesity and Severe Obesity Among Adults: United States, 2017–2018.* NCHS Data Brief. Hyattsville, MD: National Center for Health Statistics.

Hamman, Richard, Rena Wing, Sharon Edelstein, et al. 2006. Effect of Weight Loss with Lifestyle Intervention on Risk of Diabetes. *Diabetes Care* 29 (9): 2102–2107.

Harrington, Mary, Sigrid Gibson, and Richard Cottrell. 2009. A Review and Meta-Analysis of the Effect of Weight Loss on All-Cause Mortality Risk. *Nutrition Research Reviews* 22 (1): 93–108.

Harris, Sarah Ann. 2015. Overweight Haters Ltd: Police Probe 'Fat Cards' Handed out on London Underground. *The Huffington Post UK.* <https://www.huffingtonpost.co.uk/2015/12/01/overweight-haters-ltd-fat_n_8686108.html>.

Harrison, Christy. 2019. *Anti-Diet: Reclaim Your Time, Money, Well-Being and Happiness Through Intuitive Eating.* London: Yellow Kite.

Harrison, Da'Shaun L. 2021. *Belly of the Beast: The Politics of Anti-Fatness as Anti-Blackness.* Berkeley, CA: North Atlantic Books.

Haslanger, Sally. 2012. *Resisting Reality: Social Construction and Social Critique.* New York: Oxford University Press.

Haslanger, Sally. 2014. Social Meaning and Philosophical Method. *Proceedings and Addresses of the American Philosophical Association* 88: 16–37.

Haslanger, Sally. 2015. Social Structure, Narrative and Explanation. *Canadian Journal of Philosophy* 45 (1): 1–15.

Haslanger, Sally. 2017. Culture and Critique. *Aristotelian Society Supplementary Volume* 91 (1): 149–173.

Hatzenbuehler, Mark, Katherine Keyes, and Deborah Hasin. 2009. Associations Between Perceived Weight Discrimination and the Prevalence of Psychiatric Disorders in the General Population. *Obesity* 17 (11): 2033–2039.

Howard, Dana, and Sean Aas. 2018. On Valuing Impairment. *Philosophical Studies* 175 (5): 1113–1133.

Hunger, Jeffrey, Alison Blodorn, Carol Miller, and Brenda Major. 2018. The Psychological and Physiological Effects of Interacting with an Anti-Fat Peer. *Body Image* 27: 148–155.

Hunger, Jeffrey, Brenda Major, Alison Blodorn, and Carol Miller. 2015. Weighed Down by Stigma: How Weight-Based Social Identity Threat Contributes to Weight Gain and Poor Health. *Social and Personality Psychology Compass* 9 (6): 255–268.

Bibliography

Hunger, Jeffrey, Joslyn Smith, and A. Janet Tomiyama. 2020. An Evidence-Based Rationale for Adopting Weight-Inclusive Health Policy. *Social Issues and Policy Review* 14 (1): 73–107.

Jaglo, Kirsten, Shannon Kenny, and Jenny Stephenson. 2021. *From Farm to Kitchen: The Environmental Impacts of U.S. Food Waste.* U.S. Environmental Protection Agency.

Janssen, Ian, Peter Katzmarzyk, and Robert Ross. 2004. Waist Circumference and Not Body Mass Index Explains Obesity-Related Health Risk. *The American Journal of Clinical Nutrition* 79 (3): 379–384.

Jha, Prabhat. 2020. The Hazards of Smoking and the Benefits of Cessation: A Critical Summation of the Epidemiological Evidence in High-Income Countries. *eLife* 9: e49979.

Judge, Timothy, and Daniel Cable. 2011. When It Comes to Pay, Do the Thin Win? The Effect of Weight on Pay for Men and Women. *Journal of Applied Psychology* 96: 95–112.

Kelly, Erin. 2013. What Is an Excuse? In *Blame: Its Nature and Norms*, edited by D. Justin Coates and Neal A. Tognazzini, 244–262. Oxford: Oxford University Press.

Kenchaiah, Satish, Jane Evans, Daniel Levy, Peter W.F. Wilson, Emelia Benjamin, Martin Larson, William Kannel, and Ramachandran S. Vasan. 2002. Obesity and the Risk of Heart Failure. *New England Journal of Medicine* 347 (5): 305–313.

Kessler, David 2009. *The End of Overeating: Taking Control of the Insatiable American Appetite.* Emmaus, PA: Macmillan.

Keys, A., A. Menotti, M.J. Karvonen, C. Aravanis, H. Blackburn, R. Buzina, B.S. Djordjevic, A.S. Dontas, F. Fidanza, and M.H. Keys. 1986. The Diet and 15-Year Death Rate in the Seven Countries Study. *American Journal of Epidemiology* 124 (6): 903–915.

Keys, Ancel et al. 1950. *The Biology of Human Starvation.* 2 volumes. Minneapolis: University of Minnesota Press.

King, Barbara J. 2013. The Fat-Shaming Professor: A Twitter-Fueled Firestorm. NPR. <https://www.npr.org/sections/13.7/2013/06/06/188891906/the-fat-shaming-professor-a-twitter-fueled-firestorm>.

Kirkland, Anna. 2008. *Fat Rights: Dilemmas of Difference and Personhood.* New York: NYU Press.

Kirkland, Anna. 2011. The Environmental Account of Obesity: A Case for Feminist Skepticism. *Signs* 36 (2): 463–485.

Kitahara, Cari, Alan Flint, Amy Berrington de Gonzalez, et al. 2014. Association Between Class III Obesity (BMI of 40–59 kg/m2) and Mortality: A Pooled Analysis of 20 Prospective Studies. *PLoS Medicine* 11 (7): e1001673.

Kolata, Gina. 2007. *Rethinking Thin: The New Science of Weight Loss—And the Myths and Realities of Dieting*. New York: Picador/Farrar, Straus and Giroux.

Kolata, Gina. 2016a. After 'The Biggest Loser,' Their Bodies Fought to Regain Weight. *The New York Times*. <https://www.nytimes.com/2016/05/02/health/biggest-loser-weight-loss.html>.

Kolata, Gina. 2016b. Why Do Obese Patients Get Worse Care? Many Doctors Don't See Past the Fat. *The New York Times*. <https://www.nytimes.com/2016/09/26/health/obese-patients-health-care.html>.

Kolata, Gina. 2016c. The Shame of Fat Shaming. *The New York Times*. <https://www.nytimes.com/2016/10/02/sunday-review/the-shame-of-fat-shaming.html>.

Kolata, Gina. 2017. A Lesson from The Biggest Losers: Exercise Keeps off the Weight. *The New York Times*. <https://www.nytimes.com/2017/10/31/health/biggest-losers-weight-loss.html>.

LaRosa, John. 2022. U.S. Weight Loss Market Shrinks by 25% in 2020 with Pandemic, but Rebounds in 2021. *Market Research.com*. <https://blog.marketresearch.com/u.s.-weight-loss-market-shrinks-by-25-in-2020-with-pandemic-but-rebounds-in-2021>.

LeBesco, Kathleen. 2004. *Revolting Bodies? The Struggle to Redefine Fat Identity*. Amherst, MA: University of Massachusetts Press.

Leboeuf, Céline. 2019. Anatomy of the Thigh Gap. *Feminist Philosophy Quarterly* 5 (1): 1–22.

Levine, James, Norman Eberhardt, and Michael Jensen. 1999. Role of Nonexercise Activity Thermogenesis in Resistance to Fat Gain in Humans. *Science* 283 (5399): 212–214.

Levine, Morgan, and Eileen Crimmins. 2016. A Genetic Network Associated with Stress Resistance, Longevity, and Cancer in Humans. *The Journals of Gerontology* 71 (6): 703–712.

Lewis, Sophie, Samantha Thomas, R. Warwick Blood, David Castle, Jim Hyde, and Paul Komesaroff. 2011. How Do Obese Individuals Perceive and Respond to the Different Types of Obesity Stigma That They Encounter in Their Daily Lives? A Qualitative Study. *Social Science & Medicine* 73 (9): 1349–1356.

Look AHEAD Research Group. 2013. Cardiovascular Effects of Intensive Lifestyle Intervention in Type 2 Diabetes. *New England Journal of Medicine* 369 (2): 145–154.

Look AHEAD Research Group. 2014. Eight-Year Weight Losses with an Intensive Lifestyle Intervention: The Look AHEAD study. *Obesity* 22 (1): 5–13.

Lupoli, Roberta, Erminia Lembo, Gennaro Saldalamacchia, Claudia Kesia Avola, Luigi Angrisani, and Brunella Capaldo. 2017. Bariatric Surgery and Long-Term Nutritional Issues. *World Journal of Diabetes* 8 (11): 464–474.

Lupton, Deborah. 2013. *Fat*. New York: Routledge.

Maciejewski, Matthew, David Arterburn, Lynn Van Scoyoc, Valerie Smith, William Yancy Jr, Hollis Weidenbacher, Edward Livingston, and Maren Olsen. 2016. Bariatric Surgery and Long-Term Durability of Weight Loss. *JAMA Surgery* 151 (11): 1046–1055.

Madsen, Kristine, Hannah Thompson, Jennifer Linchey, Lorrene Ritchie, Shalika Gupta, Dianne Neumark-Sztainer, Patricia Crawford, Charles McCulloch, and Ana Ibarra-Castro. 2021. Effect of School-Based Body Mass Index Reporting in California Public Schools: A Randomized Clinical Trial. *JAMA Pediatrics* 175 (3): 251–259.

Magkos, Faidon, Inge Tetens, Susanne Gjedsted Bügel, Claus Felby, Simon Rønnow Schacht, James O. Hill, Eric Ravussin, and Arne Astrup. 2020. The Environmental Foodprint of Obesity. *Obesity* 28 (1): 73–79.

Major, Brenda, Dina Eliezer, and Heather Rieck. 2012. The Psychological Weight of Weight Stigma. *Social Psychological and Personality Science* 3 (6): 651–658.

Major, Brenda, Jeffrey Hunger, Debra Bunyan, and Carol Miller. 2014. The Ironic Effects of Weight Stigma. *Journal of Experimental Social Psychology* 51: 74–80.

Major, Brenda, A. Janet Tomiyama, and Jeffrey Hunger. 2017. The Negative and Bidirectional Effects of Weight Stigma on Health. In *The Oxford Handbook of Stigma, Discrimination, and Health*, edited by Brenda Major, John F. Dovidio, and Bruce G. Link, 499–519. New York: Oxford University Press.

Mann, Traci, A. Janet Tomiyama, Erika Westling, Ann-Marie Lew, Barbra Samuels, and Jason Chatman. 2007. Medicare's Search for Effective Obesity Treatments: Diets Are Not the Answer. *The American Psychologist* 62 (3): 220–233.

Manolopoulos, K.N., F. Karpe, and K.N. Frayn. 2010. Gluteofemoral Body Fat as a Determinant of Metabolic Health. *International Journal of Obesity* 34 (6): 949–959.

Marmot, Michael. 2004. *The Status Syndrome: How Your Social Standing Affects Our Health and Longevity*. New York: Holt.

Martin, Judith, Nicholas Martin, and Jacobina Martin. 2021. Miss Manners: My Wife Keeps Fat-Shaming Our Dog. *The Washington Post*. <https://www.washingtonpost.com/lifestyle/advice/miss-manners-my-wife-keeps-fat-shaming-our-dog/2021/01/13/8796caf2-4641-11eb-b0e4-0f182923a025_story.html>.

Mayes, Christopher. 2015. The Harm of Bioethics: A Critique of Singer and Callahan on Obesity. *Bioethics* 29 (3): 217–221.

Mehta, Tapan, Daniel Smith, Josh Muhammad, and Krista Casazza. 2014. Impact of Weight Cycling on Risk of Morbidity and Mortality. *Obesity Reviews* 15 (11): 870–881.

Ministry of Health NZ. 2022. *Obesity Statistics*. <https://www.health.govt.nz/nz-health-statistics/health-statistics-and-data-sets/obesity-statistics>.

Mokdad, Ali, James Marks, Donna Stroup, and Julie Gerberding. 2004. Actual Causes of Death in the United States, 2000. *JAMA* 291 (10): 1238–1245.

Mollow, Anna. 2015. Disability Studies Gets Fat. *Hypatia* 30 (1): 199–216.

Mollow, Anna. 2017. Unvictimizable: Toward a Fat Black Disability Studies. *African American Review* 50 (2): 105–123.

Monteiro, Carlos, Geoffrey Cannon, Renata Levy, et al. 2019. Ultra-Processed Foods: What They Are and How to Identify Them. *Public Health Nutrition* 22 (5): 936–941.

Moss, Michael. 2021. *Hooked: How Processed Food Became Addictive*. London: Random House.

Muennig, Peter. 2008. The Body Politic: The Relationship Between Stigma and Obesity-Associated Disease. *BMC Public Health* 8: 128.

Musich, Shirley, Stephanie MacLeod, Gandhi Bhattarai, Shaohung Wang, Kevin Hawkins, Frank Bottone, and Charlotte Yeh. 2016. The Impact of Obesity on Health Care Utilization and Expenditures in a Medicare Supplement Population. *Gerontology and Geriatric Medicine* 2: 2333721415622004.

Myers, Jonathan, Paul McAuley, Carl J. Lavie, Jean-Pierre Despres, Ross Arena, and Peter Kokkinos. 2015. Physical Activity and Cardiorespiratory Fitness as Major Markers of Cardiovascular Risk: Their Independent and Interwoven Importance to Health Status. *Progress in Cardiovascular Diseases* 57 (4): 306–314.

Nath, Rekha. 2020. Relational Egalitarianism. *Philosophy Compass* 15 (7): e12686.

Nath, Rekha. 2024. Obesity and Responsibility for Health. In *Responsibility and Healthcare*, edited by Ben Davies, Gabriel De Marco, Neil Levy, and Julian Savulescu, 184–209. Oxford: Oxford University Press.

Nath, Rekha. n.d. Being Fat, Feeling Fat, and Reclaiming Fat: What Does Fat Mean? Unpublished manuscript.

National Cancer Institute at the National Institute of Health. 2022. *Obesity and Cancer Fact Sheet*. <https://www.cancer.gov/about-cancer/causes-prevention/risk/obesity/obesity-fact-sheet>.

Nittle, Nadra. 2019. Shopping Can Be a Struggle for Women Who Fall Between Plus and Straight Size. *Vox*. <https://www.vox.com/the-goods/2019/2/12/18222409/retailers-women-in-between-plus-straight-size>.

Ogden, Cynthia, Molly Lamb, Margaret Carroll, and Katherine Flegal. 2010. *Obesity and Socioeconomic Status in Adults: United States, 2005–2008*. NCHS Data Brief.

Parikh, Nisha, Michael Pencina, Thomas Wang, Katherine Lanier, Caroline Fox, Ralph D'Agostino, and Ramachandran Vasan. 2007. Increasing Trends in Incidence of Overweight and Obesity Over 5 Decades. *The American Journal of Medicine* 120 (3): 242–250.

Parker-Pope, Tara. 2011. The Fat Trap. *The New York Times*. <https://www.nytimes.com/2012/01/01/magazine/tara-parker-pope-fat-trap.html>.

Pascoe, Elizabeth, and Laura Smart Richman. 2009. Perceived Discrimination and Health: A Meta-Analytic Review. *Psychological Bulletin* 135 (4): 531–554.

Pausé, Cat. 2017. Borderline: The Ethics of Fat Stigma in Public Health. *The Journal of Law, Medicine & Ethics* 45 (4): 510–517.

Pausé, Cat. 2020. Ray of Light: Standpoint Theory, Fat Studies, and a New Fat Ethics. *Fat Studies* 9 (2): 175–187.

Pausé, Cat, Jackie Wykes, and Samantha Murray, eds. 2016. *Queering Fat Embodiment*. London and New York: Routledge.

Pearl, Rebecca, Rebecca Puhl, and John Dovidio. 2017. Can Legislation Prohibiting Weight Discrimination Improve Psychological Well-Being? A Preliminary Investigation. *Analyses of Social Issues and Public Policy* 17 (1): 84–104.

Personnel Today. 2005. *Obesity Research: Fattism is the Last Bastion of Employee Discrimination*. <https://www.personneltoday.com/hr/obesity-research-fattism-is-the-last-bastion-of-employee-discrimination/>.

Phelan, S.M., D.J. Burgess, M.W. Yeazel, W.L. Hellerstedt, J.M. Griffin, and M. van Ryn. 2015. Impact of Weight Bias and Stigma on Quality of Care and Outcomes for Patients with Obesity. *Obesity Reviews* 16 (4): 319–326.

Piore, Adam. 2021. Americans Are Addicted to 'Ultra-Processed' Foods, and It's Killing Us. *Newsweek*. <https://www.newsweek.com/2021/12/17/americans-are-addicted-ultra-processed-foods-its-killing-us-1656977.html>.

Pi-Sunyer, Xavier. 2014. The Look AHEAD Trial: A Review and Discussion of Its Outcomes. *Current Nutrition Reports* 3 (4): 387–391.

Platell, Amanda. 2017. Platell's People: Obesity a Sickness? No, It's Just Greed. *The Daily Mail Online*. <http://www.dailymail.co.uk/~/article-4804330/index.html>.

Polidori, David, Arjun Sanghvi, Randy Seeley, and Kevin Hall. 2016. How Strongly Does Appetite Counter Weight Loss? Quantification of the Feedback Control of Human Energy Intake. *Obesity* 24 (11): 2289–2295.

Pollock, N.J. 1995. Cultural Elaborations of Obesity—Fattening Practices in Pacific Societies. *Asia Pacific Journal of Clinical Nutrition* 4 (4): 357–360.

Popenoe, Rebecca. 2005. Ideal. In *Fat: The Anthropology of an Obsession*, edited by Don Kulick and Anne Meneley, 9–28. New York: Tarcher/Penguin.

Pratto, Felicia, Jim Sidanius, Lisa Stallworth, and Bertram Malle. 1994. Social Dominance Orientation: A Personality Variable Predicting Social and Political Attitudes. *Journal of Personality and Social Psychology* 67 (4): 741–763.

Prospective Studies Collaboration. 2009. Body-Mass Index and Cause-Specific Mortality in 900 000 Adults: Collaborative Analyses of 57 Prospective Studies. *The Lancet* 373 (9669): 1083–1096.

Puhl, Rebecca, and Chelsea Heuer. 2009. The Stigma of Obesity: A Review and Update. *Obesity* 17 (5): 941–964.

Puhl, Rebecca, and Chelsea Heuer. 2010. Obesity Stigma: Important Considerations for Public Health. *American Journal of Public Health* 100 (6): 1019–1028.

Puhl, Rebecca, Mary Himmelstein, and Diane Quinn. 2018. Internalizing Weight Stigma: Prevalence and Sociodemographic Considerations in US Adults. *Obesity* 26 (1): 167–175.

Puhl, Rebecca, and Janet Latner. 2007. Stigma, Obesity, and the Health of the Nation's Children. *Psychological Bulletin* 133 (4): 557–580.

Raves, Danielle, Alexandra Brewis, Sarah Trainer, Seung-Yong Han, and Amber Wutich. 2016. Bariatric Surgery Patients' Perceptions of Weight-Related Stigma in Healthcare Settings Impair Post-Surgery Dietary Adherence. *Frontiers in Psychology* 7: 1497.

Reiheld, Alison. 2020. Microaggressions as a Disciplinary Technique for Fat and Potentially Fat Bodies. In *Microaggressions and Philosophy*, edited by Lauren Freeman and Jeanine Weekes Schroer, 205–225. New York: Routledge.

Riley, Tess. 2017. Just 100 Companies Responsible for 71% of Global Emissions, Study Says. *The Guardian*. <https://www.theguardian.com/sustainable-business/2017/jul/10/100-fossil-fuel-companies-investors-responsible-71-global-emissions-cdp-study-climate-change>.

Rimm, Sylvia, and Eric Rimm. 2004. *Rescuing the Emotional Lives of Overweight Children.* New York: Rodale Press.

Roehling, Mark, Patricia Roehling, and Shaun Pichler. 2007. The Relationship Between Body Weight and Perceived Weight-Related Employment Discrimination: The Role of Sex and Race. *Journal of Vocational Behavior* 71 (2): 300–318.

Roehling, Patricia, Mark Roehling, Jeffrey Vandlen, Justin Blazek, and William Guy. 2009. Weight Discrimination and the Glass Ceiling Effect Among Top US CEOs. *Equal Opportunities International* 28 (2): 179–196.

Ros, Emilio, Miguel Martínez-González, Ramon Estruch, Jordi Salas-Salvadó, Montserrat Fitó, José Martínez, and Dolores Corella. 2014. Mediterranean Diet and Cardiovascular Health: Teachings of the PREDIMED Study. *Advances in Nutrition* 5 (3): 330S–336S.

Rosa, Christopher. 2018. This Victoria's Secret Model Is Being Accused of Fat Shaming for Exercising at an In-N-Out Burger. *Glamour.* <https://www.glamour.com/story/this-victorias-secret-model-is-being-accused-of-fat-shaming-for-exercising-at-an-in-n-out-burger>.

Rothblum, Esther D., and Sondra Solovay, eds. 2009. *The Fat Studies Reader.* New York: New York University Press.

Rubino, Domenica, Niclas Abrahamsson, Melanie Davies, et al. 2021. Effect of Continued Weekly Subcutaneous Semaglutide vs Placebo on Weight Loss Maintenance in Adults with Overweight or Obesity: The STEP 4 Randomized Clinical Trial. *JAMA* 325 (14): 1414–1425.

Ryan, Donna, and Sarah Ryan Yockey. 2017. Weight Loss and Improvement in Comorbidity: Differences at 5%, 10%, 15%, and Over. *Current Obesity Reports* 6 (2): 187–194.

Saguy, Abigail. 2013. *What's Wrong with Fat?* New York: Oxford University Press.

Salas-Salvadó, Jordi, Monica Bulló, Nancy Babio, et al. 2011. Reduction in the Incidence of Type 2 Diabetes with the Mediterranean Diet. *Diabetes Care* 34 (1): 14–19.

Schaper, David. 2018. Tired of Tiny Seats and No Legroom on Flights? Don't Expect It to Change. *NPR.* <https://www.npr.org/2018/07/12/628546532/airline-passenger-groups-outraged-over-faa-ruling-on-seat-sizes>.

Schapiro, Rich. 2021. 'An Ongoing Nightmare': People with Obesity Face Major Healthcare Obstacles. *NBC News.* <https://www.nbcnews.com/health/health-news/ongoing-nightmare-obese-people-face-major-obstacles-when-seeking-medical-n1272019>.

Schvey, Natasha, Rebecca Puhl, and Kelly Brownell. 2011. The Impact of Weight Stigma on Caloric Consumption. *Obesity* 19 (10): 1957–1962.

Schwartz, Marlene, Heather O'Neal Chambliss, Kelly Brownell, Steven Blair, and Charles Billington. 2003. Weight Bias Among Health Professionals Specializing in Obesity. *Obesity Research* 11 (9): 1033–1039.

Schwartz, Marlene, Lenny Vartanian, Brian Nosek, and Kelly Brownell. 2006. The Influence of One's Own Body Weight on Implicit and Explicit Anti-Fat Bias. *Obesity* 14 (3): 440–447.

Shelby, Tommie. 2003. Ideology, Racism, and Critical Social Theory. *The Philosophical Forum* 34 (2): 153–188.

Simmonds, M., A. Llewellyn, C.G. Owen, and N. Woolacott. 2016. Predicting Adult Obesity from Childhood Obesity: A Systematic Review and Meta-Analysis. *Obesity Reviews* 17 (2): 95–107.

Sims, E.A. 1976. Experimental Obesity, Dietary-Induced Thermogenesis, and Their Clinical Implications. *Clinics in Endocrinology and Metabolism* 5 (2): 377–395.

Sims, E.A., E. Danforth Jr., E.S. Horton, G.A. Bray, J.A. Glennon, and L.B. Salans. 1973. Endocrine and Metabolic Effects of Experimental Obesity in Man. *Recent Progress in Hormone Research* 29: 457–496.

Singer, Peter. 2012. Weigh More, Pay More. *Project Syndicate*. <https://www.project-syndicate.org/commentary/weigh-more--pay-more>.

Singer, Peter. 2016. *Ethics in the Real World: 82 Brief Essays on Things That Matter*. Princeton: Princeton University Press.

Smith, Angela M. 2013. Moral Blame and Moral Protest. In *Blame: Its Nature and Norms*, edited by D. Justin Coates and Neal A. Tognazzini, 27–48. Oxford: Oxford University Press.

Statistics Canada, Government of Canada. 2019. *Overweight and Obese Adults, 2018*. <https://www150.statcan.gc.ca/n1/pub/82-625-x/2019001/article/00005-eng.htm>.

Steele, Claude M., Steven J. Spencer, and Joshua Aronson. 2002. Contending with Group Image: The Psychology of Stereotype and Social Identity Threat. In *Advances in Experimental Social Psychology*, 34: 379–440.

Strings, Sabrina. 2019. *Fearing the Black Body: The Racial Origins of Fat Phobia*. New York: New York University Press.

Stunkard, Albert, Jennifer Harris, Nancy Pedersen, and Gerald McClearn. 1990. The Body-Mass Index of Twins Who Have Been Reared Apart. *New England Journal of Medicine* 322 (21): 1483–1487.

Stunkard, Albert, Thorkild I.A. Sørensen, Craig Hanis, Thomas Teasdale, Ranajit Chakraborty, William Schull, and Fini Schulsinger. 1986. An Adoption Study of Human Obesity. *New England Journal of Medicine* 314 (4): 193–198.

Sutin, Angelina, Yannick Stephan, and Antonio Terracciano. 2015. Weight Discrimination and Risk of Mortality. *Psychological Science* 26 (11): 1803–1811.

Sutin, Angelina, and Antonio Terracciano. 2013. Perceived Weight Discrimination and Obesity. *PloS one* 8 (7): e70048.

Swinburn, B., and G. Egger. 2002. Preventive Strategies Against Weight Gain and Obesity. *Obesity Reviews* 3 (4): 289–301.

Taylor, Roy, and Rury Holman. 2015. Normal Weight Individuals Who Develop Type 2 Diabetes: The Personal Fat Threshold. *Clinical Science (London, England:* 1979) 128 (7): 405–410.

Teachman, B.A., and K.D. Brownell. 2001. Implicit Anti-Fat Bias Among Health Professionals: Is Anyone Immune? *International Journal of Obesity and Related Metabolic Disorders* 25 (10): 1525–1531.

Thedinga, Hendrik, Roman Zehl, and Ansgar Thiel. 2021. Weight Stigma Experiences and Self-Exclusion from Sport and Exercise Settings Among People with Obesity. *BMC Public Health* 21 (1): 565.

Thompson, Iyonna, Jun Sung Hong, Jeoung Min Lee, Nicholas Alexander Prys, Julie Toth Morgan, and Ini Udo-Inyang. 2020. A Review of the Empirical Research on Weight-Based Bullying and Peer Victimisation Published Between 2006 and 2016. *Educational Review* 72 (1): 88–110.

Tiffany, Kaitlyn. 2019. Lean Cuisine Doesn't Want to Be Part of Diet Culture Anymore. Does It Have a Choice? *Vox.* <https://www.vox.com/the-goods/2019/7/24/20700861/lean-cuisine-body-positivity-wellness-diet-culture>.

Tomiyama, A. Janet. 2014. Weight Stigma Is Stressful. A Review of Evidence for the Cyclic Obesity/Weight-Based Stigma Model. *Appetite* 82: 8–15.

Tylka, Tracy, Rachel Annunziato, Deb Burgard, Sigrún Daníelsdóttir, Ellen Shuman, Chad Davis, and Rachel Calogero. 2014. The Weight-Inclusive Versus Weight-Normative Approach to Health: Evaluating the Evidence for Prioritizing Well-Being Over Weight Loss. *Journal of Obesity.*

U.S. Department of Agriculture. 2022. Food Loss and Waste. *FDA.* <https://www.fda.gov/food/consumers/food-loss-and-waste>.

van Baal, Pieter H.M., Johan Polder, G. Ardine de Wit, Rudolf Hoogenveen, Talitha Feenstra, Hendriek Boshuizen, Peter Engelfriet, and Werner Brouwer. 2008. Lifetime Medical Costs of Obesity: Prevention No Cure for Increasing Health Expenditure. *PLoS Medicine* 5 (2): 242–249.

Walls, Helen, Anna Peeters, Joseph Proietto, and John McNeil. 2011. Public Health Campaigns and Obesity—A Critique. *BMC Public Health* 11: 136.

Wang, Zhaoxia, and Tomohiro Nakayama. 2010. Inflammation, a Link Between Obesity and Cardiovascular Disease. *Mediators of Inflammation* 2010: 535918.

Wann, Marilyn. 2009. Foreword. Fat Studies: An Invitation to Revolution. In *The Fat Studies Reader*, edited by Esther D. Rothblum and Sondra Solovay, ix–xxv. New York: New York University Press.

Watson, Gary. 1977. Skepticism About Weakness of Will. *The Philosophical Review* 86 (3): 316–339.

Whipple, Tom. 2019. Obesity Is Bad for the Environment, Study Shows. *The Times*. <https://www.thetimes.co.uk/article/obesity-is-bad-for-the-environment-study-shows-9wknjl6kc>.

Wiedmann, Thomas, Manfred Lenzen, Lorenz Keyßer, and Julia Steinberger. 2020. Scientists' Warning on Affluence. *Nature Communications* 11 (1): 3107.

Wikler, Daniel. 1987. Who Should Be Blamed for Being Sick? *Health Education Quarterly* 14 (1): 11–25.

Wilding, John P.H., Rachel Batterham, Salvatore Calanna, et al. 2021. Once-Weekly Semaglutide in Adults with Overweight or Obesity. *New England Journal of Medicine* 384 (11): 989–1002.

Wildman, Rachel, Paul Muntner, Kristi Reynolds, Aileen McGinn, Swapnil Rajpathak, Judith Wylie-Rosett, and MaryFran Sowers. 2008. The Obese Without Cardiometabolic Risk Factor Clustering and the Normal Weight with Cardiometabolic Risk Factor Clustering: Prevalence and Correlates of 2 Phenotypes Among the US Population (NHANES 1999-2004). *Archives of Internal Medicine* 168 (15): 1617–1624.

Wilkinson, Richard, and Kate Pickett. 2011. *The Spirit Level: Why Greater Equality Makes Societies Stronger*. New York: Bloomsbury.

Wing, Rena, Jeanne Clark, Edward Gregg, et al. 2020. 143-OR: All-Cause Mortality Over 16 Years in Look AHEAD. *Diabetes* 69 (Supplement_1): 143-OR.

Wing, Rena, and James Hill. 2001. Successful Weight Loss Maintenance. *Annual Review of Nutrition* 21 (1): 323–341.

Wischhover, Cheryl. 2018. As 'Dieting' Becomes More Taboo, Weight Watchers Is Changing Its Name. *Vox*. <https://www.vox.com/the-goods/2018/9/24/17897114/weight-watchers-ww-wellness-rebranding>.

Wootson, Cleve. 2019. 'At Least They'll Keep Me Warm': Fat-Shaming Passenger Fumes About Being Seated Between 'Pigs'. *Washington Post*. <https://www.washingtonpost.com/transportation/2019/01/29/least-theyll-keep-me-warm-fat-shaming-passenger-fumes-about-being-seated-between-pigs/>.

World Health Organization. 2018. *Taking Action on Childhood Obesity*. <https://apps.who.int/iris/bitstream/handle/10665/274792/WHO-NMH-PND-ECHO-18.1-eng.pdf>.

World Health Organization. 2021. *Obesity and Overweight*. <https://www.who.int/news-room/fact-sheets/detail/obesity-and-overweight>.

World Health Organization. 2024. *Obesity and Overweight*. <https://www.who.int/news-room/fact-sheets/detail/obesity-and-overweight>.

Young, Iris Marion. 1990. *Justice and the Politics of Difference*. Princeton: Princeton University Press.

Zabinski, Marion, Brian Saelens, Richard Stein, Helen Hayden-Wade, and Denise Wilfley. 2003. Overweight Children's Barriers to and Support for Physical Activity. *Obesity Research* 11 (2): 238–246.

Zacher, Hannes, and Courtney von Hippel. 2022. Weight-Based Stereotype Threat in the Workplace: Consequences for Employees with Overweight or Obesity. *International Journal of Obesity* 46 (4): 767–773.

Zee, Renate van der. 2017. Demoted or Dismissed Because of Your Weight? The Reality of the Size Ceiling. *The Guardian*. https://www.theguardian.com/inequality/2017/aug/30/demoted-dismissed-weight-size-ceiling-work-discrimination>.

Index

Note: Endnotes are indicated by the page number followed by "n" and the note number e.g., 258n31 refers to note 31 on page 258.

Printed in the United States
by Baker & Taylor Publisher Services